A CHILD'S GEOGRAPHY
Volume 5

Explore Viking REALMS

MASTERBOOKS®
CURRICULUM

MasterBooks®
—CURRICULUM—

Editor-in-Chief:
Laura Welch

Editorial Team:
Craig Froman
Willow Meek
Judy Lewis
Carla Bradley

Art Director:
Diana Bogardus

Design Team:
Diana Bogardus
Terry White
Jennifer Bauer

First Edition: 2005
Master Books® Revised Edition: May 2024

Master Books, P.O. Box 726, Green Forest, AR 72638
Master Books® is a division of the New Leaf Publishing Group, LLC.

ISBN: 978-1-68344-373-5
ISBN: 978-1-61458-892-4 (digital)

Unless otherwise indicated, Scripture quotations are taken from the (NASB®) New American Standard Bible®, Copyright © 1960, 1971, 1977 by The Lockman Foundation. Used by permission. All rights reserved. lockman.org

Scripture quotations marked (NIV) are taken from the Holy Bible, New International Version®, NIV®. Copyright © 1973, 1978, 1984, 2011 by Biblica, Inc.™ Used by permission of Zondervan. All rights reserved worldwide. www.zondervan.com The "NIV" and "New International Version" are trademarks registered in the United States Patent and Trademark Office by Biblica, Inc.™

Verses marked KJV are from the King James Version of the Bible.

Printed in the United States of America.

Please visit our website for other great titles: www.masterbooks.com

About the Author

Terri Johnson is married to Todd and is the mother of six children. She is the author of eleven books, including the *Map Trek: Atlas & Outlines* series, the *A Child's Geography* series, and the *What Really Happened* series, which she originally published through her educational publishing company, Knowledge Quest, Inc. Terri loves to spend time with her family, to travel and write so that children can truly understand and appreciate the world we live in, and to help others develop and grow their own businesses. Having sold her publishing company to Master Books at the end of 2019, she is enjoying the life of a freelance business coach, brand strategist, and graphic designer.

Table of Contents

Image Credits

L = left, T= top, TL = top left, B=bottom, BL = bottom left, C = center, CR = center right, CL = center left, R = right, TR = top right, BR = bottom right, BC = bottom center

All images are public domain (PD-US, and PD-Art), except for:

Course Description

A Child's Geography: Exploring Viking Realms offers a year-long interactive journey with a mix of geography and history for The Baltic States, Scandinavia, The British Isles, and North Atlantic. In a unique travel-reading approach, students will learn about the five themes of geography in a sixteen-lesson course: location, place, human-environment interaction, movement, and region. Created with a variety of visuals and content, students will engage with meaningful learning resources: maps, architecture, history of countries, Viking artifacts, food experiences, historical sites, and current-day places of interest. The content is built on a faith foundation of helping the learner connect the study of geography and history with a love for the concept of neighbor.

Features

	Target Level	*Designed for grades 6 and up*
	Flexible 180-Day Schedule	*Approximately 30 to 45 minutes per lesson, three days a week*
	Open & Go	*Convenient daily schedule, Well-designed lessons*
	Engaging Application	*Reflection opportunities, Faith tie-ins, Experiential learning*
	Assessments	*Travel itineraries, Adventure challenges, Activities, Reviews, Quizzes, and Final exam*

Objectives

★ Enjoy creative activities and challenges while learning language, history, geography, and cultures.

★ Explore the region of Vikings through a mix of geography, history, and travel.

★ Demonstrate learning with map activities, reading questions, and hands-on learning activities.

★ Participate in an interactive journey that connects to loving our neighbors and applying an understanding of geography.

★ Complete a variety of assessments build understanding, application, and critical thinking.

Placement

A Child's Geography: Exploring Viking Realms is part of the A Child's Geography series that is designed for grades 6 and up. This volume includes slightly more advanced activities than the first books in the series, so students can stairstep their way through completing activities. It can be completed independently without completing other books in the series.

Students are ready to begin *A Child's Geography: Exploring Viking Realms* when they can

- 🌍 read close to a sixth-grade level or higher
- 🌍 answer reading questions
- 🌍 draw and design maps from an example
- 🌍 make connections between learning about the world today and themselves
- 🌍 create hands-on activities independently or with guided practice from a parent or teacher

Course Overview

The four geographical areas of Northern Europe are studied. Students create a travel itinerary and have a quiz at the close of each section.

1. The Baltic States
2. Scandinavia
3. The British Isles
4. North Atlantic

There are sixteen lessons, and each includes five parts.

1. Reading (part 1)
2. First Adventure Challenge
3. Reading (part 2)
4. Second Adventure Challenge
5. Closing activities related to map study and glossary terms

The course concludes with a final exam.

There are five learning outcomes to describe what students will be to be able to do.

1. On a map, locate countries, capitals, and geographic features of Northern Europe in The Baltic States, Scandinavia, The British Isles, and North Atlantic.
2. Create designs and build replicas of historic and modern sites that include castles, churches, landscapes, and more.
3. Discuss, write about, and draw images related to cultural aspects and influences of Vikings on these regions.
4. Identify features of God's creation as they relate to geography, including landforms, animals, and people.
5. Apply faith-building connections to strengthen biblical understanding and love for neighbors.

Special Features

Narrative Travel Readings engage readers in a firsthand account of traveling the region in current times. Readers will discover the magnificence of God's creation against a backdrop of the connections and conflicts among nations and people seeking to understand the One True God.

Adventure Challenges create experiential learning opportunities for learners to make connections in the world around them while writing, drawing, creating, designing, exploring, and building. Other skills will be developed, including demonstrating understanding, applying learning to other situations, and discussing meaningful reflections.

Activities help students experience some of the concepts in action, including map identification and geographic terms. Discussion guides invite students to make real-world connections.

Flashcards give students practice with writing bolded glossary terms and definitions. Students will need ruled index cards for this part of the course. A course materials list begins on page 7.

Love Your Neighbor readings offer prayers and scripture for the heart of the learner. Students will further develop their understanding of God's creation and love for people.

A Tasty Tour recipes (optional) provide an additional opportunity to explore culture and learning through hands-on learning.

Travel Itineraries are completed by students at the end of each section: The Baltic States, Scandinavia, The British Isles, and North Atlantic. This invites learners to describe and explore what was most memorable to them in their readings.

Teacher Resources

Be sure to check out the appendix for additional resources, including answer keys, reference maps, and a glossary.

Materials List

General Supplies

- ☐ Pencil
- ☐ Paper
- ☐ Colored pencils
- ☐ Scissors
- ☐ Glue
- ☐ Index cards (with lines)
- ☐ Ruler

Lesson 1:
Adventure Challenge 2

- ☐ 35 straws of one color
- ☐ 30 straws of another color
- ☐ Tape

Lesson 2:
Adventure Challenge 3

- ☐ Camera or drawing paper with drawing supplies and paper of your choosing

Lesson 3:
Adventure Challenge 5

- ☐ Large pan with edges
- ☐ 4–6 cups flour
- ☐ 1 cup dry cocoa powder or dry pudding mix
- ☐ Pieces of candy, nuts, or small fruit pieces
- ☐ Sifter

Lesson 4:
Adventure Challenge 7

- ☐ Small pitcher with two cups of water
- ☐ Empty water bottle with label removed and cap
- ☐ Mixing spoon
- ☐ Funnel
- ☐ Blue food dye
- ☐ Baby oil
- ☐ Glitter (optional)

Lesson 5:
Adventure Challenge 9

- ☐ Water
- ☐ Food coloring (various colors)
- ☐ Assorted plastic cups or bowls
- ☐ Small pan
- ☐ Tray
- ☐ Salt (approximately ¼ cup)
- ☐ Ice cube tray (optional)

Lesson 6:
Adventure Challenge 12

- ☐ Paint
- ☐ Paintbrush
- ☐ Surface or paper for painting

Lesson 9:
Adventure Challenge 17

- ☐ Chalk or 48 feet of yarn or thick string
- ☐ Tape
- ☐ Ruler, yardstick, or tape measure

Lesson 10:
Adventure Challenge 20

Basic Design:

- ☐ Two empty applesauce containers or two paper cups
- ☐ Hole punch
- ☐ Three feet of yarn or thick string
- ☐ Hanger with shoulder grooves
- ☐ Small household or outdoor items* (parent's permission or guidance)

Advanced Design:

- ☐ Various household items and art supplies available (parent's permission or guidance)
- ☐ Small household or outdoor items* (parent's permission or guidance)

Lesson 13:
Adventure Challenge 26

- ☐ Magnifying glass
- ☐ Drawing paper with drawing supplies and paper of your choosing

Lesson 13:
Activity 18

- ☐ Cardboard
- ☐ 4 cups flour
- ☐ 2 cups salt
- ☐ 2 cups water
- ☐ Mixing bowl

Lesson 13:
Activity 19

- ☐ Paint
- ☐ Paintbrushes
- ☐ Black marker

Lesson 14:
Activity 28

☐ Thin-tip black marker

Lesson 15:
Adventure Challenge 30

☐ Smooth cardstock or watercolor paper

☐ Small glass of tea

☐ Paintbrush

☐ Feather and black paint or calligraphy marker

☐ Gold marker or gold paint

☐ Markers or paint

Lesson 15:
Activity 22

☐ Cylinder-shaped objects (paper towel rolls, wrapping paper rolls, nut or potato chip container).

☐ Hot glue gun

☐ Brown paper, brown sacks, or cardboard

☐ Black marker

☐ Paintbrush

☐ Black and white paint

☐ Cornmeal

Lesson 16:
Adventure Challenge 31

☐ 2-liter bottle of soda

☐ Package of Mentos® that is shaped like a cylinder

☐ Sheet of construction paper or cardstock

☐ Tape

☐ Toothpick

A Tasty Tour Recipe Grocery List (optional)

A related recipe is included on some lessons of the course.

NOTE: Adult supervision and participation required for this part of the course!

Lesson 1:
Crepes

☐ 1 cup all-purpose flour

☐ 2 eggs

☐ ½ cup milk

☐ ½ cup water

☐ ¼ teaspoon salt

☐ 2 tablespoons butter, melted

Lesson 2:
Biezpiena Sierins

☐ 2 cups cottage cheese

☐ 5 tablespoons powdered sugar

☐ 1 tablespoon melted butter

☐ ½ teaspoon vanilla

For glaze:

☐ 8 oz dark chocolate

☐ ¼ cup butter

Lesson 3:
Marzipan

☐ 2 cups almond flour

☐ 1 cup granulated sugar

☐ ¼ cup plus 2 tablespoons water

☐ 1 egg white, lightly beaten

☐ 1 teaspoon of almond extract

☐ ½ teaspoon of rose water or orange blossom water

☐ Confectioner's sugar as needed

Lesson 4:
Cloudberry Tart

☐ Two pre-baked pie shells

☐ Batch of pastry cream

☐ 2 cups cloudberry gelatin puree (or a pre-made raspberry pie filling, low-sugar jam, or gelatin)

☐ 2 cups of whipped cream

☐ ½ cup of whole berries

☐ A sprig of mint

Cooking Supply List (optional)

☐ General kitchen cooking supplies and utensils. This can include measuring spoons, measuring cups, bowls, skillet, and a cooking sheet or baking pan. Any special equipment needed for a recipe is included in that recipe's supply list.

Lesson 5:
Swedish Meatballs

- ☐ 2½ lb ground beef
- ☐ 4 eggs
- ☐ 2 cups milk
- ☐ 1 cup dry bread crumbs
- ☐ 1 cup minced onion
- ☐ ¼ cup butter, divided
- ☐ 1 teaspoon salt
- ☐ ¼ teaspoon nutmeg
- ☐ ¼ teaspoon allspice
- ☐ ¼ teaspoon cardamom

For the gravy:

- ☐ ¼ cup flour
- ☐ 2 cups beef stock
- ☐ 1 cup light cream
- ☐ 3 teaspoons dill weed
- ☐ Salt and pepper to taste

Lesson 6:
Lefse

- ☐ 10 pounds potatoes, peeled
- ☐ ½ cup butter
- ☐ ⅓ cup heavy cream
- ☐ 1 tablespoon salt
- ☐ 1 tablespoon white sugar
- ☐ 2½ cups all-purpose flour

Special equipment:

- ☐ Potato ricer
- ☐ Pastry cloth

Lesson 7:
Frikadeller

- ☐ 1½ lb ground beef
- ☐ ½ lb ground sausage
- ☐ 1 grated or finely chopped onion
- ☐ 1 egg
- ☐ ½ cup milk
- ☐ 2 tablespoons flour
- ☐ 2 tablespoons breadcrumbs
- ☐ ¼ teaspoon pepper
- ☐ ¼ teaspoon salt
- ☐ ½ teaspoon cloves

Lesson 8:
Fish and Chips

- ☐ 4 (7-ounce) white fish fillets (usually cod or haddock)
- ☐ ½ cup of all-purpose flour
- ☐ ½ cup of cornstarch
- ☐ 1 teaspoon baking soda
- ☐ Salt and ground pepper (to taste)

Ingredients for the chips:

- ☐ 2 pounds potatoes, peeled
- ☐ 1 quart (1 liter) vegetable oil

Lesson 9:
Cream Scones

- ☐ 1¾ cup flour
- ☐ ¼ cup sugar
- ☐ 2 teaspoons baking powder
- ☐ ⅛ teaspoon salt
- ☐ ½ cup dried cranberries or chocolate chips
- ☐ ⅓ cup butter, chilled
- ☐ ½ cup whipping cream
- ☐ 1 large egg
- ☐ 1½ teaspoons vanilla or almond extract

Lesson 10:
Yorkshire Pudding

- ☐ ½ cup milk
- ☐ ⅞ cup flour
- ☐ ½ cup water
- ☐ ½ teaspoon salt
- ☐ 2 eggs

Lesson 11:
Bubble and Squeak

- ☐ 6 tablespoons unsalted butter
- ☐ 4 strips of bacon (chopped)
- ☐ 1 onion (finely sliced)
- ☐ 1 garlic clove (chopped)
- ☐ 1 whole cabbage (boiled, shredded)
- ☐ 1 pound mashed potato
- ☐ Salt and pepper (to taste)

Lesson 12:
Scottish Oatcakes

☐ 1½ cup Scottish oats

☐ ¼ teaspoon baking powder

☐ ½ cup all-purpose flour

☐ ¼ cup melted butter (½ stick)

☐ ¼ teaspoon sugar

☐ ⅓ cup hot water

☐ ¼ teaspoon salt

Lesson 13:
Rarebit

☐ 4 slices thick bread

☐ 2 egg yolks

☐ 2 tablespoons sour cream

☐ ¾ teaspoon Worcestershire sauce

☐ 1 teaspoon mustard (Dijon for spicy)

☐ 2 cups cheddar cheese, grated

Lesson 15:
Colcannon Mash

☐ 5 large potatoes

☐ 4 cloves of garlic

☐ 7 ounces of butter

☐ Whole cabbage (thinly sliced)

☐ 3 ounces of spring onions

☐ ½ cup single cream

☐ ½ ounce fresh chives (chopped finely)

☐ Salt and ground black pepper to taste

Grading

It is always the prerogative of an educator to assess student grades however he or she might deem best. The following is only a suggested guideline based on the material presented through this course. To calculate the percentage of the worksheets and tests, the educator may use the following guide. Divide total number of questions correct (example: 43) by the total number of questions possible (example: 46) to calculate the percentage out of 100 possible. 43/46 = 93 percent correct.

The suggested grade values are noted as follows:

90 to 100 percent = A

80 to 89 percent = B

70 to 79 percent = C

60 to 69 percent = D

0 to 59 percent = F

Note: The answer key starting on page 371 provides answers for the numbered questions in this course.

A Child's Geography 5: Explore Viking Realms Daily Schedule

Calendar		Assignment	Due Date	✓	Grade
		**First Semester–First Quarter**			
Week 1	Day 1	Before Embarking! • Pages 19–20			
	Day 2				
	Day 3	Lesson 1: "Lithuania" • Pages 21–24			
	Day 4				
	Day 5	Adventure Challenge 1 • Pages 25–26			
Week 2	Day 6	Lesson 1 • Pages 27–32			
	Day 7				
	Day 8	Adventure Challenge 2 • Pages 33–34			
	Day 9				
	Day 10	Activity 1 • Pages 35–36			
Week 3	Day 11	Lesson 2: "Latvia" • Pages 37–40			
	Day 12				
	Day 13	Adventure Challenge 3 • Pages 41–42			
	Day 14				
	Day 15	Lesson 2 • Pages 43–46			
Week 4	Day 16	Adventure Challenge 4 • Pages 47–50			
	Day 17				
	Day 18	Activity 2 • Pages 51–52			
	Day 19				
	Day 20	Activity 3 • Pages 53–54			
Week 5	Day 21	Lesson 3: "Estonia" • Pages 55–62			
	Day 22				
	Day 23	Adventure Challenge 5 • Pages 63–64			
	Day 24				
	Day 25	Lesson 3 • Pages 65–68			
Week 6	Day 26	Adventure Challenge 6 • Pages 69–70			
	Day 27				
	Day 28	Activity 4 • Pages 71–72			
	Day 29				
	Day 30	**Write Travel Itinerary 1: The Baltic States • Page 330**			

Calendar		Assignment	Due Date	✓	Grade
Week 7	Day 31	Review the Baltic States • Lessons 1–3 Study Tips • Page 350 The Baltic States Map • Page 381			
	Day 32				
	Day 33	**Quiz 1: The Baltic States • Pages 351-353**			
	Day 34				
	Day 35	Lesson 4: "Finland" • Pages 73–76			
Week 8	Day 36	Adventure Challenge 7 • Pages 77–78			
	Day 37				
	Day 38	Lesson 4 • Pages 79–82			
	Day 39				
	Day 40	Adventure Challenge 8 • Pages 83–84			
Week 9	Day 41	Activity 5 • Pages 85–86			
	Day 42				
	Day 43	Activity 6 • Pages 87–88			
	Day 44				
	Day 45	Lesson 5: "Sweden" • Pages 89–92			

Calendar	Assignment	Due Date	✓	Grade
	First Semester–Second Quarter			
Week 1	Day 46 — Adventure Challenge 9 • Pages 93–94			
	Day 47			
	Day 48 — Lesson 5 • Pages 95–100			
	Day 49			
	Day 50 — Adventure Challenge 10 • Pages 101–102			
Week 2	Day 51 — Activity 7 • Pages 103–104 Summer in Sweden (Optional) • Pages 105–112			
	Day 52			
	Day 53 — Lesson 6: "Norway" • Pages 113–118			
	Day 54			
	Day 55 — Adventure Challenge 11 • Pages 119–120			
Week 3	Day 56 — Lesson 6 • Pages 121–124			
	Day 57			
	Day 58 — Adventure Challenge 12 • Pages 125–126			
	Day 59			
	Day 60 — Activity 8 • Pages 127–128			
Week 4	Day 61 — Lesson 7: "Denmark" • Pages 129–132			
	Day 62			
	Day 63 — Adventure Challenge 13 • Pages 133–134			
	Day 64			
	Day 65 — Lesson 7 • Pages 135–140			
Week 5	Day 66 — Adventure Challenge 14 • Pages 141–142			
	Day 67			
	Day 68 — Activity 9 • Pages 143–144			
	Day 69			
	Day 70 — Activity 10 • Pages 145–146			
Week 6	Day 71 — **Write Travel Itinerary 2: Scandinavia • Page 331**			
	Day 72			
	Day 73 — Review Scandinavia • Lessons 4–7 Study Tips • Page 350 Scandinavia Map • Page 382			
	Day 74			
	Day 75 — **Quiz 2: Scandinavia • Lessons 4–7 • Pages 355-357**			

Calendar		Assignment	Due Date	✓	Grade
Week 7	Day 76	Lesson 8: "England: London" • Pages 147–156			
	Day 77				
	Day 78	Adventure Challenge 15 • Pages 157–158			
	Day 79				
	Day 80	Lesson 8 • Pages 159–164			
Week 8	Day 81	Adventure Challenge 16 • Pages 165–166			
	Day 82				
	Day 83	Activity 11 • Pages 167–168			
	Day 84				
	Day 85	Lesson 9: "Southern England" • Pages 169–176			
Week 9	Day 86	Adventure Challenge 17 • Pages 177–178			
	Day 87				
	Day 88	Lesson 9 • Pages 179–186			
	Day 89				
	Day 90	Adventure Challenge 18 • Pages 187–188			
		Midterm Grade			

Calendar		Assignment	Due Date	✓	Grade
		Second Semester–Third Quarter			
Week 1	Day 91	Activity 12 • Pages 189–190			
	Day 92				
	Day 93	Lesson 10: "Central England" • Pages 191–198			
	Day 94				
	Day 95	Adventure Challenge 19 • Pages 199–200			
Week 2	Day 96	Lesson 10 • Pages 201–208			
	Day 97				
	Day 98	Adventure Challenge 20 • Pages 209–210			
	Day 99				
	Day 100	Activity 13 • Pages 211–212			
Week 3	Day 101	Lesson 11: "Northern England" • Pages 213–218			
	Day 102				
	Day 103	Adventure Challenge 21 • Pages 219–220			
	Day 104				
	Day 105	Lesson 11 • Pages 221–226			
Week 4	Day 106	Adventure Challenge 22 • Pages 227–228			
	Day 107				
	Day 108	Activity 14 • Pages 229–230			
	Day 109				
	Day 110	Lesson 12: "Scotland" • Pages 231–236			
Week 5	Day 111	Adventure Challenge 23 • Pages 237–238			
	Day 112				
	Day 113	Lesson 12 • Pages 239–246			
	Day 114				
	Day 115	Adventure Challenge 24 • Pages 247–248			
Week 6	Day 116	Activity 15 • Pages 249–250			
	Day 117				
	Day 118	Activity 16 • Pages 251–252			
	Day 119				
	Day 120	Lesson 13: "Wales" • Pages 253–256			
Week 7	Day 121	Adventure Challenge 25 • Pages 257–258			
	Day 122				
	Day 123	Lesson 13 • Pages 259–262			
	Day 124				
	Day 125	Adventure Challenge 26 • Pages 263–264			

Calendar		Assignment	Due Date	✓	Grade
Week 8	Day 126	Activity 17 • Pages 265–266			
	Day 127				
	Day 128	Activity 18 • Pages 267–268			
	Day 129				
	Day 130	Activity 19 • Pages 269–270			
Week 9	Day 131	Lesson 14: "Northern Ireland" • Pages 271–276			
	Day 132				
	Day 133	Adventure Challenge 27 • Pages 277–278			
	Day 134				
	Day 135	Lesson 14 • Pages 279–282			

Calendar		Assignment	Due Date	✓	Grade
		Second Semester–Fourth Quarter			
Week 1	Day 136	Adventure Challenge 28 • Pages 283–284			
	Day 137				
	Day 138	Activity 20 • Pages 285–286			
	Day 139				
	Day 140	Lesson 15: "Republic of Ireland" • Pages 287–294			
Week 2	Day 141	Adventure Challenge 29 • Pages 295–296			
	Day 142				
	Day 143	Lesson 15 • Pages 297–304			
	Day 144				
	Day 145	Adventure Challenge 30 • Pages 305–306			
Week 3	Day 146	Activity 21 • Pages 307–308			
	Day 147				
	Day 148	Activity 22 • Pages 309–310			
	Day 149				
	Day 150	**Write Travel Itinerary 3: The British Isles • Pages 333–334**			
Week 4	Day 151	Review The British Isles • Lessons 8–15 Study Tips • Page 350 The British Isles Map • Page 383			
	Day 152				
	Day 153	**Quiz 3: The British Isles • Lessons 8–15 • Pages 359–361**			
	Day 154				
	Day 155	Lesson 16: "Iceland" • Pages 311–316			
Week 5	Day 156	Adventure Challenge 31 • Pages 317–318			
	Day 157				
	Day 158	Lesson 16 • Pages 319–324			
	Day 159				
	Day 160	Adventure Challenge 32 • Pages 325–326			
Week 6	Day 161	Activity 23 • Pages 327–328			
	Day 162				
	Day 163	**Write Travel Itinerary 4: North Atlantic • Page 335**			
	Day 164				
	Day 165	Review North Atlantic • Lesson 16 North Atlantic Map • Page 384			

Calendar		Assignment	Due Date	✓	Grade
Week 7	Day 166	**Quiz 4: North Atlantic • Pages 363–365**			
	Day 167				
	Day 168	Review maps and Lesson Review 1-3.			
	Day 169				
	Day 170	Review maps and Lesson Review 4-7.			
Week 8	Day 171	Review maps and Lesson Review 8-11.			
	Day 172				
	Day 173	Review maps and Lesson Review 12-15.			
	Day 174				
	Day 175	Review maps and Lesson Review 16.			
Week 9	Day 176	Review glossary words.			
	Day 177				
	Day 178	Study day for Final Exam.			
	Day 179				
	Day 180	**Final Exam • Pages 367–369**			
		Final Grade			

Before Embarking!

After the fall of the Roman Empire in A.D. 476 much of Europe plunged into darkness. Although the sun did not literally disappear from the sky, nor the stars fade from view, the world did change in ways that historians would describe as "dark."

The time of leisure and the pursuit of recreational activities so enjoyed during the Classical era had come to a screeching halt. No longer did the people of Europe have time to pursue education and scholarship, architectural advancements, or political debate. More pressing matters needed their attention . . . like survival.

The **Vikings** of Northern Europe were masters at survival as they were well adapted to living in harsh conditions, particularly the exceedingly cold, dark winters that lasted for months on end. They were forced to build sturdy homes; sew thick, insulated clothing; and prepare food in advance to survive the frigid arctic extremes.

For these reasons, the Vikings thrived during the period known as the "dark ages," emerging as a powerhouse. Not content to settle and populate the most northernmost region of the continent alone, they began to explore and raid other nations to expand their territory, wealth, and influence.

While other countries were weakening, the **Nordic** Vikings were gaining strength and momentum, soon to rule one of the largest realms the world has ever known. The countries to the east, south, and west would feel their fury. Rumors of fur-clad warriors in sleek ships invading peaceful settlements spread like wildfire throughout Europe. Could they be stopped?

In many regions, the Vikings encountered loosely organized barbarian hordes. Complete conquest for more territory was their ultimate goal, but that wasn't always possible. So if they couldn't raid, they would trade. The Vikings traded luxurious furs and sparkling **amber** in exchange for useful goods and valuables all the way down to the Black Sea.

But they encountered a different kind of valuable when they reached the British Isles. The people were different. Even though the dark pressed in around every other corner, here there shone a light that burned ever so brightly.

When the Roman soldiers abandoned England to fend for herself, missionaries stepped into the void to shine the light of the gospel. They built monasteries where students could pore over the Word of God and other great works of literature. Common people

Vikings: people group that settled northern Europe, conducting raids

Nordic: people groups of Northern Europe and North Atlantic

amber: fossilized valuable substance collected and traded by Vikings

learned to read, churches were filled with eager worshipers, and more missionaries were trained to take the light of the gospel to the far reaches of the world. There was light indeed!

You'll have to read on to find out what happened. Would the Vikings stamp out this light? Or would the light increase and spread and influence the invaders who came motivated by greed not religion?

And so, it is time to continue our explorations around God's glorious globe. Are you ready to go? I am!

Let's don our fur capes and lace up our tall leather boots as we venture into new territory with dramatic landscapes that are a reminder of God's creative handiwork: **The Baltic States** (Lithuania, Latvia, Estonia); **Scandinavia** (Finland, Sweden, Norway, Denmark); **The British Isles** (England, Scotland, Wales, Northern Ireland, Ireland); and **North Atlantic** (Iceland). I cannot wait to see what we will find there, and whom we will meet!

Come! Let's explore the Viking realms and the modern-day countries of **Northern Europe**. This journey is going to be quite an adventure!

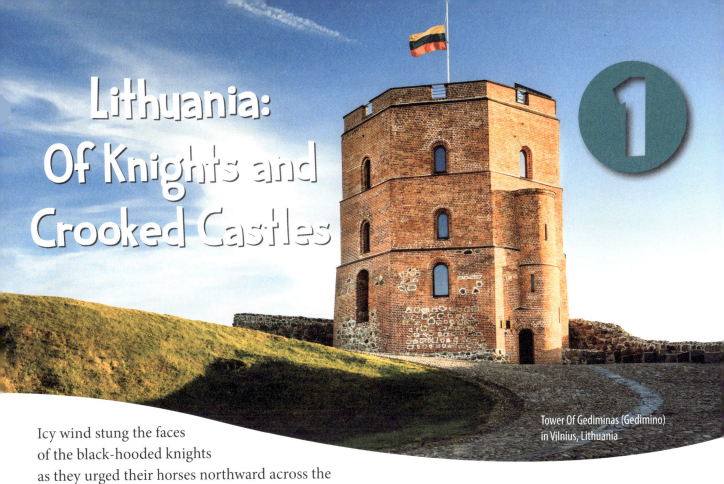

Lithuania: Of Knights and Crooked Castles

Tower Of Gediminas (Gedimino) in Vilnius, Lithuania

Icy wind stung the faces of the black-hooded knights as they urged their horses northward across the barren plain. Their next mission field was the vast and mighty empire of Lithuania. The Knights of the Teutonic Order had recently received their new assignment: convert the last **pagan** nation of Europe to Christianity or die trying. This religious mission was a daunting one — Lithuania was the largest and fastest-growing kingdom in Europe during the 13th century. Her pagan roots ran deep out of old tribal customs, Viking terrorism, and **barbarian** beliefs.

The irony of the knights' mission was not lost on these black-and-white-clad knights carrying the emblem of the cross on their **tunics**, flags, and shields. The Teutonic Order was established to save life, not destroy it. These knights were originally sent to ravaged Israel to build hospitals and attend to the wounded by nursing Christians, Jews, and Muslims alike back to health. Yet their new marching orders were clear: convert the pagans to Christianity or destroy the nation of Lithuania. With the recent death of the fierce King Mindaugus of Lithuania, leaving the empire leaderless, the knights hoped their takeover would be swift and the Christianization process easy.

pagan: a person holding religious beliefs other than those of the main world religions

barbarian: lacking social skills and manners; rough or violent

tunics: ancient Greek- and Roman-style clothing that was sleeveless and reached the knees

Present-day version of the coat of arms of Lithuania

Trakai Island Castle

The Teutonic Order: The Teutonic Order began as a military society in the Kingdom of Jerusalem around the year 1190 — a time when many Christians were taking pilgrimages to the Holy Land. This trip was very dangerous, and the knights of this order would often provide protection for the pilgrims. The Livonian Order joined the Teutonic Order and their fight.

After Christians lost control of the Holy Land, the Order began to operate in Central and Eastern Europe. They became embroiled in numerous political battles on and off the battlefield — often working to increase their own power and lands, as well as those who supported the Order.

They also initiated forced Christianization against pagans in these areas. This involved brutal oppression or death, the destruction of pagan sites, and the ruthless wiping out of any pagan worship. Often if a leader chose to become Christian, or was forced to by the knights, all the people in that area also had to become Christian.

Although these efforts brought military, financial, and political power, they did not truly save anyone spiritually. John 6:44 states, "No one can come to Me unless the Father who sent Me draws him; and I will raise him up on the last day."

A relationship with God cannot be forced. The Holy Spirit woos, or draws us, toward God. True faith comes when we realize our sin nature and choose for ourselves to truly receive Christ's gift of salvation bought by His death on the Cross. Faith forced upon someone doesn't make them believe — it only creates fear, resentment, and false displays of worship.

God doesn't want forced worship — He seeks a personal relationship with us. True faith comes from the heart that believes in Him and seeks to obey God's Word to please and honor Him.

As a military power, the Teutonic Order continued until 1810, when Napoleon Bonaparte took what was left of lands in the region. After this, the Order still existed in areas of Europe, but only as a religious order as part of the Catholic Church. In the 20th century, two world wars, as well as fascist and socialist governments, made things very difficult for the Order, yet it continues its charitable work.

The Teutonic Knights of Germany, along with cavalries from several other European kingdoms, congregated and planned their attack from the medieval fortress of Malbork in the neighboring country of Poland. The plan was simple: The horde of knights would swoop down *en mass* across the Polish plain into Lithuania using the "shock and awe" tactic of complete and utter surprise.

They were wrong. The knights' surprise attack against Lithuania turned into an all-out war, lasting over 200 years. In 1410, after the Battle of Grunwald — one of the longest and most brutal battles in medieval history — Lithuania emerged victorious, spelling the end of the Lithuanian Crusades. Lithuania came out of the war stronger and more confident than ever before. She continued her dominance in the north, conquering the surrounding nations until, ultimately, she became one of the largest countries in Europe.

In the 600 years since the Battle of Grunwald, Lithuania is no longer the largest country in Europe. In fact, she is one of the smallest. Nestled alongside the chilly Baltic Sea between Poland and Latvia, Lithuania is one of only three Baltic states. But while her land may be small, her history and culture are immense.

This great nation is where we begin our journey around the countries of the northern realm of Europe. Each of these places once served as a Viking stronghold during the Middle Ages.

So, lace up your hiking boots, strap on your backpack, and grab your camera. We have much to see and do in the beautiful, historic land of Lithuania. Let's go!

Take a peek out your airplane window. Do you see all those blue lakes? The small country of Lithuania contains over 3,000 lakes, located mostly in the east and southeast regions of the country. The capital city, Vilnius, is located in the southeast corner, where the Vilnia and Neris Rivers merge, and is within easy walking or driving distance of many of these lakes.

From this high altitude, you might also notice the many forests stretching beyond the horizon, covering over one-third of the countryside. The forested landscape gently rises and falls along the low rolling hillsides. Most of the country is comprised of low, rolling hills, none of which are very high in elevation. In fact, the tallest mountain in the "highlands" region of Lithuania is a hill at just 965 feet. It is called the Aukštojas Hill. At less than 1,000 feet, Lithuania's tallest peak is shorter than most city skyscrapers and about 100 feet shorter than the Eiffel Tower in Paris, France.

However, none of this compares to Lithuania's arguably most unique geographical feature. You can't see it from here, but soon you will have the chance to see it up close. Lithuania borders the Baltic Sea and half of its coastline sits along the Curonian Spit. A **spit** is a narrow finger of land that projects out into the water. However, this particular spit stretches from the northern coast of Kaliningrad, the Russian **enclave** that is Lithuania's southern neighbor, to the northern coast of Lithuania, forming a **lagoon**. The long spit is covered in white sand dunes — dunes high enough to slide down on sleds. Sandboarding (a.k.a. sand sledding) is a favorite pastime for Lithuanian children and is something you might enjoy as well.

Beautiful lake at Molėtai, Lithuania

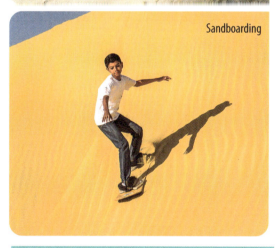
Curonian Spit

Sandboarding

spit: a narrow point of land projecting into the sea

enclave: a country, or portion of a country, that is entirely surrounded by another country

lagoon: a pool of water that is separated from the main body of water by a reef, sandbar, or other barrier

Time to buckle up and prepare for landing. We'll be arriving in Vilnius in just a few short minutes.

From the Largest Country in Europe to One of the Smallest

Medieval and Middle Ages:	✔ Lithuania was previously a Viking stronghold.
	✔ With the Crusades, the Knights of the Teutonic Order fought paganism.
	✔ The Battle of Grunwald drastically shrank the land of Lithuania.
Lithuania:	✔ Nestled between Poland and Latvia, the Baltic Sea is to the west.
	✔ The Capital city is Vilnius.
	✔ Waterways include Vilnia and Neris Rivers, along with more than 3,000 lakes.
	✔ Landscape is mainly low, rolling hills with the highest altitude being only 965 feet.
	✔ The Curonian Spit stretches into the sea and is covered in white sand dunes.

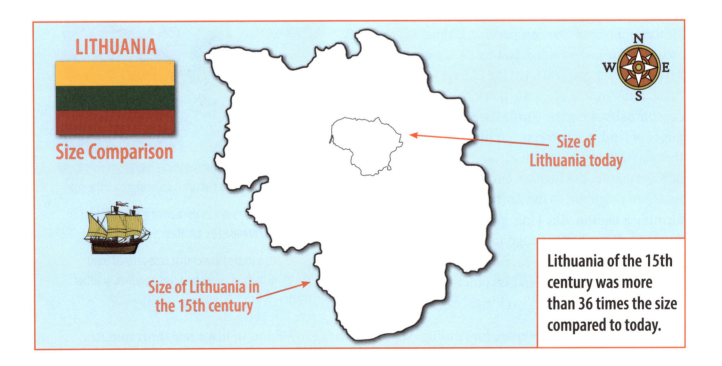

LITHUANIA

Size Comparison

Size of Lithuania today

Size of Lithuania in the 15th century

Lithuania of the 15th century was more than 36 times the size compared to today.

24 🌐 Lesson 1, Day 3

A Child's Geography. Vol. 5: Explore Viking Realms

Draw a Flag or Coat of Arms

As a person who is part of a family and community, we each have a choice of how we represent who we are and where we live.

In the blank spaces, you will either draw a flag or design a coat of arms.
(Or you may choose both!)

The Lithuanian flag has
three horizontal stripes.

Yellow = prosperity and sun

Green = land, hope, and forests

Red = courage and blood of those who have died for Lithuania

There is also a Christian flag with a cross
that you may have seen in some locations.

White = purity of faith

Blue = baptism waters and Jesus' faithfulness

Red cross = blood that Jesus shed at Golgotha

Draw a flag that represents your community, state, or country. Use colors and symbols. With your parent's permission or guidance, research to label the meaning of symbols and colors.

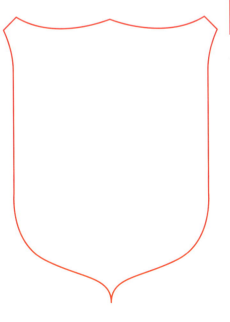

We learned about the Teutonic Order, a military power during the Middle Ages that sought control through forced religion. Like other armed troops, knights played an important role — Teutonic Knights fought in the Crusades. Influence or power can be used for either good or harm (sometimes even when it is intended to help). A knight's coat of arms — often on their shield, coat, and even horse — was a design unique to the user. It often contained symbols to represent their family. Design your own coat of arms to represent yourself as part of your family's history. Use colors to add to the design and meaning. Be sure to include a motto (saying) on the banner that reflects your family's values!

Share What You Remember About Lithuania

Answer the questions about Lithuania.

1. Why did the Teutonic Knights invade Lithuania? _____
_____

2. Was the mission successful for the Teutonic Knights when they invaded Lithuania? _____
_____

3. Who won the Battle of Grunwald? _____

4. What is one of the most remarkable geographical features of Lithuania? _____
_____

5. What is a popular recreational pastime people enjoy in Lithuania? _____

Explore Sand Dunes

Optional: Teacher's Discretion ☐ No ☐ Yes Due Date: _____

The Curonian Spit is a protected area with an abundance of sand and forest space along the coast of Lithuania. Sand dunes offer remarkable views. With the permission of your parent, explore books or online resources to learn about the Curonian Spit. Discover more about sand dunes in Lithuania and discover sites with sand dunes in your home country or beyond.

Complete the table by including the Curonian Spit in Lithuania and two locations with sand dunes from your home country or beyond. Complete each row in the table by including the name of the site, the country, and a unique feature that you find interesting.

Sand Dune Site	Country	Unique Feature
Curonian Spit	Lithuania	

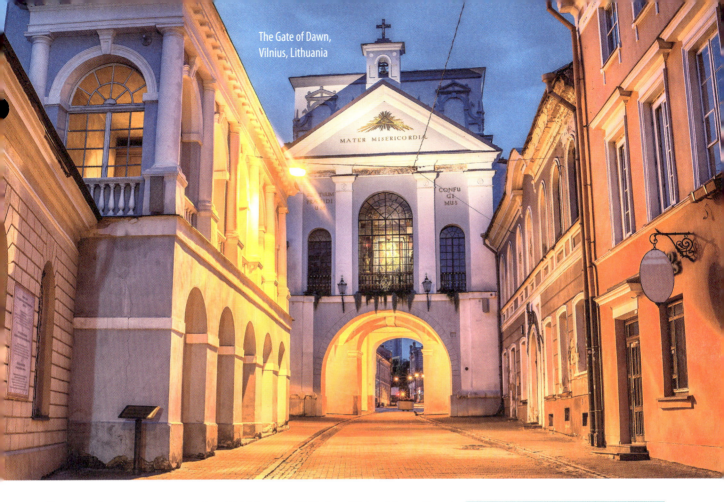
The Gate of Dawn, Vilnius, Lithuania

➜ Our adventure starts in the Old Town of Vilnius. This old medieval center inside the capital city is preserved as a **UNESCO World Heritage Site**. This means that the cultural and architectural elements are protected from destruction or misuse so that current and future generations can appreciate what medieval Lithuania was like.

UNESCO World Heritage Site: a place designated by the United Nations Educational, Scientific and Cultural Organization as a place of historical or cultural significance

We'll enter through the Gate of Dawn, the only gate remaining of the nine original gates located along the medieval stone wall that once encircled this fine city. Most of the buildings inside the wall are considered new by Lithuanian standards, having been built in the last 500 years. Before that, the town's buildings were made of wood, which meant the buildings were vulnerable to fire. The entire city center burned to the ground twice during the Middle Ages. Now the buildings are constructed with stone to better withstand natural disasters.

Interestingly enough, most of the original buildings had basements or cellars, so while the rebuilt structure above ground may only be a few hundred years old, the basement below is often much older. Many of these cellars have been converted into places where people gather, including casual eateries.

Let's walk to the top of Bleak Hill — also known as the Three Crosses Hill — where Crooked Castle stands overlooking the Vilnia River.

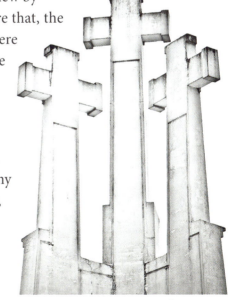
Crosses on Three Crosses Hill

Remember, all the hills are gentle here, so it isn't too strenuous of a hike. The castle is called "crooked" because its layout is awkward and misshapen. Back in 1390, Welsh raiders stormed the castle using a demolition weapon known as the **Welsh cat**. According to surviving documents, this wooden weapon was pushed close to a defensive wall and then, with its movable arm, the "cat" clawed away at the castle wall, hence the name.

Not far from here is the surprisingly beautiful Church of St. Peter and St. Paul. While it is magnificent on the outside, the exterior doesn't hold a candle to what you will see inside. If you've come along on our travels in earlier volumes of *A Child's Geography*, then you've seen many cathedrals. After a while, they may all start to look the same. But this one is unique. There is no other church in Europe that looks like this. Let's go inside!

What is perhaps most surprising about the interior of this church is its near-blinding whiteness. It almost feels as if you have ascended into the clouds when you enter the **nave**. Most of the decorative elements in the church are white, punctuated by the occasional brightly colored painting. In fact, there are thousands upon thousands of

Nave of the Church of St. Peter and St. Paul

Welsh cat: similar to a battering ram, only a Welsh cat clawed away at a defensive wall rather than ramming it

nave: the long central part of a church

pure-white stucco figures and ornamental finishes decorating the entire interior of the church. The masters who created this incredible artwork were Italian Renaissance artists, both named Giovanni. Although designed by Italians, the Church of St. Peter and St. Paul is considered a Polish-Lithuanian masterpiece of the baroque period.

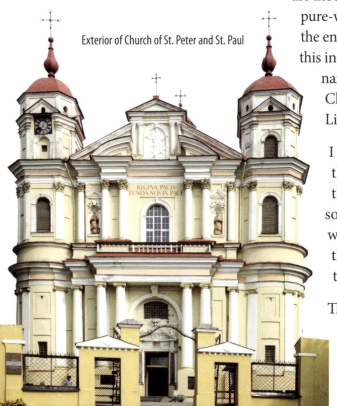
Exterior of Church of St. Peter and St. Paul

I don't know about you, but I'm famished. The only thing we've eaten today is a little package of cookies on the airplane. Let's step into this sidewalk cafe and order something to eat. We should stop at a bakery and see what delectable creations they have inside. I've heard they serve the best cappuccino in town, but maybe they'll also offer something more substantial for lunch.

The menu board reads that they serve the traditional menu of Lithuanian fare — puff pastries, yeasty buns, **kybyns**, crepes, soups, salads, and pizza. I'll have the pizza. How about you? The seating is limited, so we'll have to share a table with an older couple who are waiting for their meal. In many cultures, it is not unusual to share a table with people you do not know, especially if the seating is tight.

Kybyns

"You look like a happy lot of adventure-seekers! What's the most interesting thing you've seen today?" asks the woman in a clear British accent.

Surprised that she speaks English, we rattle on about the Crooked Castle and the Church of St. Peter and St. Paul.

She and her husband smile at the excitement we share with them.

"What brings you here to Lithuania?" I ask.

"Oh, our daughter and son-in-law live here, and we have been visiting with them and our grandchildren this past week and a half. We head home to London tomorrow."

After mentioning that we have just arrived, Mr. Scott, a European history professor, asks us if we'd like a little history lesson about the country of Lithuania.

"Yes, please!" we answer in unison as our food arrives at the table. The pizza is piping hot, so it looks like we've got plenty of time.

"Lithuania is a very old country with an exciting past." He smiles and continues animatedly, "Not much is known about Lithuania from the Dark Ages, except that it was inhabited by barbarian Baltic tribes. At that time, a powerful warlord named Mindaugas united the fragmented tribes into one country and was crowned the first King of Lithuania on July 6, 1253. He ruled for only ten years before he was **assassinated**. This was a tragic blow to the Lithuanians, who now found themselves without a leader.

kybyns: a Lithuanian pastry, often stuffed with chopped mutton or beef. However, this versatile pastry can also be filled with mushrooms, vegetables, curd, nuts, or even chocolate.

assassinate: to murder an important person in a surprise attack for political or religious reasons

crusaders: fighters for political, social, or religious causes during medieval times

The Battle of Grunwald

"Remarkably, the situation worsened. After the fall of Jerusalem in 1291, the **crusaders** set their sights on Lithuania, the last pagan territory in Europe, and now vulnerable without a strong leader. The goal of the crusade was to subdue Lithuania and convert her subjects to Christianity. That didn't turn out to be easy. Then, in 1385, almost a hundred years later, Jogaila, a Christian, was crowned king of Poland and grand duke of Lithuania. Now allied with Poland, Lithuania was finally able to defeat the Teutonic Knights at the Battle of Grunwald.

"However, Lithuania's victory did not lead to peace. Surrounding countries, like Norway and Sweden, felt threatened by the Polish-Lithuanian alliance and attacked in 1655. This series of battles became known as the Northern Wars. Less than 150 years later, there was another war — the Great North War — involving many of the same neighboring countries. And this time, Lithuania did not win. The Swedish army destroyed the land and destroyed the economy. A famine followed these two wars, then the **plague**, and then another war. Lithuania's population was reduced by 40%. Nearly half of her citizens died from battle, sickness, or starvation. Lithuania was left weak and vulnerable.

plague: a contagious disease that spreads rapidly and kills many people

"Foreign powers swooped in, divided the territory into thirds, and gave it to Russia, Prussia, and Austria (formerly Habsburg Austria). Most of Lithuania was swallowed up by Russia to the east. Unhappy with their lot, the Lithuanians protested and revolted against the Russian government. Russia fought back by closing Lithuanian schools and banning Lithuanian newspapers. The Russians believed that if they could keep Lithuania ignorant and isolated, they stood a chance at keeping her down. But their attempts to subdue the Lithuanian people failed. An underground network of book smugglers was formed, and Lithuanians began homeschooling their children in secret. How clever is that?"

We smile, because homeschooling is a topic we are familiar with.

30 Lesson 1. Day 6

A Child's Geography. Vol. 5: Explore Viking Realms

"That's really amazing! You know, some of us homeschool as well," I chime in. "It's great to have the freedom to choose how we learn rather than being forced to keep it secret."

"Really? Good for you. Then pay attention, because this is when the ping pong match starts." Mr. Scott smiles, knowing he has captured our attention again. "Lithuania was passed back and forth between Russian and German control for the next 200 years. Yes, that is a long time. It continued right up through the 20th century, the two world wars, and the **communism** of Eastern Europe. This was perhaps the darkest season of Lithuanian history.

"The ping pong match continued until 1990, when East Germany declared an end to communism in their country and the people of Lithuania were encouraged to do the same. After decades — even centuries — of oppression, Lithuania declared her independence on March 11, 1990. The Soviets tried to squelch the succession but failed. Iceland was the first nation to recognize Lithuania's independence, and the United Nations recognized the newly independent nation of Lithuania the following year."

> **communism:** a government in which all property is publicly owned and shared equally

"That's quite a history, now, isn't it?" Mr. Scott sighs, but in a satisfied history professor sort of way. He and his wife begin to stack their dishes.

As they stand and prepare to leave, Mrs. Scott smiles. "I hope you weren't too bored by a couple of old-timers like us! We've certainly got the gift of gab."

We wave goodbye and decide that it's time we too get on our way. We've got tickets to a basketball game tonight. The Lithuanians are world-renowned for their basketball teams, having won several medals at world events, including the Olympics. After the game, we'll spend the night in a small historic hotel in the town square. Tomorrow, we'll take a train west to the coast so we can see those pristine, sparkling sand dunes of the Curonian Spit for ourselves.

→ Chasing away dreams of knights in crooked castles and fanciful pastries, the sun peeks its cheery face over the horizon. We are ready for another exciting day in Lithuania. Within an hour, our packs are on, maps are handy, and stomachs are full of the delicious complimentary breakfast served downstairs. Let's ask for directions from the hotel host so we can make the most of our day.

Before stepping through the door, our host kindly tells us which train to board, which station to get off, and the best place to rent sandboards and sand sleds. Then he wags his finger at us and warns us sternly, "Now keep your eyes and your mouth closed tightly when you sled down the dunes. Otherwise, you will spit sand at the sand spit." He chuckles at his English-language pun, points us in the direction of the train station, and we are off on our next adventure.

Lithuania is a fascinating country of contradictions — old and new, somber and friendly, fiercely independent and yet blending well with the surrounding nations. Lithuania is still actively creating her own identity as a small but free country, with a unique culture and language all her own.

"*Sudie*, goodbye, Lithuania! It has been a pleasure getting to know you!"

A Ping Pong Match of a History

Landmarks:
- ✔ The remaining Gate of Dawn stands as one of the original nine gates around Lithuania.
- ✔ Known as the Three Crosses Hill, the Crooked Castle towers are at the top of Bleak Hill.
- ✔ The entire city burnt to the ground twice in the Middle Ages.
- ✔ Cellars or basements are now casual eateries.
- ✔ The Church of St. Peter and St. Paul stands out among churches in Europe.

Cultural Contrasts:
- ✔ Cuisine includes sweet pastries along with kybyns (pastries with mutton and onion).
- ✔ Although there is pagan history, Christian influences have also shaped the land.
- ✔ The defeat of the Teutonic Knights led to more fighting with the Great Northern War.
- ✔ Lithuania was bounced between Russian and German control for 200 years.
- ✔ Basketball and sandboarding both capture the interests of sports fans.

TIMELINE

1253 ▶	King Mindaugus of Lithuania crowned the first king of Lithuania.
1291 ▶	Lithuanian Crusades begin.
1390 ▶	Welsh raiders stormed the Crooked Castle using a weapon called the Welsh cat
1395 ▶	Jogaila, a Christian, became king of Poland and grand duke of Lithuania.
1410 ▶	Battle of Grunwald takes place in Lithuania.
1655 ▶	Sweden attacks Poland and Lithuania.
1795–1990 ▶	Two hundred years of back and forth between Germany and Russian occupation of Lithuania.
1990 ▶	Lithuania declares her independence.

Build a Dome

The Church of St. Peter and St. Paul in Vilnius, Lithuania, is unique in its design of awe-inspiring beauty and decor. It also shares a characteristic of some other famous churches with its dome feature. In the center of the dome at the Church of St. Peter and St. Paul, God the Father is represented, which shows us that He is omniscient, meaning He can see all. The artistic placement of God in the center of the dome reminds us to place Him in the center of our lives above all else.

Materials needed:

☐ 65 straws

☐ Scissors

☐ Tape

☐ Ruler

Although there are different variations of domes, they share architectural features that rely on engineering and math. Where have you encountered domes in photos or travels? Let's build a dome! With your parent's permission, follow the step-by step instructions about how triangles are used to construct a dome (adapted from Science Museum Group).

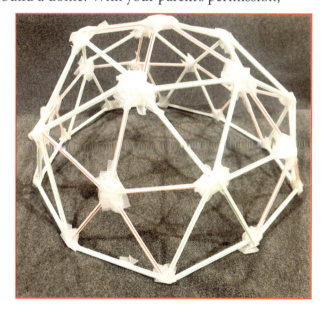

Step 1: Cut 35 straws to be 13 cm each. Cut 30 straws to be 11 cm each. Discard any straw scraps from workspace.

Step 2: With tape, attach 10 of the longer straws together to form a round shape.

Step 3: With tape, build triangles up from the base by alternating between short straws and long straws until all straws are used and a dome is formed.

Dome on the Church of St. Peter and St. Paul in Vilnius

Dome of St. Peter's Basilica in Rome

Fill in the Blank

Fill in the answers.

1. In 1655, Sweden attacks _____ and Lithuania.

2. Two hundred years were endured of back and forth between _____ and Russian occupation of Lithuania.

3. In 1990, Lithuania declares her _____.

4. King _____ of Lithuania was crowned the first king of Lithuania.

5. The year _____ was when the Lithuania Crusades began.

6. Welsh raiders stormed the Crooked Castle using a weapon called the _____ _____.

7. Jogaila, a _____, became king of Poland and grand duke of Lithuania in 1395.

8. In 1410, the Battle of _____ takes place in Lithuania.

9. Write a question about Lithuania and answer it.

   Question: _____

   _____

   Answer: _____

   _____

Share What You Remember About Lithuania

Answer the questions about Lithuania.

1. What makes the Church of St. Peter and St. Paul in the city of Vilnius so different from the "average" cathedral? _____

2. Lithuania is world famous for which sport? _____

One generation will praise Your works to another.

And will declare Your mighty acts.

– Psalm 145:4

Mapping It Out!

Complete the map of the country of Lithuania in the box below. Refer to the map on page 381.

Label the following places on your map. You can use colored pencils to shade areas of land or water, draw rivers and mountains, etc.

☐ Lithuania

☐ Baltic Sea

☐ Curonian Spit

☐ Lake Galvė

☐ Add a star ★ for the capital city of Vilnius.

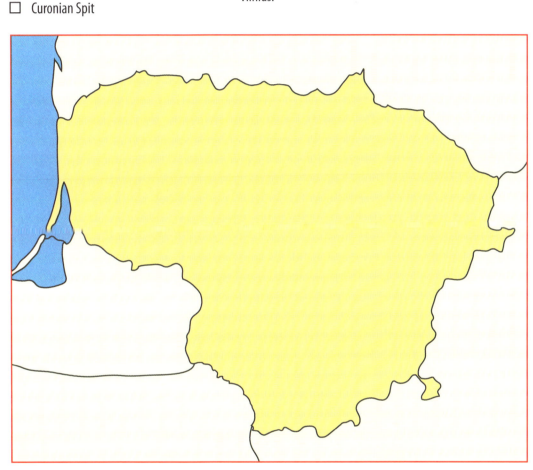

Lithuanian hound

Flashcards

Make flashcards of the bolded glossary words from this lesson. Then, add drawings of the terms. Be creative!

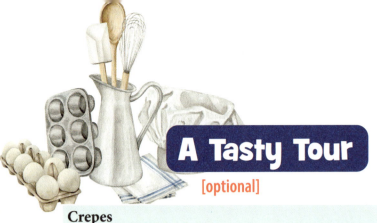

A Tasty Tour

[optional]

Crepes

Ingredients:

1 cup all-purpose flour

2 eggs

½ cup milk

½ cup water

¼ teaspoon salt

2 tablespoons butter, melted

NOTE: This recipe requires adult supervision and participation.

Optional: Teacher's Discretion

☐ No   ☐ Yes

Due Date: _____

Directions:

1. In a large mixing bowl, whisk together the flour and the eggs. Gradually add in the milk and water, stirring to combine. Add the salt and butter; beat until smooth. (Alternately, combine all in a blender.)

2. Have an adult heat a lightly oiled griddle or frying pan over medium-high heat. Pour or scoop the batter onto the griddle, using approximately ¼ cup batter for each crepe. Tilt the pan with a circular motion so that the batter coats the surface evenly.

3. Cook the crepe for about 2 minutes, until the bottom is light brown. Loosen with a spatula, turn, and cook the other side. Serve these right away, taking care not to burn yourself as you add a filling. Fill with jelly, pie filling, or fresh fruit. Top with a drizzle of chocolate sauce and whipped cream.

Learn Geography Terms

Page 342 is a reference page for understanding the terms geographers use to describe landforms.

Love Your Neighbor

We learned about the use of power that caused devastating harm during the Teutonic Order and Crusades. Let's pray for people today who have been hurt by forces in the name of religion. Let's also pray for people to experience a relationship with the One true God. Lord, please draw us closer to you. Psalm 145:21a: "My mouth will speak in praise of the LORD."

2

Old castle ruins in Cesis, Latvia

Latvia: The Great Amber Way

A quick bus ride north along the Baltic Sea whisks us out of Lithuania and into Latvia. We are tired from sandboarding but have very little time to rest before we arrive in Liepaja, a seaside resort town on the Baltic Sea. Latvia is similar to Lithuania in some ways but very different in others. I can't wait to explore it with you.

The park-like landscape of Latvia is very flat and dotted with clear blue lakes, much like Lithuania. Over half of its vast, unspoiled countryside is blanketed in dense forests of birch, oak, and pine. Latvia may be a small country in the northern Baltic region of Europe and often overlooked by her big neighbors, yet the natural beauty of this land is grand indeed. This is hiking and cycling territory with only one real cosmopolitan city, Latvia's capital city of Riga.

Baltic Sea coastline, Liepaja

Latvia is well known for its pristine white beaches, which are desolate in the winter and overcrowded during the summer. Like clockwork, Rigans and other Baltic city dwellers escape to the seashore for their summer holiday retreats.

Liepaja is our first stop in Latvia. At this time of year, the desolate beach is eerily unforgettable with its beauty as the churning waves crash upon the glistening white sand and the mournful cries of seabirds echo overhead. We are meeting new friends here today. Levi and Grace Russell, members of my parents' church, will join us at the beach before taking us on a scenic hike and later, a grand tour of their beautiful city of Riga. There they are now!

Liepaja beach

"Hello, hello!" Levi and Grace call, waving their hands to draw our attention to them sitting on a large blanket high upon the sand dunes. They jump up to meet us halfway and give us hugs even though we have never met. "It's so good to see faces from home and hear you speak native English. We have been a bit homesick lately."

The Russells are Christian missionaries in Latvia, serving the Lutheran church, which has long been established here. They both teach English in local high schools during the day and lead Bible studies at the church a couple evenings per week. Grace is expecting their first baby.

The Lutheran Church: the first Protestant church that was established in Latvia. It expanded north from Germany after Martin Luther tacked his *95 Theses* to the Wittenberg door. A number of other churches have established thriving congregations as well in the country.

"How are your parents? Please tell them hello from us. But please, come, sit down and tell us all about your travels. Where have you been so far and where are you going?" Levi asks enthusiastically.

We tell them that Latvia is our second stop and that we will be traveling all around the northern Scandinavian countries on the mainland of Europe and then the island nations of the United Kingdom and beyond. Suddenly, Grace squeals in delight. At first, we think her enthusiasm is in

response to our travel plans, yet we quickly discover it has nothing to do with our adventure, but with something she discovered in the sand.

While listening to us speak, she was moving sand with her bare feet when suddenly she hit something hard and very smooth. She lifts the yellow stone-like object from the fine white sand and polishes it on her sweater.

"It's **amber**!" she cries.

We all crowd close to appreciate her beautiful find and then pass it around to inspect for natural **inclusions**, such as an insect of some sort. No, this piece of amber is crystal clear. In fact, its honey color is translucent in the brilliant Baltic sunshine.

Grace asks us, "Do you know how amber is formed?"

"No," we answer, hoping we may get a mini science lesson right here on the beach.

Grace holds the smooth, organic gem out toward the sun and explains, "Amber is created by trees, such as those pine trees on the far side of the beach. When a tree is cut or scratched, by a woodpecker or a beaver for instance, the tree releases **resin** to protect itself, much like our bodies produce a scab when we are injured. Sometimes insects or small animals ambling by get trapped in the sticky resin. If this resin is buried, over time it can become fossilized and is called amber."

"If amber comes from trees, then why did you find this piece in the sand?"

"Strange, huh?" Levi chimes in. "But this is the most fascinating part to me. At some point in history, large glaciers moved through this region, knocking down whole forests and dragging them into the sea. Over the years, the resin fossilized and became amber. Amber floats, so once fossilized, the pieces drift to the top of the sea and eventually wash ashore. The perfect combination of vast forests and massive glaciers in the Baltic region is the reason why more amber is found here than in any other region in the world.

"In fact, amber has always played a critical role in Latvia's culture and history. During ancient and medieval times, amber found along the Baltic coast was so prized that the Vikings who lived here in the north used it to barter for riches found farther south in Greece, Egypt, and even Rome. Because of the lively and active trade of amber, the Amber Road, a major trade route in ancient times, was built."

"But you're starting to look sunburnt," Grace notices. "Let's put on our hiking boots and see some of the beautiful landscape of Latvia."

With cameras in our pockets and water bottles in hand, we set out on a trail that leads up from the beach and into the lush coastal woodlands. Under the shade of the trees, it feels cooler than on the

amber: hard, translucent fossilized resin produced by coniferous trees, typically yellowish in color. Amber has been used in jewelry since antiquity. It is found chiefly along the southern shores of the Baltic Sea; pieces often contain the bodies of trapped insects. When rubbed, amber becomes charged with static electricity: the word electric is derived from the Greek word for amber.

inclusions: a plant, insect, or other item found within amber.

resin: a sticky flammable organic substance, insoluble in water, exuded by some trees and other plants

beach, even though the temperature rarely rises above 70 degrees Fahrenheit even during the warmest months of the summer. In the wintertime, the temperature is usually below freezing, but today is a lovely day to hike through the forests of Latvia.

Black stork

Grace tells us to keep our eyes open for wildlife that, although common here, is endangered throughout the rest of Europe, such as the Eurasian beaver and the European wolf and lynx. She also tells us about some of the rare birds which live only in these Latvian woods, such as the corncrake, black stork, white-backed woodpecker, and spotted eagle. Hollow tapping sounds echo through the forest, and we look up to find woodpeckers busy at work. We also see several white wagtails, the national bird of Latvia, and daisies, her national flower.

After about an hour of hiking along wooded trails, over lazy creeks, and behind cascading waterfalls, our trail circles back around to the parking lot. And just before reaching the Russells' car, a spotted eagle soars over our heads. Its majesty is awe-inspiring. Imagine the lofty view of the dense forest, the sparkling beach, and the deep blue waters of the Baltic Sea this king of birds beholds every day!

Finding a Gem in Latvia

Outdoor Beauty:
- ✔ Latvia is known for its pristine white beaches.
- ✔ Latvia is one of the three Baltic countries by the Baltic Sea.
- ✔ Biking and hiking are well suited along Latvia's lush landscape, trails, and waterfalls.
- ✔ A variety of wildlife includes the national bird, the white wagtail.

Amber:
- ✔ The Vikings bartered with the gemstone amber.
- ✔ Amber is created from the resin of pine trees and is exceptionally known in Latvia.
- ✔ A close examination of amber may reveal inclusion of an insect within the amber.
- ✔ In the past, glaciers moved through forests, pulling them to sea, adding more amber.

40 Lesson 2. Day 11

A Child's Geography. Vol. 5: Explore Viking Realms

The Amazing Outdoors in Latvia

We learned about the landscape and wildlife of Latvia. Using the list of words with the clues provided, write the correct letter on the line to match each image.

1. _____ **Daisy** — national flower of Latvia with white petals and yellow disk

2. _____ **Black stork** — bird with long, pointed red bill and long, reddish legs

3. _____ **Eurasian beaver** — largest living rodent species native to Eurasia

4. _____ **Birch** — tree with multicolored or white bark

5. _____ **Corncrake** — bird with a short bill and long body with dark streak marks

6. _____ **White wagtail** — national bird of Latvia; small in stature and marked with gray, black, and white

7. _____ **White-backed woodpecker** — bird that uses its beak to drill holes in trees to eat sap and bugs

8. _____ **Glacier** — large body of ice that moves slowly

9. _____ **European lynx** — wildcat with spots that is native to Eurasia

10. _____ **Oak** — tree that is known for a thick, sturdy trunk and long lifespan

11. _____ **Sand dune** — tall formation of sand that is shaped by wind

12. _____ **Amber** — known for its beauty, a translucent honey-colored substance from fossilized tree resin

13. _____ **Pine** — type of evergreen tree with pine cones and no leaves

14. _____ **Waterfall** — moving water that goes over an edge to drop to a waterway below

15. _____ **European wolf** — thick-furred mammal with a bushy tail; typically lives in a pack (group)

Fill in the Blank

1. The rare gem _____ can be found along the coast of Latvia and is formed from tree _____.

2. The Bronze Age refers to the materials created from various objects, such as tools and jewelry, from stone and _____.

3. The Eurasian beaver is an endangered mammal in Latvia along with the European _____ and _____.

4. Some _____ are endangered in Latvia: corncrake, black stork, white-backed woodpecker, and spotted eagle.

5. Latvia has been invaded by various countries through the years, including Poland, Sweden, and _____.

Blessed be the LORD God, the God of Israel,
Who alone works wonders.
And blessed be His glorious name forever:
And may the whole earth be filled with His glory.
Amen and Amen.

—Psalm 72:18-19

View of the old city of Riga

→ The road to Riga is short, flat, and straight as an arrow. The capital city lies a little more than a meter above **sea level** on a flat and sandy plain. Riga is not only the largest city in Latvia, it is also the largest city in all the Baltic states combined, with over 600,000 inhabitants. About a third of all Latvians live in this historic city situated on the southern shore of the Gulf of Riga.

The city of Riga is well over 800 years old. It began as a Viking fishing village but grew into an important trading center. Situated at the mouth of the Daugava River, the Vikings traded amber and other valuables up and down the Daugava-Dvina-Dneiper river system all the way to Greece and the Byzantine Empire thousands of miles to the south.

> **sea level:** the average height of the sea's surface; often used as the baseline for measuring elevation
>
> **bishopric:** led by bishop; diocese

During the 12th century, crusaders were dispatched to Christianize the pagans, and in 1200, Bishop Albert arrived with 23 ships and 500 crusaders to establish Riga as the new seat of the Livonian **bishopric** by force. In plain language, the leaders of the church invaded the town of Riga and made it a new capital for the Christian Church. This declaration was made in the year 1201, and that year is now considered Riga's founding date, even though it existed and thrived for many, many years prior to that event.

"How do you like our city?" Grace asks from the front seat.

"First stop is the city center!" Levi announces. "It is so well preserved that the entire center is listed as a UNESCO World Heritage Site. It's truly beautiful. In fact, Riga was officially recognized as a European Capital of Culture. We are proud to call it our 'home away from home.'"

After parking the car, we wander through the old quarter, admiring the historic buildings, some dating back to the 13th century when Riga joined the **Hanseatic League**, a community of merchant guilds that formed their own set of laws to ensure free trade among the cities of Northern Europe. Riga provides a striking contrast of old and new architecture laced with lush green public parks filled with people and their pets enjoying this bright spring day. It's a perfect day for a picnic. At the outdoor market, we buy Latvian black bread, smoked fish, smoked Gouda, strawberries, and a paper sack filled with *biezpiena sierins*, a sweetened cheese curd snack. Now we have all the essentials for the perfect Latvian picnic!

Hanseatic Seal

Out on the green lawn, soaking up the warmth of the waning sun, our gracious hosts tell us more about the Latvia we are learning to love.

Latvia's past has not been a peaceful one. After the crusades, the pagans of Latvia were Christianized and modernized for the times. Fortifications such as ramparts and town walls were built to protect Riga and the nearby communities, after which peace and prosperity abounded for a few hundred years, until the Reformation. The majority of Latvians protested the Catholic Church and embraced Protestantism. However, this left the country divided and therefore weak. And so began the invasions. First, Poland invaded, followed by Sweden, and finally Russia.

Hanseatic League: group formed to protect and control trade

The first Russian occupation of Latvia lasted just over 200 years from 1710 to 1917. During the first few years under Russian control, more than 40% of all Latvians died from either famine or plague. At the end of the 200 years, the territory of western Russia, which included the state of Latvia, had been devastated by World War I. With a weakened Russian Empire and the general chaos of the war's aftermath, Latvia declared its independence from Russia in 1918. However, her independence didn't last long.

Latvian black bread

In 1939, the Germans and Russians made a secret agreement to divide the countries of northern and eastern Europe into two "spheres of influence." Latvia, along with the other Baltic states, was assigned to Russian control. Two years of misery and devastation passed under the dictatorship of Russia. Not surprisingly, neither Germany nor Russia kept their end of the bargain and were soon fighting it out for countries previously assigned to the other party. First, they fought over Poland, then, in 1941, fought

Biezpiena sierins

over Latvia. Germany prevailed, placing Latvia under equally miserable domination, as Germany's goal for Latvia was to reduce her population by 50%.

Under both countries' regimes, over 200,000 Latvians were either deported or killed, including 75,000 Jews who were murdered in Nazi **extermination camps**. The end of the Second World War brought no less hardship. Once again under the control of Russia, hundreds of thousands of terror-stricken Latvians fled to Sweden and Germany for **refuge**.

Thankfully, this story is coming to a happy ending. Fifty years after Russia's second occupation and **sovietization**, Latvia regained her independence in 1991. Latvia was finally free to rule herself once again! Today, many Russians still live in Latvia, but the Latvian language is the national tongue, and the traditional Latvian culture that existed before the Russian occupation is being slowly restored. The last hundred years have been extremely difficult and tragic for this small country, but Latvians are a strong and resilient people, rising from the ashes of domination and despair to become a beautiful, welcoming country, with Riga serving as her crowning capital of culture.

"That's a depressing history, isn't it?" asks Levi. "It may seem so very different from your own country's history if yours has experienced freedom for many hundreds of years. But it is a history that we must learn so that we, as citizens of God's world, do not repeat such mistakes or commit such atrocities going forward. How about we walk back to the square and get some ice cream before we drive to our apartment?"

Oh yes, we are happy to jump up from the grass and get some exercise after our delicious picnic. After topping off the meal with some refreshing ice cream and additional sightseeing through Riga's old town, including St. Peter's Church and the Riga Cathedral, we hop back into their car and drive to the Russells' third-floor apartment not far from the city center.

extermination camp: a type of prison where many people are held, often under terrible conditions

refuge: a condition of being safe or sheltered from pursuit, danger, or trouble

sovietization: under the control and influence of the Soviet Union

City Hall Square with House of the Blackheads and St. Peter's Church

Latvian black bread

We talk late into the night about their work here in Latvia and their future plans to return to the United States sometime in the next year or two. Grace and Levi have classes to teach tomorrow, so they give us their best tips for what else to see before we leave Latvia to drive north to Estonia.

Turaida Castle

There are some lovely medieval castles they insist we see. One is Turaida Castle, which is not far from Riga. The other place they insist we visit is the town of Cesis, one of Latvia's oldest townships. Running through its charming city center are cobbled lanes lined with historic wooden buildings and a few impressive castles.

As we drift off to sleep on mattresses laid out on the Russells' living room floor, we are thankful for new friends, the beautiful countryside, an exciting city in which to spend the night, and delightful plans to continue our explorations tomorrow.

Oh Latvia, neither tragedy nor triumph can hold you down, fade your inner beauty, or destroy your tenacious spirit. May your hard-fought and well-earned independence last for many centuries to come!

From Vikings to Castles and More

Travel Log

Riga:
- ✔ It began as a Viking fishing village well over 800 years ago.
- ✔ Known as a location for trade, the Vikings traded amber and other items of value.
- ✔ As the capital of Latvia, it is on a sandy plain barely above sea level.
- ✔ Located on the southern shore, it is located along the Gulf of Riga.
- ✔ It is the largest city in Latvia and in all the Baltic states.
- ✔ The Turaida Castle and other castles are nearby.

Struggle for Freedom:
- ✔ Latvia faced control from the Crusades.
- ✔ Other countries invaded, including Poland, Sweden, and Russia.
- ✔ Plague and famine struck the land between the early 1700s into the early 1900s.
- ✔ After a German battle with Russia, Germany gained control of Latvia.

TIMELINE

1800 B.C. ▶	Maarahvas build fort settlements.
1201 ▶	Bishop Albert claimed Riga, Latvia, as the new capital for the Christian Church.
1710 ▶	Russian occupation of Latvia begins.
1917 ▶	Russian occupation of Latvia ends.
1918 ▶	Latvia declares her independence from Russia.
1941 ▶	Germany conquers Latvia.
1991 ▶	Latvia regains her independence.
2014 ▶	Riga recognized as a European Capital of Culture.

Fill in the Blank

1. Soviet control and influence, called _____, was a result of occupation.

2. In the year _____, Latvia regained her independence.

3. Originally a Viking fishing village, Riga is the capital city and is at the mouth of the

    _____ River.

Take a Hike!

Optional: Teacher's Discretion   ☐ No   ☐ Yes Due Date: _____

With your parent's permission or guidance, take a foot hike or virtual hike to explore an outdoor space in nature. Discover some of the types of wildlife and the landscape. Also, search for resin on trees.

1. Take photos to document your discoveries or create a drawing on paper. (Or you may try both!)

2. Write what you located.

Materials needed:

☐ Camera
or
☐ Colored pencils
☐ Paper of your choosing

Wildlife	
Landscape	
Evidence of resin	

Design a Latvian Folk Outfit

Traditional Latvian clothing may be described as folk costume attire that relates to a region. The styles have adapted through time and in different areas of Latvia. For example, the fabric was once flax and fleece. After German influence, materials were a cross between knitting or crocheting, called needle-binding. Then, linen became a popular choice.

Belts with designs set the fashion for both men and women in Latvian folk clothing. Bold choices of jewelry are also included. (Remember the trade during the Bronze Age? Jewelry at that time was often made of bronze.) Women's attire is marked by more vibrant colors of reds, yellows, greens, and oranges with stripes sometimes used for skirts. Vests or shawls help layer for warmth. Men's choices often include blacks, browns, dark blues, and muted tans.

In the images, observe the details of hats, boots, belts (or sashes), and other elements of design. Note how intricate patterns create a bold, distinctive look.

Design, draw, and color a Latvian folk costume.

48 Lesson 2. Day 16

A Child's Geography. Vol. 5: Explore Viking Realms

Read and Reflect

The people of Latvia struggled for many years after being invaded and controlled by outside forces. The Book of Psalms expresses words of disappointment, frustration, or a call to the Lord for help. At other times, the Psalm reflects songs or poems of praise and thanksgiving. Psalm 77 is a song of comfort in times of difficulty that also remembers God's mighty works.

Observe: Some translations include the Hebrew word *selah* (meaning to pause or reflect) in the right margin of some chapters of the Psalms.

Read Psalm 77 in the Bible. Then answer the questions.

In what verse does the song turn from one of grief and mourning to one of remembering the works of God? _____

What is one of the verses that describes the mighty power of God's creation? Write it out.

_____

_____

_____

_____

When is a time that you have experienced anger or disappointment?

_____

_____

_____

_____

For what can you give thanks to God?

_____

_____

_____

_____

_____

Dārte Lutheran Church, Latvia

Mapping It Out!

Complete the map of the country of Latvia in the box below. Refer to the map on page 381.

Label the following places on your map. You can use colored pencils to shade areas of land or water, draw rivers and mountains, etc.

☐ Latvia

☐ Cesis

☐ Liepaja

☐ Gulf of Riga

☐ Daugava River

☐ Add a star ★ for the capital city of Riga.

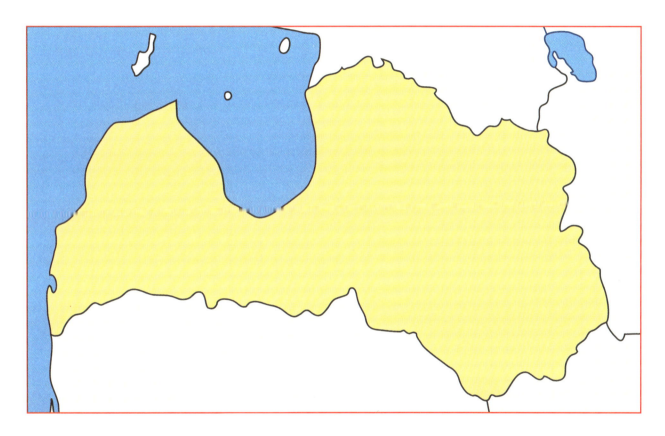

Flashcards

Make flashcards of the bolded glossary words from this lesson. Then, either add drawings of the terms or act them out in charades. Be creative!

Latvian hound

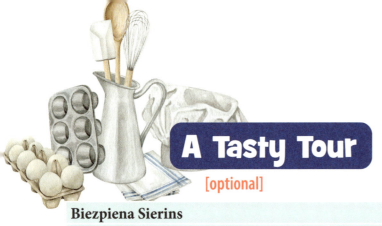

A Tasty Tour

[optional]

Biezpiena Sierins

Ingredients:

2 cups cottage cheese

5 tablespoons powdered sugar

1 tablespoon melted butter

½ teaspoon vanilla

For glaze:

8 oz dark chocolate

¼ cup butter

NOTE: This recipe requires adult supervision and participation.

Optional: Teacher's Discretion
☐ No   ☐ Yes   Due Date: _____

Directions:

1. Combine the first four ingredients. Mixture should be quite thick. If soupy, squeeze out extra liquid using a cheese cloth or add graham cracker crumbs. Either roll into balls or press mixture into molds then chill in the refrigerator for 3 hours.

2. Once cheeses are chilled, melt the chocolate and butter in a double boiler or in the microwave.

3. Dip cheeses into the melted chocolate using a fork or a large toothpick and return to the refrigerator for 30 minutes more.

4. Enjoy!

Trade and the Amber Road

The European Amber Road was a well-established trade route for the precious gem of amber.

With a marker or highlighter, trace the route of the European Amber Road, noting the importance of Riga, Latvia, for the trade of amber.

Material needed:

☐ Marker or highlighter

The European Amber Road

Talk About It

Talk with your family or a friend about today's trade or commerce.

Conversation starter ideas:

Locate 5 items in your home and see if you can determine their origin.

Identify objects that are created by someone in your home or community.

Describe something that is of great value to you or your family.

Learn Geography Terms

Page 342 is a reference page for understanding the terms geographers use to describe landforms.

Love Your Neighbor

As we explored Lithuania and now Latvia, we learned about the long struggle for independence both countries endured. Even today, while we are citizens of this world, we remember that Ephesians 2:19 says, "So then you are no longer strangers and foreigners, but you are fellow citizens with the saints, and are of God's household." This reminds us that through the Spirit of God, we have His citizenship available to us. Lord, we thank You for Your eternal kingdom of true, eternal peace and citizenship. We pray for those in this world who struggle for freedom in their lands, and we pray that all people may fully know You.

On the glorious splendor of

Your majesty

And on Your wonderful works,

I will meditate.

—Psalm 145:5

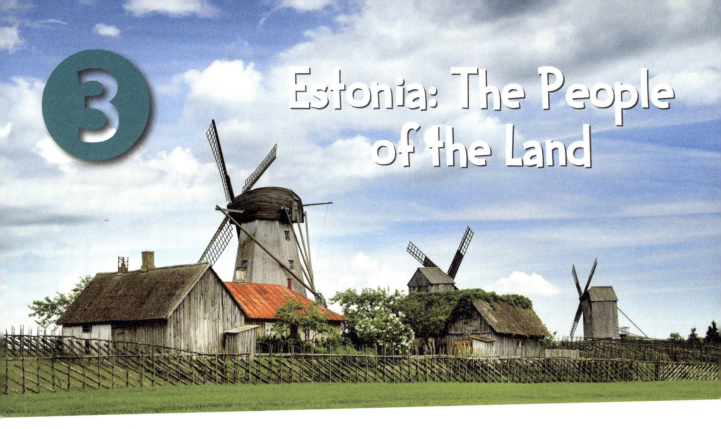

3 Estonia: The People of the Land

After a thrilling day exploring several dark and drafty castles around the Latvian countryside, we scoot across the northern border of Latvia and arrive in Pärnu, a seaport city in Estonia. It's been a long day; I suggest we grab some dinner so we can turn in early. Over dinner, I can bring you up to speed on Estonia's history before we drift off to sleep in our hotel and begin our adventures anew tomorrow.

The word "Estonia" comes from an ancient Scandinavian saga, and it means "east land." But the earliest Estonians did not use this word to describe themselves or their land. They referred to themselves as *maarahvas,* which means "country people" or "people of the land," and they called this region Maavald, meaning "Country Parish." The maarahvas were not a Baltic Tribe, like the ancient peoples of Lithuania and Latvia; they were a people of Finno-Ugric descent, which means they were more closely related to the Finnish people and other northern tribes who lived west of the Ural Mountains.

The ancient maarahva people fished in the deep blue waters off the coast and along the icy glacial streams flowing off the mountains for their survival. They also hunted bear, beaver, and wolf for their meat and ultra-warm fur.

The Bronze Age: In history, you will often read about different ages like the Stone Age, the Bronze Age, and others. These periods represent estimated time periods that are known by the kinds of materials that were being used at the time. Before the Bronze Age, people created all sorts of objects from stone. When bronze was discovered from a mix of melted tin and copper, it became the predominant material used by a number of civilizations.

Not everyone discovered bronze at the same time. The knowledge of it could have taken some civilizations longer to discover or even be aware of its existence. That is why terms like "Bronze Age" represent a general period of time versus a very exact one.

We know in the Bible that before the Flood, there were tools made of bronze and iron (Genesis 4:22). Some also think that when the people groups left Babel, not all may have had the skills or the materials to create metal tools in the areas they resettled and so may have had to rely on using stone tools for a time.

Around 1800 B.C., the maarahvas began to build fort settlements for their tribes upon the higher hills, which were surrounded by single and multi-family farms. The hill forts, led by a group of elders, were called "parishes." Artifacts from the Bronze Age have been discovered that tell a small piece of their story — that they lived in harmony and traded frequently with their western neighbors across the Baltic Sea and with their southern neighbors in Germany.

Eventually, relations with their neighbors turned sour as the once peaceful tribes around the Baltic Sea prepared for battle. Several Scandinavian sagas tell tales of war — especially the one about how the Estonians defeated and killed King Ingvar of Sweden.

A few years later, barbarian hordes from Russia poured in and defeated the Estonians, establishing a Russian foothold in the region now known as Tartu. This foothold in Estonia lasted about 30 years, until the Estonians counterattacked in 1061 and sent the invaders running back to Russia. While the Vikings are traditionally thought to have only resided in Scandinavia, Iceland, and Greenland, Vikings also dwelt in the Baltic region. And it was at this time that the era of the mighty Baltic Vikings had officially begun.

The fearsome Vikings ruled the land and sea of the north. Tales of their might and destruction swept through medieval Europe like a plague. The Danes tried to stamp out the Estonians but were unsuccessful. In 1199, Pope Innocent III ordered a crusade from faraway Rome to establish Christianity as the dominant religion way up here on the northern fringe of Europe. The German Livonian Brothers of the Sword were dispatched from nearby Poland and Lithuania in 1208 to tame the wild Vikings of Estonia. After ten years of raiding and counterraiding, the Estonians suffered defeat at the Battle of St. Matthew's Day and their leader of the resistance, Lembitu, was killed.

Ivangorod Fortress on the Narva River

The surrounding countries jumped into the fray, and with the help of the Danes and Swedes, the Vikings of Estonia were subdued in 1227 by the crusaders.

Following the crusade, the territories of present-day Estonia and Latvia were merged and named Terra Mariana, later renamed Livonia, until Estonia reclaimed her original name back in the 18th century. The king of Denmark would now rule Northern Estonia, while the remaining regions were divided up between the Knights of the Teutonic Order, simultaneously receiving their new identity as the Sword Brothers of the Livonian Order, which was formerly Livonia Brothers of the Sword.

The crusade was unsuccessful in bringing about peace, as wars against foreign powers continued for generations. However, it did bring about the founding of Reval, now named Tallinn, the capital city of Estonia. Reval joined the Hanseatic League that controlled trade on the Baltic Sea and became a powerful ally with the other towns in the league farther south, bringing some organization out of the chaos of the Baltic region during the Middle Ages.

Livonia Brothers of the Sword: A German Catholic military order created in the 12th century by the Bishop of Riga, the Livonian Brothers of the Sword was formed. They became the military presence in what is now Latvia and Estonia. The Livonian Brothers, like the Teutonic Order, were essentially warrior monks who fought pagan tribes and crusaded to turn these populations into Christians.

To join the Livonian Brothers of the Sword, each knight promised to be obedient and not to seek personal wealth, among their other vows. Founded in 1202, their ranks were decimated in 1236 in the Battle of Schaulen. Those who survived became an autonomous (independent) part of the Teutonic Order of Knights the following year.

Many of the pagan practices eventually died out over time or were ended in some areas sooner by the zealous efforts of the knights. Today, the majority of Latvians identify as Christians, though religious oppression and state atheism in the 20th century helped contribute to continued low attendance at churches.

You look sleepy. Let's get some rest and we'll see what adventures tomorrow holds for us. Close your window and pull down the shade. The sea breeze smells nice, but it is getting chilly outside. We are very far north here in Estonia. That's why it's still light outside at such a late hour. But even in summer, the nights can get quite cold. Grab an extra blanket from the closet so that you can stay nice and toasty warm throughout the night. See you in the morning.

———◆———

And a good morning it is! Pulling back the heavy curtains, we welcome the bright sunlight into the room. With the window now cracked open, we can hear boat horns off in the distance and the screech of seagulls overhead. What an exciting day we have ahead! Let's pack up our things quickly so we can catch the morning ferry that will take us out to the island of Saaremaa.

Estonia has over 1,500 islands, but Saaremaa is the largest of them all. The islands have a culture all their own. Let's begin our Estonian explorations there.

Driving aboard a ferry can take some time. For the crew, it is like putting together a giant jigsaw puzzle. They must make sure all the cars, trucks, and trailers fit perfectly on the car decks and that the cargo load is correctly balanced. Hot chocolate and coffee are available for passengers in the cabin. Grab a cup and let's climb the stairs to find seats near a window so we can see the island as we approach. We say a quick prayer of thanks for our hot drinks as we find a perfect spot at the bow of the ship to enjoy the 60-mile journey from Pärnu to Kuressaare, the only city on the island.

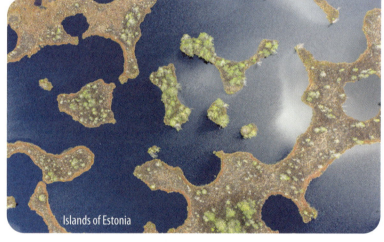
Islands of Estonia

Lighthouse on the island of Saaremaa

Saaremaa in Estonian means "island land" or "the land on the island." From the way the Estonian people refer to themselves and their land, they are either extremely matter of fact or have a very dry sense of humor. We may discover they are both by the end of today's journey.

According to archaeological finds, people have been living on this island for thousands of years. In fact, pre-Viking era ships have been found on Sörve Peninsula. This particular ferry will not head out into the Baltic Sea at all for this leg of the journey but will stay within the more placid Gulf of Riga. The island of Saaremaa with its long Sörve Peninsula provides a protective barrier between the gulf and the sea, which created an ideal location for a network of busy fishing villages to emerge during ancient and medieval times.

Aerial photo of Pärnu

Hands down, the most exciting event that occurred on the island during ancient history was the fiery collision of nine meteorites into the earth near the town of Kaali. Imagine going about your everyday business, when the sky explodes overhead with the entry of several meteorites from outer space, violently slamming against our planet just outside your town. It must have been a frightening experience. Those meteorites that crashed into the ground left nine large craters on the island. Scientists estimate that this event occurred sometime around 1500 B.C.

Meteorite crater in the village of Kaali

Windmills on Saaremaa Island

There's Saaremaa ahead! We'll be there soon. As we pull into port, notice the working windmills on our left. Those windmills have been in operation for hundreds of years. Aren't they both rustic and magnificent at the same time?

Because of Saaremaa's unique location and isolation from the mainland, the island has retained a great deal of medieval charm. The closer we get to shore, the more clearly you will see the stone fences separating individual homesteads and the thick thatched roofs capping the centuries-old stone cottages that dot the coastline. The islanders' lives have been bound to the sea for as long as

Guests from Overseas by Nicholas Roerich

people have lived here. Much of what you see here is the result of hardworking families whose womenfolk toiled the land while their men were out to sea, fishing and fighting.

Tribal sagas retell stories of ancient battles between the islanders and other Viking tribes around the Baltic Sea, unfolding the details that led to either glorious victory or agonizing defeat. The island of Saaremaa was the wealthiest region of ancient Estonia because it was the home of the notorious Estonian Pirates, sometimes referred to as the Eastern Vikings. One such tale recounts a landmark event when a fleet of 16 ships carrying 500 Estonian Pirates landed on the shores of southern Sweden, which belonged to Denmark at the time, who then pillaged and plundered the area, carrying even more wealth back to Saaremaa.

These Vikings, like all Vikings, were an adventurous people who not only thoroughly explored the northern region of Europe but also discovered many new lands to the west, such as Iceland, Greenland, and parts of North America. Around the year A.D. 1000, a notorious Viking named Gunnar Hámundarson of Iceland journeyed back to Europe and participated in a grand-scale raid on tiny but rich Saaremaa. It was on this island that he obtained his favorite weapon, the **atgeir**, by taking it from a man who was defending his home.

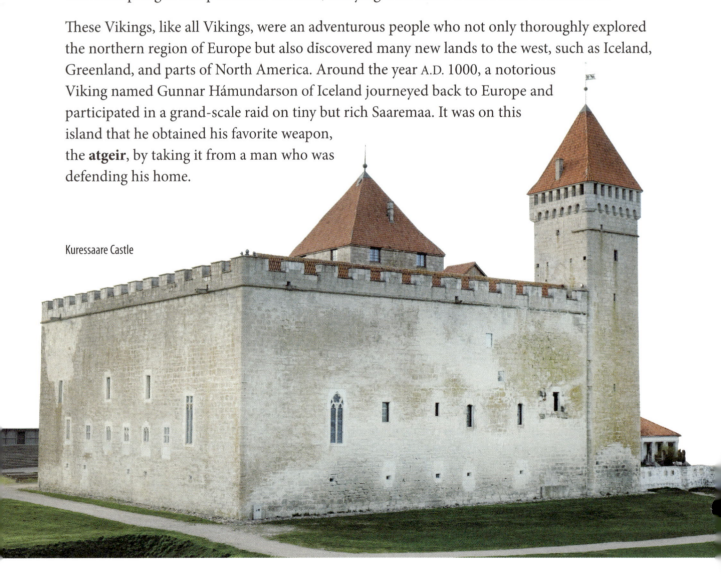
Kuressaare Castle

60 Lesson 3. Day 21

A Child's Geography. Vol. 5: Explore Viking Realms

From the 14th to 16th centuries, the people of Saaremaa began to move away from the island to escape frequent pirating raids and find more peaceful habitation on the mainland. However, the entire country of Estonia has been fought over for centuries as Denmark, Sweden, and Russia fought to claim it. For a long time, there truly was no peaceful region of Estonia to retreat to. Even in more recent times, the people of Saaremaa fled their island, crossed the gulf, and established villages along the western and northern coasts of mainland Estonia.

atgeir: a type of polearm, or spear-like weapon, used during the Viking Age in Scandinavia and Norse colonies in the British Isles and Iceland

After wandering through the old city center of Kuressaare and meandering through its medieval castle, we'll drive east on Highway 10 to witness the meteorite craters for ourselves. The sheer size and magnitude of the craters are evidence of the catastrophic crash and violent shaking of the earth that must have happened upon impact. It's rather mindblowing to see evidence of this rare and frightening phenomenon. The intensity of meteorites is a reflection of God's almighty power over all.

On the far side of this island is a smaller island called Hiiumaa, which is also accessible by ferry. While Saaremaa is famous for its windmills and craters, Hiiumaa is known for its lighthouses. Both islands are sparsely populated, which allows us to enjoy the unspoiled nature found in this part of the world.

Besides the towering lighthouses, there is another unique site on the island of Hiiumaa called the Hill of Crosses. However, it's not much of a hill. The Hill of Crosses is more like a small rise of earth with rustic, homemade crosses set in the ground. It also happens to be located right along the road we are traveling! The first crosses date back to 1781 when Tsarina Catherine II forced the Swedes

Aerial view of the city of Tallinn

living on this island to resettle in the Ukraine. This site marks the place where the Swedish residents spent their last evening on the island, making crosses and worshiping the Lord. Since then, every visitor is encouraged to build a crude cross and stake it into the ground here on this "hill."

Would you like to make a cross to stake into the ground as proof that you too have been here?

We have one more day in Estonia and we'll spend it in the capital city of Tallinn. Both islands — Saaremaa and Hiiumaa — have airports with quick hopper flights to the capital. Once we board, we'll be there in no time at all.

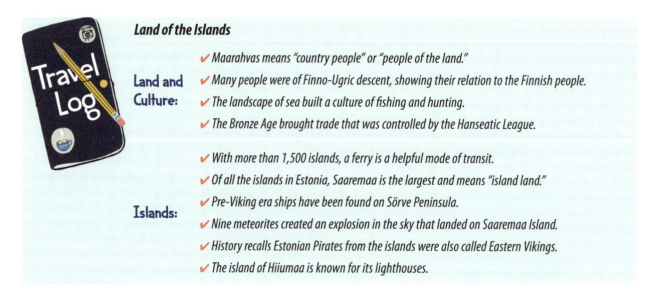

Land of the Islands

Land and Culture:

✔ *Maarahvas means "country people" or "people of the land."*

✔ *Many people were of Finno-Ugric descent, showing their relation to the Finnish people.*

✔ *The landscape of sea built a culture of fishing and hunting.*

✔ *The Bronze Age brought trade that was controlled by the Hanseatic League.*

Islands:

✔ *With more than 1,500 islands, a ferry is a helpful mode of transit.*

✔ *Of all the islands in Estonia, Saaremaa is the largest and means "island land."*

✔ *Pre-Viking era ships have been found on Sörve Peninsula.*

✔ *Nine meteorites created an explosion in the sky that landed on Saaremaa Island.*

✔ *History recalls Estonian Pirates from the islands were also called Eastern Vikings.*

✔ *The island of Hiiumaa is known for its lighthouses.*

62 Lesson 3. Day 21

A Child's Geography. Vol. 5: Explore Viking Realms

Draw Crosses

Do you remember the Hill of Three Crosses in Lithuania made from concrete? At the Hill of the Crosses on the Island of Hiiumaa, Estonia, crosses are made from natural materials, such as sticks, branches, twigs, hay, and bark.

Hill of Three Crosses (Lithuania)

Hill of Crosses (Estonia)

Draw either the Hill of Three Crosses in Lithuania or the Hill of Crosses in Estonia.

Short Answer

Answer the questions.

1. What does maarahvas mean?

_____

2. What does Saaremaa mean?

_____

3. What catastrophic event happened on the island of Saaremaa approximately 3,500 years ago?

_____

Make Craters with Meteorites

We learned about the meteorites that struck the island of Saaremaa nine times. When a meteor strikes ground, it is called a meteorite, and it often makes a crater on the surface. Now it's our turn to create mini-meteorites that make craters.

1. Fill the large pan with flour about one inch deep and smooth the top.

2. With a sifter, dust the top of the flour with the dry cocoa or dry pudding mix.

3. Drop or throw a "meteor" (candy, nut, or small fruit piece) into the pan.

4. Experiment with throwing or dropping different shapes and sizes of "meteors" into the pan at different angles, speeds, and distances.

Take time to clean up the space when you are finished!

Adapted from *Scientific American*.

Materials needed:

☐ Large pan with edges

☐ 4–6 cups flour

☐ 1 cup dry cocoa powder or dry pudding mix

☐ Pieces of candy, nuts, or small fruit pieces

☐ Sifter

Write about your observations about the meteor craters.

What I observed: _____

Angle: _____   Speed: _____   Distance: _____

What I learned: _____

Tallinn at sunrise

→ That was a quick flight with little time to rest! The weather is perfect today in the capital city of Estonia — warm enough to be outdoors most of the day but cool enough to wear a sweater. Let's explore.

Tallinn is a new name for an old city. It was established in 1248 by the Danes and originally given the name Lyndanisse, then later, Reval. As with the rest of the Baltic states, Estonia was at one time under Danish, then Swedish, rule, but after the Great Northern War, the Russians gained control and kept it for 200 years. In 1918, Estonia declared her independence from Russia and renamed her capital Tallinn, which means "Danish town," possibly in honor of her roots. Interestingly, the word *Tallinn* in Estonian can also be translated to mean "snow fortress." Independence was short-lived; however, it was later regained in 1991.

St. Olaf's Church

Tallinn is the oldest capital city in Northern Europe and, despite the political upheaval this region has experienced over the centuries, has never been attacked, pillaged, or bombed. For this reason, her old town, encased within a thick medieval wall, is perfectly preserved.

Let's walk across the ramparts and through the wide gates of Old Tallinn. See there? That is St. Olaf's Church with its skyscraping spire stretching toward the heavens. St. Olaf's was possibly the tallest building in the world from 1549 to 1625. According to legend, the steeple has been hit by lightning at least ten times and it may have been even taller before it was reconstructed. Shall we go inside?

This church reflects Estonia's religious history. It was named for King Olaf II of Norway, who lived during the tenth century; after his

Estonia: The People of the Land

death, he was honored as a **saint**. St. Olaf's was originally a Roman Catholic Church. But when the Reformation swept through Europe in the 1500s, Estonia protested against the Catholic Church, along with many other European countries, and this church became Lutheran. In 1950, it became a Baptist church.

Kiluvõileib

Since it's a beautiful sunny day here in Tallinn, let's not hide inside. Even though there are many museums we could visit and old buildings we could wander through, I suggest we get some lunch at an outdoor cafe to experience something one can only experience in Estonia. Would you like to try an Estonian delicacy known locally as *vürtsikilud*, or spicy sprats? Sprats are small silvery fish found in the Baltic Sea, marinated in a mixture of black pepper, allspice, cloves, nutmeg, coriander seeds, bay leaves, salt, and sugar.

Marzipan creations

The best way to enjoy *vürtsikilud* is to order *kiluvõileib*, an open-faced sandwich on dark rye bread layered with butter, sprats, hardboiled eggs, and red and green onions. It's delicious! The world's largest *kiluvõileib*, created here in Tallinn's Town Hall Square in 2014, was 20 meters (over 65 feet) in length.

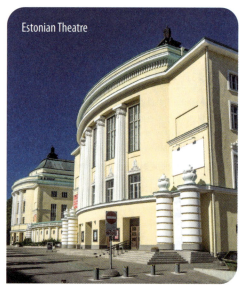
Estonian Theatre

Tallinn has also created some of the largest **marzipan** structures in the world. Marzipan is a sweet confection made from two basic ingredients — sugar or honey, and almond meal made from ground almonds. The marzipan industry in Tallinn began long ago during the Middle Ages, but it was originally sold as a medicine. Eventually, it became popular to mold the putty-like dough into an edible decoration to adorn a dessert or be rolled thin to top a celebration cake for royalty and commoners alike. Medieval marzipan crafters typically molded miniature imitations of fruits and vegetables, but today's artisans create larger and more unique creations, such as a 26-pound (12 kilogram) model of the Estonian Theatre.

This afternoon, we are going to do something you've likely never done before. Our destination is about an eight-mile drive outside of town — the

saint: a person who is holy and set apart for God's work; or canonized by the Catholic Church

marzipan: a sweet, yellowish paste of ground almonds, sugar, and egg whites, often colored and used to make small cakes or confections

Kõnnu Suursoo bogs of Estonia. A **bog** is a stretch of wet, spongy ground with soil that is composed mainly of decayed vegetable matter. Wooden pathways have been built so that visitors can walk through the bogs without getting wet and dirty. But that sounds tame, doesn't it? Let's try something a little more invigorating — **bog-shoeing**. We'll get to strap on shoes that resemble snowshoes, but — created from rubber — are especially suited for getting soaked in the bogs. With bog-shoes on, we won't have to follow the path.

Kõnnu Suursoo bogs

Bog shoes

After trekking a short distance into the forest along the narrow, two-plank-wide path, we come to a perfect place for strapping our bog shoes over our rubber boots and gingerly lowering ourselves down into the marshy bog. As we wobble and mush our way through the bog, our guide, Urmas, tells us that without bog shoes, we would surely sink right down into the muck. Yuck! Urmas is an enthusiastic guide as he tells us about the mosses and lichen found in the bog that Estonians use to make a tea to soothe sore throats, and about the wild tart cranberries that can be found growing in the muddy swamp. God's created world has an abundance of beauty and purpose. We can be thankful for all that He provides us!

bog: wet, muddy ground too soft to support a heavy object or body. It is a wetland that accumulates peat, a deposit of dead plant material. Other names for bogs include mire, quagmire, muskeg, and fen.

bog-shoeing: wearing special footwear so as to walk along the top of the bog without sinking into it

Urmas points to a tower with a flag waving in the distance and tells us that is our destination. Then he tells us this story:

"Two bog rangers were staring up the flag pole, scratching their heads. A really old farmer in his really old truck pulled up and asked them, 'What's the problem, boys?' One of them answered, 'Our boss wants us to measure the height of the flag pole, but we cannot climb up this skinny pole.' The farmer walked back to his truck to fetch a monkey wrench and a tape measure. He loosened a couple bolts, lowered the pole to the ground, and then measured it. 'Seven and a half meters, my friends.' Then he picked up his tools and drove away. The bog rangers looked at one another and laughed. 'What was he thinking? We wanted the height, and he gave us the length.' "

Urmas looks at us intently, his eyes twinkling, but he doesn't smile. We do, though, because Americans, like Estonians, enjoy a good joke.

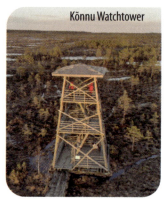
Kõnnu Watchtower

After our strenuous hike sloshing through the murky bog, we find another plank trail, which leads us back to the Kõnnu Watchtower. A climb up several flights of stairs to the top of the tower provides us with an incredible view of the vast wetlands as the sun dips low in the western sky. The bog lands stretch as far as the eye can see. One can literally bog-shoe for days before coming out the other side.

Estonia is a curious country of contrasts. Her people are straightforward yet funny. Her land is untamed and wild yet has experienced oppression for all but 20 years of the past millennium at the hands of the Danes, Swedes, Russians, and Germans. Her history, similar to Latvia's, could have crushed her culture, yet it has not diminished the Estonian people. The heart of Estonia is lovely, full of light, laughter, and song. She is as beautiful as a delicate snowflake yet as strong as a glacier. She is beauty indeed.

Miles and Miles of Bogs

Tallinn:
- ✔ Tallinn is the capital city and was previously called Reval and originally Lyndanisse.
- ✔ "Danish town" is the meaning of Tallinn.
- ✔ As the oldest capital city in Northern Europe, it preserves its medieval history.
- ✔ It's been said that St. Olaf's Church has been struck by lightning 10 times or more.
- ✔ Museums and old buildings fill the landscape of the area.

Food and Fun:
- ✔ A favorite food delicacy is spicy sprats, also called vürtsikilud.
- ✔ Kiluvõileib is a spicy sprat served on an open-faced sandwich with eggs and green onions.
- ✔ Sprats are marinated small silvery fish from the Baltic Sea.
- ✔ The marzipan industry started making sweet treats in the Middle Ages.
- ✔ Bog-shoeing is similar to snowshoeing except that it is across wet, spongy ground.

 TIMELINE

1800 B.C. ▶	Maarahvas build fort settlements.
1500 B.C. ▶	Nine meteorites crash into the island of Saaremaa in Estonia.
1000 ▶	A Viking named Gunnar Hámundarson of Iceland raids the island of Saaremaa in Estonia.
1061 ▶	Estonians prevail against barbarian invaders from Russia.
1199 ▶	Pope Innocent III orders a crusade to Estonia to establish the Christian Church in the north.
1208 ▶	A crusade is dispatched to subdue the Vikings in Estonia.
1227 ▶	Crusaders defeated the Estonian Vikings.
1248 ▶	The capital city of Estonia, Tallinn, is established by the Danes.
1549–1625 ▶	St. Olaf's Church in Tallinn is the tallest building in the world.
1918 ▶	Estonia declares her independence from Russia.
1991 ▶	Estonia again declares independence.

Short Answer

Answer the questions.

1. The tallest building in the capital city of Tallinn was once the tallest building in the world between 1549 and 1625. What is it?

   _____

2. What is a bog?

   _____

   _____

   _____

3. Instead of walking on the wooden planks, we can walk through it wearing what type of shoes?

   _____

Matching

In front of each vocabulary word, write the correct corresponding letter for each definition.

1. _____ atgeir
2. _____ saint
3. _____ bog
4. _____ marzipan

a. holy person set apart for God's work
b. a type of polearm, or spear-like weapon
c. small cakes or confections made from almond paste
d. wet, muddy ground too soft to support a heavy object

Write a Song of Freedom

25th Estonian Song Celebration, 2009

Like her neighbors, Estonia fought for freedom for more than 200 years. Leading up to gaining independence in 1991, the Estonian Song Festival was started in 1869 to gather and sing songs that expressed a longing for independence. Estonians continue the tradition of gathering to sing and celebrate freedom.

A line from one Estonian freedom song, "One Day No Matter What," is "The desire for freedom crackling in our hearts like flames in the fireplace."

A line that is in the Estonian freedom song "Dawn" is "Song, our song of victory, will resound."

A line from the Estonian national anthem, "My Fatherland, My Happiness and Joy," is "My native land, my joy – delight."

Often tied to political freedom is spiritual freedom. Before World War II, a large majority of people in Estonia identified as Christian, but the Soviet occupation and resulting efforts weakened the influence and growth of the faith. Sadly, today, a small portion of Estonians identify as Christian or consider religion as something important in their life.

We are reminded in Galatians 5:1 that "It was for freedom that Christ set us free; therefore keep standing firm and do not be subject again to a yoke of slavery."

Write your own lyrics to describe what spiritual freedom means to you.

_____

_____

_____

_____

_____

_____

_____

_____

_____

_____

Optional: Teacher's Discretion ☐ No ☐ Yes Due Date: _____

With a parent's permission, locate an Estonian freedom song on video or audio online and listen.

Mapping It Out!

Complete the map of the country of Estonia in the box below. Refer to the map on page 381.

Label the following places on your map. You can use colored pencils to shade areas of land or water, draw rivers and mountains, etc.

☐ Estonia

☐ Pärnu

☐ Saaremaa Island

☐ Hiiumaa Island

☐ Gulf of Riga

☐ Lake Peipus

☐ Add a star ★ for the capital city of Tallinn.

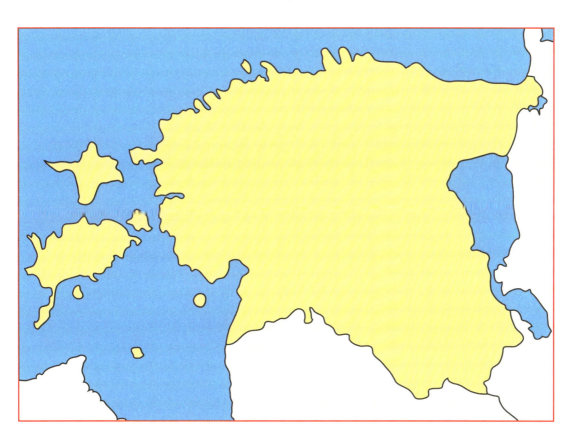

Estonian hound

Flashcards

Make flashcards of the bolded glossary words from this lesson. Then, either add drawings of the terms or act them out in charades. Be creative!

A Tasty Tour

[optional]

Marzipan

Ingredients:

2 cups almond flour

1 cup granulated sugar

¼ cup plus 2 tablespoons water

1 egg white, lightly beaten

1 teaspoon of almond extract

½ teaspoon of rose water or orange blossom water

Confectioner's sugar as needed

NOTE: This recipe requires adult supervision and participation.

Optional: Teacher's Discretion

☐ No   ☐ Yes

Due Date: _____

Directions:

1. In a pan, gently heat sugar and water over medium heat, stirring constantly, until sugar is dissolved. Stop stirring and bring to a boil, brushing down the sides of the pan with a wet pastry brush to wash down stray sugar crystals. Increase the heat to medium-high and boil until the syrup reaches 238° F (116° C) on a candy thermometer. Remove from heat and stir until syrup becomes slightly cloudy.

2. Stir in the ground almonds. Add lightly beaten egg white and return to low heat, cooking gently for a minute or two until the marzipan firms up slightly. Remove from heat and mix in orange blossom water and almond extract.

3. Turn out marzipan onto a work surface dusted with confectioner's sugar. Let sit until cool enough to handle. Knead until smooth and pliable, kneading in a few tablespoons of confectioner's sugar as needed if mixture is too sticky. Knead in color and flavor while still warm.

4. Store marzipan and finished candies wrapped in plastic wrap or wax paper, refrigerated in a airtight container or zip-top bag, for up to 1 month, or frozen for up to 6 months.

Learn Geography Terms

Page 342 is a reference page for understanding the terms geographers use to describe landforms.

Love your neighbor

As we conclude our time in the Baltic states, or countries of Lithuania, Latvia, and Estonia, let's pray for the people! We pray for the bakers in Vilnius, sandboarders, historians in Riga's city center, bikers, hikers, museum guides, and anglers around the island of Saaremaa. Thank you, Lord, for creating each person. Genesis 1:27 reminds us, "So God created man in His own image, in the image of God he created him; male and female He created them."

72 Lesson 3. Day 28

A Child's Geography. Vol. 5: Explore Viking Realms

4

Finland: King of the Wood

Old Town pier in Helsinki

Having boarded another ferry, this one from Tallinn to Helsinki, we are now crossing the Gulf of Finland to the great northern country it was named after. This is the same journey that thousands of Jewish Estonians traveled during World War II when they fled German-occupied Estonia to escape the horrors of the Holocaust. Thankfully, many Jewish families found refuge and safety in their neighboring country of Finland.

If we were flying in an airplane at a 30,000-foot altitude, we would be able to see that Finland is a land of thousands and thousands of lakes — 188,000 lakes to be exact. It has 179,000 islands offshore with the greatest concentration of rocky outcroppings, large and small, located between southern Finland and Åland in the Archipelago Sea off the southwest coast of Finland.

When you think of Finland, what comes to mind? Ice caverns and palaces, glaciers and frozen lakes, long nights and dark days. Finland has all these things, but this is just the tip of the iceberg, so to speak. Finland is cold, yes, but it is so much more than a frozen landscape. In fact, you will be surprised to learn that Finnish summers can be quite hot because of an intriguing phenomenon happening

Aulanko Observation Tower, Hameenlinna, Finland

deep down in the ocean by a gigantic current. Finland is close enough to the Atlantic Ocean to be warmed by the **Trans-Atlantic Gulf Stream**.

The Gulf Stream current carries warm water up from the equator, which then cools while it is up north before its return to the southern hemisphere. With warm water swirling out at sea, Finnish summers are more than pleasant. They can be unusually hot, even if they are short compared with other regions that share the same latitude on the globe, such as Alaska, Siberia, and Greenland.

Finland, one of the world's most northern countries, lies between latitudes 60° and 70° north. In fact, Finland's capital of Helsinki is the second-northernmost capital in the world, lying south of Reykjavík, Iceland, alone.

Trans-Atlantic Gulf Stream: a warm and swift Atlantic ocean current that originates in the Gulf of Mexico and stretches to the tip of Florida, and follows the eastern coastlines of the United States and Newfoundland before crossing the Atlantic Ocean

The ferryboat is pulling into the massive harbor of Helsinki now. It is dwarfed by the huge cruise ships that look like floating cities and the gigantic cargo ships loading and offloading their goods. Finland is the largest producer and exporter of wood in Europe and one of the largest in the world as well. That means that shiploads of pine, spruce, and birch logs are being transported across the world from this port. Of the total land area of Finland, 10% is covered by lakes, rivers, and ponds, and nearly 80% is blanketed by **taiga** forests. That leaves just 10% of the total area that isn't water, **fen**, or forest.

A friend of mine lives in Finland. Her name is Anya, and she's going to show us around her beautiful country. Anya trained in the United States to become a world-class pole vaulter. She has won many international competitions, but she no longer competes in her sport. Today, she runs her own business, which manufactures and sells natural cosmetics. She is the face and model for her own company's product line.

"*Hei*," Anya waves from the dock as we alight from the ferry. "Shall we drive in your car or mine?" she asks.

We agree to follow her in her car to the city center and then begin our tour from there.

taiga: the sometimes swampy coniferous forest of high northern latitudes

fen: a low and marshy or frequently flooded area of land

We park in a parking garage and then come out into the daylight alongside a beautiful city park dotted with large evergreen and deciduous trees. Anya opens her arms wide and says, "Welcome to Finland and my hometown of Helsinki! Let me show you around."

As we stroll through the park and along the chic waterfront streets of downtown Helsinki, Anya proudly shares a little history and Finnish culture with us.

"One out of five Finns lives here in the capital city, which is actually built on a network of 316 islands. That's why there are so many bridges! Finland is the least populated country in Europe yet one of the largest by land area."

Cold in the Winter and Unusually Hot in the Summer

Land and Resources:

✔ There are 188,000 lakes and 179,000 islands in Finland.
✔ In the summer months, there is a warming effect from the Trans-Atlantic Gulf Stream.
✔ Lying between latitudes 60° and 70° north, it is one of the most northern countries.
✔ Helsinki is the capital.
✔ It is one of the largest exporters of wood in the world with nearly 80% of land in taiga forests.

Navigating the Land:

✔ As one of the largest land countries in Europe, it is the least populated country in Europe.
✔ Bridges and islands help with navigating the landscape of lakes and islands.
✔ During the Holocaust, Jewish Estonians fled German-occupied Estonia across the Gulf of Finland.

Helsinki was built on many islands.

Exports and the Economy

Just south of the Arctic Circle, taiga forests are made of thick growths of pine, spruce, and birch trees. According to figures from the United Nations, in 2022, exports related to wood from Finland were over $4 billion.

Exports are products sent to another country for sale.

Imports are products or services brought into a country from another.

An example of a product is an object, such as wood. An example of a service is a type of work performed, like telecommunications (transfer of information electronically).

Trade surplus is when the value of a country's exports is greater than the imports.

Trade deficit is when the value of a country's imports is greater than its exports.

As you can likely guess, a trade surplus can be beneficial to a country's economy. One part of achieving this is to have popular or in-demand services and products to export. Other things influence trade, such as trade agreements and currency rates. Simply put, when a nation has a trade surplus, it is because of positive net exports — a higher amount gained on exports than spent on imports.

1. Use the list of Finland's exports to fill in the chart.

2. In the second column, label the export amount for each item from highest to lowest. Include the name of the good in the first column.

3. Total the amount and complete the answers that follow the chart on the next page.

Finland's Exports

Wood — $4.3 billion
Woodpulp — $3.01 billion
Plastics, plastic articles — $3.05 billion
Machinery, including computers — $10.3 billion
Vehicles — $5.1 billion

Paper, paper items — $8.1 billion
Iron, steel — $6.8 billion
Electrical machinery and equipment — $7.2 billion
Optical, technical, and medical apparatus — $3.6 billion
Mineral fuels, including oil — $9.5 billion

Top 10 Finland Exports for a Year

Exports	U.S. Dollar Amount

1. Total export for a year = _____ billion U.S. dollars

2. If Finland imported more value in products than it exported, it would have a trade

   _____.

3. If Finland exported more value in products than it imported it would have a trade

   _____.

In the past, Vikings often bartered (or traded) for valuables, including amber, iron, and, sadly, even slaves. Eventually, Vikings traded silver and Arabic coins to buy goods, which had also expanded to pottery, jewelry, cloth, and more.

Fill in the Blank

Fill in the blanks to answer the question or complete the sentence.

1. Does Finland have more lakes or islands? _____

2. The Trans-Atlantic Gulf Stream carries warm water up from the _____,

   which cools in the northern hemisphere and then returns to the southern hemisphere.

Sea in a Bottle

Finland's shoreline is at the Baltic Sea. Finland is surrounded by the Gulf of Bothnia, Gulf of Finland, and Archipelago Sea. Let's create a sea in a bottle!

Materials needed:

☐ Small pitcher with two cups of water
☐ Mixing spoon
☐ Empty water bottle with cap (label removed)
☐ Funnel
☐ Blue food dye
☐ Baby oil
☐ Glitter (optional)

1. Add some blue food dye to pitcher and stir.

2. Place the funnel on the water bottle and slowly fill the water bottle halfway with the blue water. Place the cap on the watter bottle.

3. Set the water bottle aside for a few minutes until any bubbles disappear.

4. Using the funnel if needed, fill the water bottle to the top with baby oil.

5. When you turn the bottle on its side and move it, you will observe what appear to be waves.

78 Lesson 4. Day 36

A Child's Geography. Vol. 5: Explore Viking Realms

→ "According to archaeological evidence, the history of Finland dates back thousands of years," Anya tells us. "It was settled during the Stone Age when the last sheet of ice receded from the Ice Age. Various stone tools and pottery have been found in and around Helsinki, like the artifacts found in neighboring Russia and Sweden.

"But we Finns are nothing like the Russians or the Swedes, just so you know. In fact, we have a saying, 'We are not Swedes and we do not want to become Russians, let us therefore be Finns.' Yes, we are a very proud and independent people."

Anya tells us that the name *Finland* comes from *finlandi*. This word was carved into three ancient stones discovered in the area. The name refers to an old northern tribe known as the Finns, pre-dating the Vikings. The Finns dwelt here 2,000 years ago, around the same time Christ walked upon the earth.

"Later, Swedish kings gained more power in the north and Swedish-speaking settlers colonized this entire region during the Middle Ages. Most Finns began to speak Swedish, the dominant language of the nobility, and Finnish was cast out to be spoken only by peasants. Thankfully, the Finnish language has been revived, and 90% of all Finns now speak their native tongue once

Finland: King of the Wood

again. Finnish is completely unrelated to Swedish and the other Scandinavian languages. It is more like Hungarian and considered to be as difficult to learn as Chinese.

"Over the centuries, the people of Finland have worked hard to create their identity as separate and unique from our closest neighbor, Sweden. However, Finland has many times been caught in the middle of skirmishes between Sweden and our other next-door neighbor, Russia, twice falling into the hands of Russia during the 18th century. Finns refer to these times as the Greater Wrath (1714–1721) and the Lesser Wrath (1742–1743). It is estimated that an entire generation of young men was lost during the Greater Wrath, due to the mass destruction of homes and farms, as the Russians razed Helsinki and the surrounding countryside to the ground.

The Attack. The Russian double-headed eagle is attacking the maiden symbolizing Finland, tearing a law book.

"Finnish nobility and peasants alike had had enough of being caught in the middle. Due to Sweden's and Russia's repeated use — or shall I say, abuse — of Finland as a battlefield, Finland declared her independence from both."

Anya stops walking suddenly and spins around to look at us. "All this talk of wars and arguments is making me hungry. Let's grab a bite to eat before I show you the real Finland. The 'behind-the-scenes' Finland," Anya says with a wink.

"This is one of my favorite places to take my cosmetic buyers to lunch. They have a good beef dish that is served with a creamy mushroom sauce. It's delicious. There are several types of fish to choose from as well. But I think the reason why I like this restaurant so much is because they serve the best

Aurora borealis (northern lights) over Finnish Lapland

80 Lesson 4. Day 38

A Child's Geography. Vol. 5: Explore Viking Realms

coffee and Finnish pastries. They make a yummy cardamom coffee bread. I also really like the cloudberry tart; it's heavenly and tastes great with their coffee! Did you know that Finns drink more coffee per capita than any other country in the world?

"After we finish our meal, I have the rest of the day planned out for us," Anya smiles. "I would like to take you up to my house to meet my family. It is about an hour drive north of here. Most days I work from home, which I love, but our house is close enough to Helsinki for the days when I do need to drive into the office for work. My husband, Jan, and our two teens, Aava and Mattic, would love to meet you. Plus, I have a Finnish tradition to show you!

"In the United States, it seems there are many neighborhoods or backyards with swimming pools. That is not the case here. Finns only like to swim in heated indoor pools. As you can imagine, most families can't afford one or don't have the space needed to build one inside their home, but most Finnish homes have a built-in sauna.

"The sauna is a Finnish invention. In case you have never seen one, it is a small room or outbuilding designed to warm you up quickly. Saunas can deliver wet or dry heat, but the purpose of the high heat and steam is to cause you to sweat. Finns believe that perspiration leads to better health and longer life.

Finnish sauna

"Healthwise, the Finns believe that saunas are good for cleansing the body of toxins and relieving symptoms of the common cold or reducing other pain and discomfort in the body. Saunas are also used for social gatherings. Families gather in the sauna to spend time together several times a week. Friends congregate at one another's homes and enjoy conversation in the sauna.

Patch of cloudberries

"Would you like to experience a Finnish sauna?"

"Oh, yes!" we reply. "That sounds like a perfect thing to do while we are in Finland."

"Perfect, we'll drive to my home after we finish eating. We have a guest room, and I would love it if you could stay the night. Tomorrow my family will be going berry picking. It is a favorite activity of ours. There is a farm near our home where we can pick our own berries — lingonberries, bilberries, cloudberries. Then, perhaps we can make a cloudberry tart from the berries we pick!

Cloudberry tart

My daughter, Aava, is an excellent baker. I'm sure we can talk her into a little Finnish baking lesson for you before you leave."

What an incredible opportunity! Make note of this: Whenever you are offered the gift of spending time in a friend or relative's home in another country, do take it. While our world can feel awfully big sometimes, and Finland can feel extremely far away when we look it up on the globe, spending time in a new place allows us to notice the uniqueness of other cultures while enjoying the similarities of our hearts.

God bless you, Anya, for giving us a unique, inside glimpse of Finland.

A Sauna in Finland Does Sound Relaxing!

Influences:
- ✔ Before the Vikings, a tribe called the Finns populated the area.
- ✔ Finland came from finlandi, referring to a tribe that existed when Jesus walked the Earth.
- ✔ Due to the influence of Swedish kings, the Swedish language was spoken by nobles.
- ✔ People were often squeezed in the middle of skirmishes of Russia and Sweden.

Behind the Scenes:
- ✔ Cloudberry tarts and cardamom coffee bread are enjoyed with coffee.
- ✔ Finns drink more coffee per capita than any other country in the world.
- ✔ Saunas are a Finnish invention believed to cleanse the body of toxins and relieve health symptoms.

TIMELINE

1714–1721 ▶	Greater Wrath
1742–1743 ▶	Lesser Wrath

Introduce Yourself in Finnish

Let's try introducing yourself in Finnish. Begin by slowly reading the following introduction aloud and inserting your name. The word "hei" is pronounced "hey" and "tu" is pronounced "too."

Hei, minun nimeni on [your name].
(Hi, I'm [your name]).

Hauska tutustua.
(Nice to meet you.)

Now practice it three more times at a slow pace.

And try it three more times.

And again three times!

Keep practicing!

Say it aloud to a parent or someone around you.

Finnish Lapphund

Fill in the Blank

Fill in the blanks.

1. The two countries of _____ and _____ used Finland as their battleground.

2. Finns drink more _____ per capita than any other people group in the world.

3. The sauna was invented in Finland because it is believed to lead to better _____ while requiring less space than an indoor _____.

4. Write a question about Finland and answer it.

   Question: _____

   _____

   Answer: _____

   _____

Personal Journal

The people of Finland championed having their own culture, free from the control and influence of Russia and Sweden. Write about yourself and what describes you. This can include your faith and beliefs, the country or location you live in, and your unique personality.

_____

_____

_____

_____

_____

_____

_____

_____

_____

_____

_____

_____

_____

_____

_____

_____

_____

_____

_____

_____

Throughout the Bible, there are reminders of having our identity in God for those who follow Him.

See how great a love the Father has given us, that we would be called children of God: and *in fact* we are.

For this reason the world does not know us: because it did not know Him.

—1 John 3:1

Mapping It Out!

Complete the map of the country of Finland in the box below. Refer to the map on page 382.

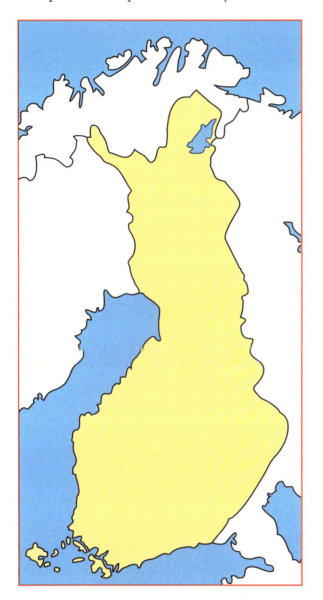

Label the following places on your map. You can use colored pencils to shade areas of land or water, draw rivers and mountains, etc.

- ☐ Finland
- ☐ Gulf of Finland
- ☐ Archipelago Sea
- ☐ Gulf of Bothnia
- ☐ Turku
- ☐ Vaasa
- ☐ Rovaniemi
- ☐ Kuopio
- ☐ Add a star ★ for the capital city of Helsinki.

Finnish
Lapphund
puppy

Flashcards

Make flashcards of the bolded glossary words from this lesson. Then, either add drawings of the terms or act them out in charades. Be creative!

Love your neighbor

As the people of Finland wrestled for freedom, they wanted their own identity. Lord, we thank you for letting us choose to have our identity in you. We also thank you for your love. John 3:16 tells us, "For God so loved the world, that He gave His only Son, so that everyone who believes in Him will not perish, but have eternal life." Thank You for sending Your Son, Jesus.

Learn Geography Terms

Page 342 is a reference page for understanding the terms geographers use to describe landforms.

Lapland Finland

86 Lesson 4. Day 41

A Child's Geography. Vol. 5: Explore Viking Realms

Trans-Atlantic Gulf Stream Map

Complete the activity by labeling and coloring the map.

Materials needed:
☐ Colored pencils

1. Color in green and label the continents of North America, South America, Europe, and Africa.

2. Color in blue and label the Atlantic Ocean.

3. Label and circle Finland.

4. Draw in red and label the Trans-Atlantic Gulf Stream.

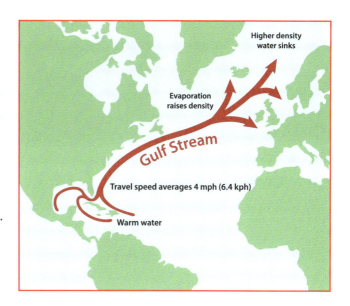

The Trans-Atlantic Gulf Stream affects the weather in Finland. Observe its pattern and effects on regions.

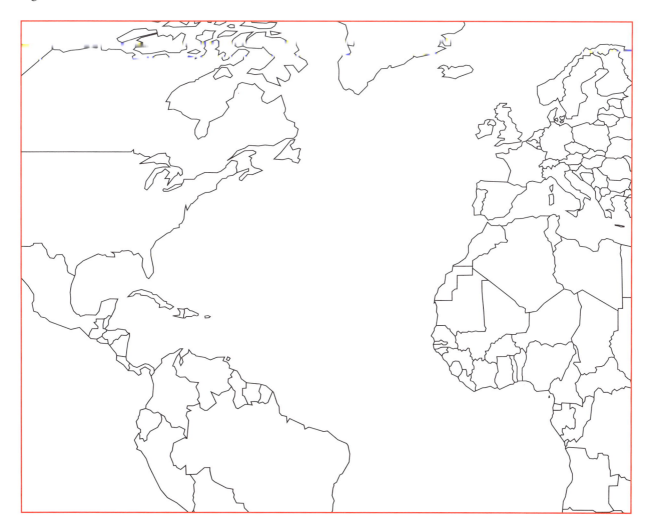

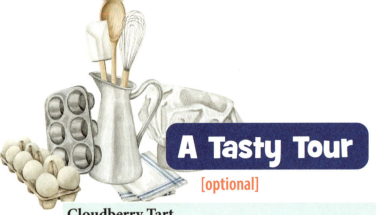

A Tasty Tour

[optional]

Cloudberry Tart

Ingredients:

Two pre-baked pie shells

Batch of pastry cream

2 cups cloudberry gelatin puree (or a pre-made raspberry pie filling, low-sugar jam, or gelatin)

2 cups of whipped cream

½ cup of whole berries

A sprig of mint

NOTE: This recipe requires adult supervision and participation.

Optional: Teacher's Discretion
☐ No   ☐ Yes   Due Date: _____

Directions:

1. Divide pastry cream equally between two tart shells (you may have leftovers); smooth surface and chill 30 minutes, or more.

2. Gently spoon half the puree over pastry cream on each tart; smooth surface and chill 2 hours.

3. Decorate each tart with whipped cream (pipe from a pastry bag), fresh berries, and mint. If presenting whole, mound cream in middle, piling berries on top of each, garnishing with mint OR plate each slice with a dollop of whipped cream, garnishing each with berries and mint.

88 🌐 Lesson 4. Day 43

A Child's Geography. Vol. 5: Explore Viking Realms

5

Sweden: The City Between the Bridges

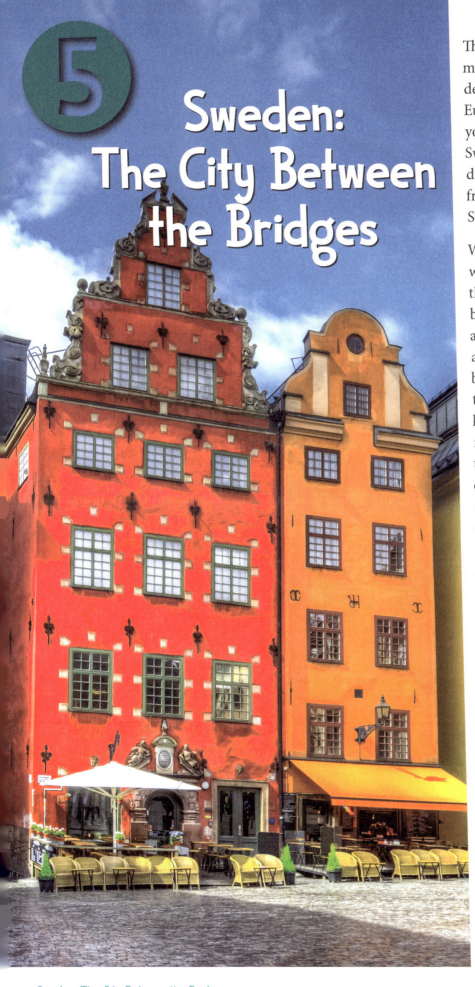

The beautiful land of my ancestors is our next destination on this Northern European adventure. Can you guess where that is? It's Sweden! There are a few different ways we can travel from Helsinki, Finland, to Stockholm, Sweden.

We could take the long way, which would involve driving through northern Finland beyond the **Arctic Circle**, around the Bay of Bothnia, across the Finland-Sweden border, and then back down through northern Sweden, known as Lapland. This route would take us at least three or four full days of driving! However, we would see some spectacular sights along the way that you can't see anywhere else. Did you know there is a place on earth where there is a glittering ice castle? Sweden's glittering palace isn't just a castle — it is a hotel.

Icehotel is an actual hotel in the village of Jukkasjärvi

Arctic Circle: the parallel of latitude 66° 33' north of the equator. It marks the northernmost point at which the sun is visible on the northern winter solstice and the southernmost point at which the midnight sun can be seen on the northern summer solstice.

where you can sleep overnight in frosty, sub-zero rooms carved from real ice. The fanciful rooms and sparkling ice sculptures captivate guests from all over the world. The jaw-dropping carvings were created by skilled, artistic hands that have brought the ice to life. In fact, the artists who create this wintry palace will watch it all melt come late spring, but they look forward to creating a new fanciful frozen hotel each year when Sweden returns to its wintery paradise.

Northern Sweden, like all land located above the Arctic Circle, is home to a spectacular phenomenon I want to share with you. The Arctic Circle is a line of latitude that marks the southernmost point on the planet where the sun never dips below the horizon for a full 24 hours on at least one day of the year, known as the **summer solstice**. This also means that the lands above the Arctic Circle experience at least one full day of darkness six months later in the year, known as the **winter solstice**, a dark day when the sun never peeks over the horizon. A day with no sun! Sounds a little dreary, doesn't it? But there is a trade-off for the people who live in northern Sweden as well as many of the other countries above the Arctic Circle. God has given them the gift of witnessing the spectacular northern lights.

summer solstice: also known as midsummer, the summer solstice occurs when one of Earth's poles has its maximum tilt toward the sun.

winter solstice: also known as midwinter, the winter solstice occurs when one of Earth's poles has its maximum tilt away from the sun.

On cold, wintry nights above the Arctic Circle, a natural light show of green, blue, and purple swirls may appear in the night sky. This phenomenon is called **aurora borealis**, meaning "northern dawn," named by Galileo Galilei, who witnessed the incredible light display on September 12, 1621. It was so named because Gregory of Tours, who lived a thousand years before the famous scientist, wrote, "The lights are so bright that you might have thought the day was about to dawn."

The light show displays can be difficult to predict, so you may end up losing some sleep waiting for one to appear. But if you ever do catch a glimpse of this wondrous shimmering curtain of light in the night sky, you will never forget it.

An aurora happens when solar flares from the sun's surface fling out into space at speeds of over a million miles per hour and crash into our earth's atmosphere. The incredible part is that a layer of our atmosphere — the ionosphere — was set in place by God to shield our earth from this explosive electrical charge from the sun. When these sun particles, called ions, smash into the ionosphere, the collision creates a glorious display of glowing lights.

> **aurora borealis:** a natural electrical phenomenon characterized by the appearance of streamers of reddish or greenish light in the sky seen near the North Pole. The effect is caused by the collision of charged particles from the sun with atoms in the ionosphere, the upper atmosphere.

Another faster way to travel from Helsinki to Stockholm is to island hop, skip, and jump our way across the Bay of Bothnia. This route would require that we take a ferry to the islands of Åland, drive across those beautiful islands by way of an interconnected series of bridges, then take a second ferry to Stockholm, the capital city of Sweden. This would be a different kind of scenic drive than the more northerly route and would take us about 12 hours to complete. That's better than four days but still a long journey.

Our third option is to fly from capital city to capital city across the waters where the Baltic Sea and the Gulf of Bothnia meet. If we go this route, we'll be in Sweden in less than an hour. Which option would you prefer? Since it's not wintertime, we'd miss much of what makes northern Sweden so spectacular anyway, so maybe we'll skip the long way this time around. Flying it is!

Blue lakes with islands and green forests in Finland

Now that we have settled into our airplane seats, let's pull out our maps again and become acquainted with our next country. Sweden is the fourth largest country on the European continent and has one of the longest coastlines. Sweden is bordered by Finland to the east, connected to Denmark by the Öresund Bridge to the south, and shares the longest uninterrupted border in Europe with Norway, her neighbor to the west.

Now that we are in the air, you can see some of the islands that belong to Sweden. As we approach the airport in Stockholm, you'll also catch a glimpse of some of the forest groves which blanket the land. While most of the land in southern Sweden is agricultural — used to grow crops — the forests grow thicker and thicker the farther north you travel. In fact, 65% of Sweden's total land area is covered with dense forests of birch, maple, alder, larch, beech, and oak trees.

Sweden is also home to two of Europe's largest lakes, Vänern and Vättern, outsized only by two massive lakes in Russia. In fact, these lakes are laced together by canals, much like the Great Lakes in the United States. Besides these two mammoth lakes, however, Sweden is home to more than 101,000 additional lakes that dot the landscape and over 24,000 islands sprinkled along the coast.

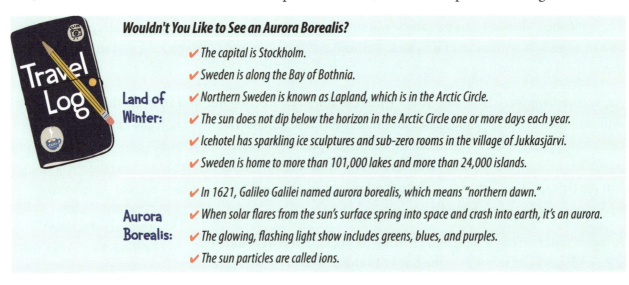

Wouldn't You Like to See an Aurora Borealis?

Land of Winter:
- ✔ The capital is Stockholm.
- ✔ Sweden is along the Bay of Bothnia.
- ✔ Northern Sweden is known as Lapland, which is in the Arctic Circle.
- ✔ The sun does not dip below the horizon in the Arctic Circle one or more days each year.
- ✔ Icehotel has sparkling ice sculptures and sub-zero rooms in the village of Jukkasjärvi.
- ✔ Sweden is home to more than 101,000 lakes and more than 24,000 islands.

Aurora Borealis:
- ✔ In 1621, Galileo Galilei named aurora borealis, which means "northern dawn."
- ✔ When solar flares from the sun's surface spring into space and crash into earth, it's an aurora.
- ✔ The glowing, flashing light show includes greens, blues, and purples.
- ✔ The sun particles are called ions.

92 Lesson 5. Day 45

A Child's Geography. Vol. 5: Explore Viking Realms

Create an Ice Sculpture

Materials needed:
- ☐ Water
- ☐ Food coloring (various colors)
- ☐ Assorted plastic cups or bowls
- ☐ Small pan
- ☐ Tray
- ☐ Salt (approximately ¼ cup)
- ☐ Ice cube tray (optional)

Icehotel in Sweden is a unique place — known as the first and largest of its kind. With the furniture made from snow and ice blocks, it is also adorned with ornate ice sculptures.

Artisans often work under a tight time frame to keep the ice from melting, or they may even work in a walk-in freezer. To carve the ice, tools can include chisels, knives, picks, and even power tools like chainsaws. We don't have to use those dangerous items to make an ice sculpture, and it doesn't take years of experience and craftsmanship to develop. Let's create a safe, easy, and colorful ice sculpture!

1. Pour water into a small pan and various shapes and sizes of small bowls, cups, ice cube trays, or other plastic shapes.

2. Drop your choice of different food colorings into the small pan and shapes. Then mix.

3. Place your small pan and shapes in a freezer until solid (four hours or more).

4. Remove ice shapes from the freezer.

5. Place your tray on your workspace. (Your tray will be where you will build your sculpture.)

6. Begin by placing your pan of ice on top of the tray first and removing the pan to create a base. (If needed, run some cool water under the small pan to loosen the ice.)

7. Sprinkle salt in the area where you will then arrange different shapes and sizes of ice onto the base and onto each other to create a sculpture. Continue sprinkling salt as you arrange each piece onto your sculpture.

Adapted from PBS.

The melting ice sculpture is also a miniature demonstration of a glacier or iceberg (part of a broken-off glacier) melting. If you want to study more about how it melts, you could take photos every 10 to 15 minutes to show the sequence of how it melted or you could create a short time-lapse video of the melting process.

Galileo Galilei and Aurora Borealis

The pronunciation of aurora borealis sounds like *uh-roar-uh-baw-ree-a-luhs.* Try saying aurora borealis aloud a few times!

Galileo Galilei, from the country of Italy, named the aurora borealis (meaning "northern dawn") in 1621. All around him, he recognized the magnificence of God's creation, giving Him the credit and the glory. The aurora borealis can be viewed in northern Sweden (or Lapland), especially during the cold, winter months.

Galileo Galilei

Galileo was also known for claiming that the earth rotated around the sun, which was a bold and unwelcome statement at the time. Galileo believed in God's magnificent creation of the universe, and he said that eventually science would reveal more about God's creation — and it did and continues to do so! In fact, today, we understand the earth rotates around the sun just as Galileo said. However, at the time, he faced persecution, even from others who professed to believe in God, yet much later, they came to agree and apologized — even if it was after his death. (Sometimes it can take us time to realize what we need to learn.)

What is a verse from the Bible that reminds you of God's amazing displays in creation?

_____

_____

_____

_____

Optional: Teacher's Discretion ☐ No ☐ Yes Due Date: _____

What is the science behind the aurora borealis (also called northern lights)? With a parent's permission or guidance, refer to books or online sources to write about aurora borealis.

Other Names for Aurora Borealis	_____
Where to View in the World	_____
Colors and Display	_____
Other Information I Learned	_____

→ That was a quick flight! We are coming in for a landing in the capital city of Stockholm. The city stretches across 14 islands, all connected by bridges and subway tunnels. Over two million people call Stockholm home (say that 5 times fast!), making it the most populated city in the entire Nordic region. In fact, one in five Swedish citizens live in or around their capital city. Stockholm is located on Sweden's third-largest freshwater lake, Lake Mälaren, where it flows out and mingles with the briny Baltic Sea.

Stockholm is a city drenched in sunshine during the daylight hours. The rainiest months occur in late summer — August and September. Like Helsinki in Finland, Stockholm enjoys a very moderate climate. Summers can become quite warm despite its northern latitude, and winters are cold but not unbearable. Stockholm's temperate climate is due in part to the warm Gulf Stream that flows up from the southern hemisphere, but also because Stockholm is one of the sunniest cities in Northern Europe, receiving more than 1,800 hours of sunshine per year.

The city of Stockholm is both beautiful and historic. It was founded all the way back in 1252 by the Swedish ruler Birger Jarl. It is interesting to note that "Jarl" wasn't his last name but his title, and is similar in rank to an earl or count in other parts of Europe. Immediately after its founding, Stockholm joined the Hanseatic League, a union that regulated trade throughout Northern Europe, allowing the city to grow rapidly. Known as the Queen of the North, she was fought over by the Danes and the Swedes for the next 300 years, but after liberation from Denmark in 1523 and from that time forward, Stockholm was widely regarded as the capital city of Sweden.

The old center of town is known as Gamla Stan, which means "the city between the bridges." Let's stroll through this old capital and see some of her sights up close. We'll definitely want to walk through a handful of Stockholm's most beautiful and historic buildings, such as the Royal Palace, the House of Lords, and the Storkyrkan, the Cathedral of St. Nicolas.

Palace Square

Oh, and there's the famous Stock Exchange painted in the classic yellow color that we associate with Sweden. Stockholm is a colorful city with buildings in all shades of yellow, blue, orange, and green. Copper rooftops gleam bright green when the sun pokes out between the gathering clouds. The Swedish flag waves proudly from many government and non-government buildings alike. This truly is a cheery and beautiful city.

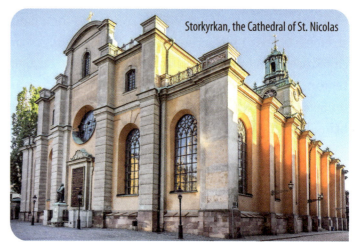
House of Lords

Without warning, the clouds above us collide and large drops of water begin falling from the sky and splattering the sidewalk, drenching the city and attempting to wash away her vibrant color. Quick! Let's duck inside this building. Oh look, it's a grocery market and it's crowded with people. Step out of the way over here by the window and we can wait out the rain shower. I wonder why there are so many people in the store shopping for groceries.

Storkyrkan, the Cathedral of St. Nicolas

We don't have to wait long to find out. Everyone is friendly and talking with each other and saying the word *midsommar*. The English translation is "midsummer," and it's a very important holiday in Sweden, second only to Christmas.

Originally a pagan celebration at the end of winter to celebrate the time of planting, once Christianity came to Sweden, the tradition was changed into a Christian celebration of the birth of John the Baptist. These cultural changes happened when people groups converted from worshiping many false gods to instead worshiping the One true God of the Bible. There was no longer a place for false gods in these Christian communities.

However, today in the 21st century, Midsommar is a secular national holiday, and it turns out that **Midsommar** will be celebrated tomorrow. All the stores and businesses are closing early so that families and friends can begin their celebration of Midsommar's Eve tonight.

A young couple stops to talk with us before leaving the market with their two bags full of groceries.

"You look a little lost. Can we help?" the young man asks.

"We are not lost, just waiting out the rain," I reply quickly. "We are travelers who are exploring your beautiful city."

"Yes, our city is beautiful indeed, but it will be closing down soon. You see, tomorrow is Midsommer, and everyone takes to the countryside to celebrate this joyful holiday. The celebration of Midsommar revolves around nature, so there will be no one left in the city by morning."

Midsommar: the middle part of summer; a Scandinavian holiday

"Oh, that is a shame. We planned to do some sightseeing," I respond.

"You can still do some sightseeing, but perhaps of a different kind," the young woman chimes in. "On Midsommar in Sweden, everyone is family. And we celebrate together as a family — friends and strangers alike. The entire population of Sweden will be gathering around the great lakes, and the smaller ones too, to join in the festive celebration. You are welcome to come. Everyone is welcome to come! This is all you need to do: Buy some picnic food and meat for the grill and drive out to the lake tomorrow. Or even better, buy or borrow some camping gear and come a day early. Join our group at the Kristinehamn Beach on Lake Vänern. But remember this, even if you cannot find us, it will be all right. Another group will surely welcome you to their gathering. You are family when it is Midsommar in Sweden."

Pike fishing on Lake Vänern

"Glad Midsommar," they call in unison as they wave goodbye and stroll out the sliding glass doors to the shiny wet streets of Stockholm.

"Glad" in Swedish means happy, so they just wished us a "Happy Midsommar!" We'll have to give that phrase a try in the upcoming festivities.

Pickled herring

Should we join our new friends at the lake to celebrate Midsommar? There's not too much to consider. The city will be closing down soon and all the city dwellers will be escaping to the countryside in a matter of hours. Let's purchase some food and be on our way! Pickled herring, a small briny fish, is a popular Swedish delicacy. Let's buy a jar along with some sour cream to make a simple side dish. We can also buy some rye bread, fruit, and sausages for the grill.

There's a sporting equipment store on the way back to the car. We might as well pick up a tent and a few sleeping bags so we can head for the lake tonight rather than waiting for tomorrow.

Back in the car, we are pretty excited to be driving out to the biggest lake in Sweden, Lake Vänern. Fortunately for us, we'll be passing by an archaeological dig where hundreds of **rune stones** have been excavated. These stones were used to record everything from honoring a friend or family member to bragging about yourself! Some were also used as part of pagan practices or false god worship, but when conversions to Christianity began, these new believers used the stones to proudly proclaim their new and life-changing faith in God.

rune stone: a large stone carved with runes by ancient Scandinavians or Anglo-Saxons

Sunset over Lake Vänern

More stones have been found that have a Christian symbol or theme than any others.

Such stones have been found by the thousands strewn across Scandinavia. Carved with runic inscriptions and serpentine illustrations, rune stones date as far back as the Bronze Age, the majority dating around the 11th century, otherwise known as the Viking Age.

Rune stone

Although rune stones were used for many purposes, they were often carved to commemorate the dead.

However, they did not serve as grave markers. They were placed along roadsides and pathways where they could be seen and appreciated by passersby. Over time, these memorials were knocked over, buried, and lost to civilization until there was a resurgence of interest in Swedish history about a hundred years ago.

In the early 20th century, many Swedish historical societies excavated the earth to restore these **monoliths**. Over 2,500 rune stones have been recovered in just Sweden alone. As you can see, the Swedes are proud of their Viking heritage.

Aren't the history of rune stones and the excavations unique? We've received a glimpse into two different cultures at the same time — the runic communication of the adventurous Vikings through stone and the exuberant discovery by the Swedes in the early 1900s.

monoliths: large, single upright blocks of stone serving as pillars or monuments

It's getting late. We'd better hurry to Kristinehamn on the lake. We still need to set up camp and we won't want to do that in the dark. The Swedish people love being outdoors and especially enjoy easy access to nature. For this reason, the Swedish tradition of freely walking wherever one likes has become law. It is called the "right to public access" and means that you can essentially walk anywhere in Sweden, even if that means crossing someone's private property, to arrive at your destination.

Kristinehamn underpass

Still, I'd rather arrive early enough to know that I'm not wandering around or pitching a tent in someone's backyard. Let's get going!

Travel Log

Yellow and Other Bright Colors of Sweden

Stockholm:
✔ Stockholm spans 14 islands that are connected by bridges and subway tunnels.
✔ The population is more than two million people.
✔ It is located on Lake Mälaren, which flows into the Baltic Sea.
✔ One of the sunniest cities in Northern Europe, it gets more than 1,800 hours of yearly sunshine.
✔ Gamla Stan, meaning "the city between the bridges," is the old town center.
✔ Stockholm is a colorful city with rooftops made of copper and vibrantly painted buildings.

Historic Happenings:
✔ Popular historic sites include the Royal Palace, the House of Lords, and the Cathedral of St. Nicolas.
✔ The Stock Exchange is painted the bright yellow associated with Sweden.
✔ Midsommar is a secular national holiday.
✔ Archaeological digs reveal rune stones, many with Christian markings signaling the cultural change from false gods to the One true God.

TIMELINE

283 ▶	Lucia, Sweden's patron saint, is born into a wealthy Italian family.
1252 ▶	Birger Jarl founded Stockholm, Sweden.
1500 ▶	Denmark rules all of Norway and much of Sweden.
1523 ▶	Stockholm is liberated from the Danes.
1621 ▶	Galileo Galilei witnesses and names the aurora borealis.
1953 ▶	Midsommar became an official national holiday.

100 Lesson 5. Day 48

A Child's Geography. Vol. 5: Explore Viking Realms

Find the Dates in the Royal Palace

In the sketch of the famous Royal Palace in Stockholm are hidden dates for the timeline. Circle the dates. Write each date next to the matching event.

1. _____ Midsommar became a national holiday.

2. _____ Birger Jarl founded Stockholm, Sweden.

3. _____ Denmark rules all of Norway and much of Sweden.

4. _____ Stockholm is liberated from the Danes.

5. _____ Galileo Galilei witnesses and names the aurora borealis.

Unscramble the Locations

Use the hints to unscramble the words of the locations.

1. Sweden's biggest lake:

    eLak nänVer   _____

2. Sweden's second-largest lake:

    Laek äternVt   _____

3. Sweden's third-largest lake:

    kLae äleMnar   _____

4. Country that borders Sweden to the east:

    inFdlan   _____

5. Country to the south of Sweden across the Öresund Bridge:

    reknDam   _____

6. City that spans across 14 islands:

    mockStohl   _____

Symbols and Messages

Viking messages or inscriptions were often carved in stone. Because writing on stone, metal, or wood is a difficult task, symbols could represent entire words. Eventually, a visual alphabet was formed that the Vikings used.

After some became Christians, they left Christian messages and symbols on the stones as a sign of their faith.

Draw one of the symbols of Christianity and shade it in to appear like a stone, metal, or wood.

Materials needed:
☐ Colored pencils

Latin Cross

Fish

Bible

Dove

Crucifix

Malta Cross

Lamb

Cross of Saint Andrew

Three Crosses

Stone markings were also used throughout history because of how long they would last. We see one example of this in the Bible, though Moses broke the first set and God wrote the commandments again:

Now the LORD said to Moses. "Cut out for yourself two stone tablets like the former ones. and I will write on the tablets the words that were on the former tablets which you smashed."

–Exodus 34:1

102 Lesson 5. Day 50

A Child's Geography. Vol. 5: Explore Viking Realms

Mapping It Out!

Complete the map of the country of Sweden in the box below. Refer to the map on page 382.

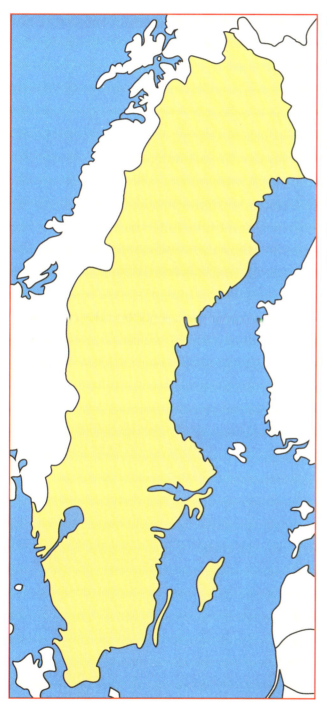

Label the following places on your map. You can use colored pencils to shade areas of land or water, draw rivers and mountains, etc.

☐ Sweden

☐ Arctic Circle

☐ Lapland

☐ Bay of Bothnia

☐ Vänern Lake

☐ Vättern Lake

☐ Add a star ★ for the capital city of Stockholm.

Swedish Vallhund

Flashcards

Make flashcards of the bolded glossary words from this lesson. Then, either add drawings of the terms or act them out in charades. Be creative!

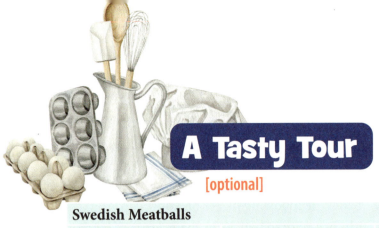

A Tasty Tour

[optional]

Swedish Meatballs

For the meatballs:

2½ lb ground beef

4 eggs

2 cups milk

1 cup dry bread crumbs

1 cup minced onion

¼ cup butter, divided

1 teaspoon salt

¼ teaspoon nutmeg

¼ teaspoon allspice

¼ teaspoon cardamom

NOTE: This recipe requires adult supervision and participation.

Optional: Teacher's Discretion

☐ No   ☐ Yes   Due Date: _____

For the gravy:

¼ cup flour

2 cups beef stock

1 cup light cream

3 teaspoons dill weed

Salt and pepper to taste

Directions:

1. Beat eggs slightly, add milk and crumbs and allow to stand while cooking the onion in 2 tablespoons of the butter. Remove onion with a slotted spoon, add to the crumbs with the seasonings and meat and mix thoroughly. The mixture will be soft. Chill for one hour to blend flavors, then shape into 1-inch balls and brown slowly in the remaining butter, turning carefully so that balls retain their shape. Add more butter if necessary. Arrange in a large baking dish or Dutch oven.

2. Add flour to the drippings in the pan and stir. Cook until the flour begins to brown. Add beef broth and cook, while stirring, until smooth and thickened. Add cream, salt, pepper, and dill. Sauce is thin. Strain sauce over meatballs, then bake in slow oven at 350 degrees for 30 minutes.

Learn Geography Terms

Page 342 is a reference page for understanding the terms geographers use to describe landforms.

Love your neighbor

The colorfully painted yellow, blue, orange, and green homes of Sweden remind us of the brilliant displays of the aurora borealis. Lord, we thank You for the beauty and power of Your creation. In the words of David in Psalm 8:1, "Lᴏʀᴅ, our Lord, How majestic is Your name in all the earth, You who have displayed Your splendor above the heavens!" May the colors of your creation invite us to also bring colorful artistry into our surroundings.

SUMMER IN SWEDEN

In this bonus optional reading section, more memories of summer in Sweden are shared. Author Terri Johnson's Swedish family heritage helps create a close-up look at traditions as the travel story continues. Parent should review the optional text and assign it to the student if needed.

Optional: Teacher's Discretion
☐ No   ☐ Yes   Due Date: _____

It's a glorious morning on the shore of Lake Vänern. This lake is so vast that you cannot see the other side. It almost looks like the ocean. Crawling out of our tent, we see that others have woken up early too and are busy with preparations for the day ahead. There is a buzz in the air as toddlers run and squeal in the gathering sunlight, parents enjoy their first sips of strong black coffee, teens reluctantly rise and gaze out on the sparkling lake, and amateur fishermen shove their boats out from shore to see what treasures can be pulled out of the cool water with their fishing lines.

We have heard that Midsommar is similar to our 4th of July in the United States, only Sweden celebrates their national birthday a couple weeks earlier. Instead of a national birthday party, this celebration is for the welcoming of summer weather, a favorite season for Swedes after the long, cold winter they have endured through snow and ice.

The children have begun to gather wildflowers for wreaths. Wild blackberry and lingonberry bushes cluster in fields not far from the lakeshore, and pickers are now arriving, wearing buckets tied around their waists with twine. Let's go join the berry pickers.

Midsommar (Midsummer): There were many celebrations originating in ancient times that were often associated with a season of the year. The holiday of Midsommar (Midsummer) began as a time of gathering for festivities in summer. Seek direction and wisdom for an understanding of some secular holidays. Talk about how your family celebrates holidays and traditions. What is important to you and your family?

Look! There's the couple we met in the market in Stockholm! We wave and walk their way, meeting them at the wall of prickly blackberry vines where they are picking.

"Hey, you made it!" the young man shouts. "*Valkommen*! Welcome! My name is Anders and this is my wife, Ingrid. Our baby's name is Astrid. We are glad to meet you and even more glad that you have joined us on this special day."

"Thank you for inviting us and making us feel so welcome," we reply.

Ingrid is carrying baby Astrid on her back, who smiles at us under her sunbonnet. Anders hands us extra containers so that we can pick berries too.

"We'll make beautiful berry tarts from these berries when we get back to the cabin," Ingrid tells us. "The more berries, the more tarts!"

Ingrid's parents own a cabin by the lake where their friends and family gather every Midsommar. We have been invited to join them. How fortunate we are!

"Why is this such an important holiday in Sweden?" I ask.

Anders puts his hands on his hips and considers his answer. "Well, it was first known as *Midsommar*, an ancient holiday that has been celebrated for as long as people have been living in these northern parts. The Vikings celebrated it and so did the barbarian tribes that lived here before them. In other words, this holiday has been celebrated for thousands of years. As the ancient holiday continued through the years, it shifted from a pagan focus to a Christian celebration of joy, and over time, a secular one today.

"Seasons are fairly extreme in Sweden. The winters are very long, very dark, and very cold. Snow stays on the ground until April or May. Then springtime arrives and the ground and trees are awakened with new life. The birds sing for joy and animals return in droves to graze and raise their families. While the Swedish people love their northern wintry climate and the frosty snow and ice that glitter during the winter months, they also rejoice when summer arrives with long, warm days full of sunshine and promise. The people of Sweden embrace summer and squeeze as much recreation and relaxation out of it as possible. We have perfected the idea of outdoor living."

"Oh yes, you will see outdoor living at its finest when you are at my parents' cabin today!" smiles Ingrid.

After filling our buckets to the brim with berries, we stroll back toward the lakeshore and the cabin. Ingrid's parents' home is small but quaint, painted bright yellow with a deck facing the lake. It's modest but very homey — and bustling with activity. Children are laughing and running across the deck, through the cabin, and back out to the pebbly beach. Adults are swinging peacefully in hammocks or talking quietly in groups on the lawn, by the water, and in the doorway of the cabin. A silvery blonde–haired woman rushes out the kitchen door to greet us as she wipes her hands on a colorful apron.

"Ingrid, Anders, who are your friends? I am Inge Holmgren. Welcome to our home away from home! Thank you for the beautiful berries," she coos, collecting as many containers as she can hold. "Please, please make yourselves at home. There is a variety of water and other beverages in the cooler on the deck, hammocks strung among the trees in the yard, lawn chairs along the lakeshore, and coffee brewing in the coffeepot."

"Thank you, Mrs. Holmgren, for opening up your home to us," I reply. "You are so generous and kind. I'll definitely take you up on a nap in a hammock later, but for now, we'd like to be put to work. What can we do to help you?"

"Well then, come, come. Let's go in the kitchen so you can help me bake the berry tarts!"

We follow her past the **kaffee-klatsch** groups on the deck and in the doorway to her small but bright and super tidy kitchen. "You two can sit at the counter and help with mixing the dough. But first let's start washing the berries," Inge says as she calmly and expertly puts everyone to work.

kaffee-klatsch: an informal social gathering at which coffee is served

"You know, this time of year is my favorite holiday outside of Christmas and Santa Lucia Day."

"Santa Lucia Day? What's that?"

"Oh, you don't know who Santa Lucia was? Oh my, you are in for a great story. Lucia was a young Italian woman who was born into a very wealthy and noble family in Syracuse in the year A.D. 283. As Lucy grew, she became very burdened in her soul for people less fortunate than herself. When she became a teenager, she declared to her mother that she would remain single and give her dowry to help feed the poor. Her family became enraged — so much so, that they killed sweet Lucy for her faith in God and her devotion to the poor. She has been remembered ever since!"

"Excuse my confusion, but why do people in Sweden celebrate an Italian girl?"

"During the Middle Ages, the people of Sweden adopted Lucia as our patron saint. The traditional story goes that she appeared in Sweden during a famine and carried food to the farmers around this very lake, Lake Vänern, to sustain their families during the long ordeal. She has been our dear Santa Lucia ever since. Even if some people don't believe the story, she represents light and goodwill to all the people of Sweden during the darkest days of winter. That's why we celebrate her life in December.

"On the morning of the 13th, the oldest daughter carries a tray with coffee and special saffron bread, known as Santa Lucia Bread, which she serves to the family. It's such a beautiful day, and Santa Lucia Bread is scrumptious! But the food we'll be having today is nearly as good," Inge winks.

The sun is high in the sky. The tables are covered with brightly checked tablecloths, big bunches of wildflowers, and small wooden horses. The food is laid out on the sideboard, and the smells lure nearby loungers and talkers toward the banquet. It's nearly time to enjoy a classic Swedish smorgasbord.

Santa Lucia

Santa (or Saint) Lucia: Santa Lucia is a holiday to celebrate a girl, Lucia, who was named a saint by the Catholic Church. By some definitions, a saint is anyone who chooses to follow the One true God, and by other definitions, it is a person who is harmed or killed because of their strong faith in God.

Parents: Talk as a family about what being a saint means and how you celebrate. Continue to seek wisdom and direction for understanding.

Santa Lucia Bread

108 Lesson 5. Day 51

A Child's Geography. Vol. 5: Explore Viking Realms

Mr. Holmgren whistles and calls everyone within earshot to gather on the lawn for the blessing. Young and old alike clasp hands, forming a large circle, while the patriarch of the family booms out a loud prayer of thanksgiving and blessing.

Swedish meatballs with lingonberry jam

"Our Lord, we thank you this day for friends, old and new, for food that nourishes us, and for faith that sustains us. And together, we pray…."

At this point in the prayer, everyone chants in unison, *"I Jesu namn till bords vi gå, välsigna Gud den mat vi få. Gud till ära, oss till gagn, så få vi mat i Jesu namn. Amen."*

Garlic beet salad

Everyone releases hands and moves in the direction of the buffet line. Seeing our curiosity, Ingrid kindly translates for us. "My father said, 'In Jesus' name to the table we go, God bless the food we receive. To God the honor, us the gain, so we have food in Jesus' name.' "

Young and old, groups and individuals, all make their way toward the food and load their plates with delicious main courses and side dishes, such as Swedish meatballs with lingonberry jam, garlic beet salad, sliced ham, gravlax (dried salmon) on rye crackers, and a rich gratin of potatoes, onions, cream, and anchovies. And there's our pickled herring! Pickled herring is an acquired taste, which has most certainly been acquired here as we watch children scoop heaping piles of it onto their plates. What will you try?

Gravlax on crackers

Let's pull up a chair at one of the tables on the deck. From here, we have a sweeping view of the lake where children are splashing farther down the shore and adults are peacefully floating by on rafts, air mattresses, and boats. Swedes have perfected the outdoor summer lifestyle. It doesn't get much better than this. The food is delicious, the mood is light, and everyone is looking forward to even more festivities as the day continues. Secretly, every heart wishes for as long and as warm a summer as possible.

Dessert is served. The tarts we helped make turned out perfectly — sweet yet tart berry jam is surrounded by a golden crust topped with fluffy whipped cream. Glorious. Mr. Holmgren carries his dessert bowl over to our table and sits down. He asks about our adventure and where we have been so far. We tell him about the beautiful and resilient people we met in the Baltic countries — Lithuania, Latvia, and Estonia — and about the interesting things we learned while in Finland.

Then I ask, "Why do you have little painted horses on each table?"

"Ah, the **dala horses**," he exclaims. "The dala horse has become the iconic symbol of Sweden. But they may be even more popular in the United States. Did you know that during the 19th century, there were more Swedes living in the U.S. than in the mother country?"

"No, we didn't know!"

"A group of Swedish families moved to the United States, looking for adventure, good jobs, and a fresh start. After a few years, more families moved across the ocean to join them. And then more and more went so they could be reunited with their extended families. Over the course of a few decades, more Swedish families lived in your country than mine. But I digress; I haven't answered your question about the dala.

"During Viking times, the horse was a revered animal. In many northern countries throughout history, wooden horses have been carved for decoration or for children to play with. In central Sweden, craftsmen used wood scraps thrown out by local furniture-makers along with pigments from nearby copper mines to create the iconic dala.

"As far as we can tell, the dala horse made its first appearance in a small log cabin deep in the forest of Dalarna in central Sweden. During the long winter nights, a furniture maker whittled in front of a log fire, carving out toys for his children using the simplest of tools, a carving knife. It was only natural that many of these toys were horses, because the horse was invaluable in those days, both as a trusty friend and as a co-worker who could pull great loads of

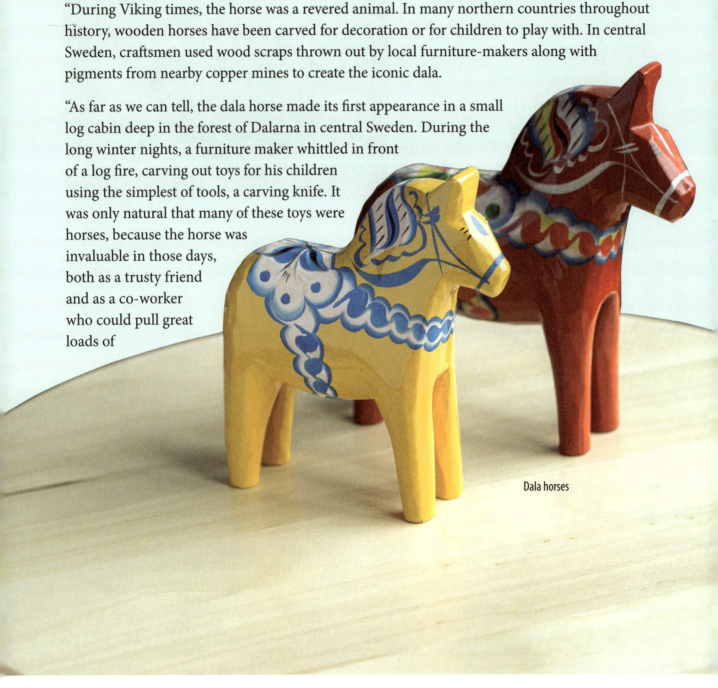

Dala horses

110 Lesson 5. Day 51

A Child's Geography. Vol. 5: Explore Viking Realms

timber from the forests during the winter months. In the summer, a family horse was invaluable on the farm.

"The little wooden toys became quite popular, and other woodcarvers began making the horses for their children and to sell in the marketplace. The toy trade began to flourish, and the dala were even used to barter for other household goods. Over time, the iconic Swedish horses were brought across the ocean to Swedish families in the U.S., who loved them and wanted more. The art of carving and painting the small horses blossomed into a full-fledged cottage industry. In fact, the rural families of Dalarna depended on toy horse production to help keep food on the table. The skills of horse carving and painting were passed on from generation to generation.

"Many early dala horses were not painted at all, but in the beginning of the 19th century, painting them in a single color, white or red, became common practice. The decoration of the dala horse has its roots in furniture painting and was perfected over the years. According to a local tale, a wandering painter came across one of these dala horses at a farmhouse he was painting. One of the children asked if he would paint the horse while he was there. 'Of course,' answered the delighted painter, who added some colorful flourishes across the back and sides of the horse, which pleased the children greatly. The design he painted was inspired by the biblical story of Jonah, who sat outside the city of Nineveh where the Lord caused a vine to grow up beside him to shade and protect him from the scorching sun. Although you may see slight variations in the shape of the toys or the painted designs across their backs, most dala horses look generally the same.

Dala Horses: The tradition of the dala horse holds special meaning in Sweden, and some Swedes may continue the tradition of decorating their home with a brightly painted dala horse or even adding a full-sized carving to an outdoor space. Continue talking with your family about how some objects and traditions can have strong cultural meanings. What is important to your family's culture? Also, talk about biblical influence. As you seek wisdom and understanding, ask your family about verses in Proverbs that talk about wisdom.

"Dala horses are still handcrafted in central Sweden, but there are just as many created in Kansas too."

We all laugh at the thought.

The afternoon proceeds just as planned. With no real schedule for the afternoon, we have time to splash in the lake, relax in the hammock, and play games with new friends, while sipping on more coffee and snacking on rich, buttery cookies.

Glad Midsommar! We welcome summer to Sweden. May you experience many warm and happy days to follow this one.

As for us, we must say farewell to this beautiful nation with the big, generous heart. What a delight it has been to get acquainted with you, Sweden. Your people are like family now, and your country has become like our second home.

"Hejdå!" We say goodbye to our friends in Swedish and then pile back into our car for the next adventure awaiting us.

112 Lesson 5. Day 51

A Child's Geography. Vol. 5: Explore Viking Realms

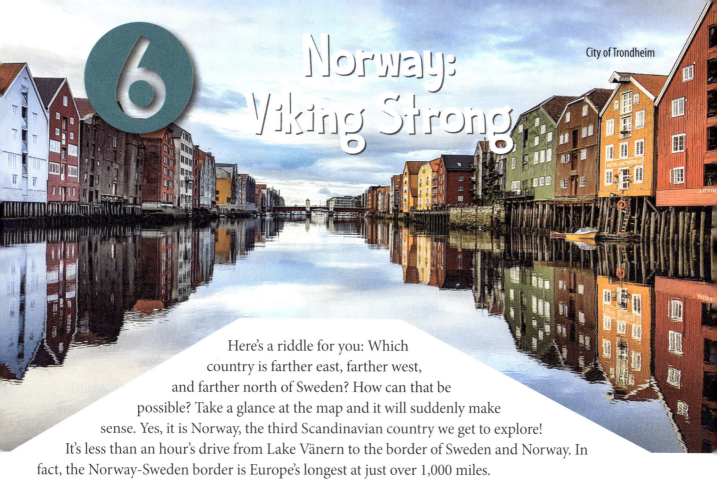

6

Norway: Viking Strong

City of Trondheim

Here's a riddle for you: Which country is farther east, farther west, and farther north of Sweden? How can that be possible? Take a glance at the map and it will suddenly make sense. Yes, it is Norway, the third Scandinavian country we get to explore! It's less than an hour's drive from Lake Vänern to the border of Sweden and Norway. In fact, the Norway-Sweden border is Europe's longest at just over 1,000 miles.

The nation of Norway also includes the islands of Svalbard, which are halfway between the mainland and the North Pole. No one lives farther north in the world than the residents of the tiny community of Ny-Ålesund (population of only 35 people) and the slightly larger town of Longyearbyen (population 2,000), who live in Svalbard, Norway.

Northernmost Scandinavian country … longest European border … northernmost city in the world…. These are not the only extremes when it comes to Norway. Norway is packed full of features unparalleled anywhere else in the world. It is the most mountainous, most picturesque, and most prosperous of all the Scandinavian countries. The days stay lighter longer, get darker earlier, and are sunnier yet rainier than every other European country. Some people would argue that Norway's natural beauty is the most dramatic and breathtaking in all of Europe and perhaps even the world. The length of its western coast is bejeweled by a long necklace of stunning deep fjords, or narrow inlets, artistically shaped and carved out by glacial ice.

The beauty of Norway is a reminder of the words in Isaiah 42:10: "Sing to the LORD a new song, Sing His praise from the end of the earth! You who go down to the sea, and all that is in it; You islands, and those who live on them."

Norway was once Viking land, and its Viking heritage can still be seen and enjoyed today. Viking remnants dot the region in the form of ruins, ships, churches, and artifacts. Thankfully, we'll get to see some of them today.

The Vikings were great traders, shipbuilders, and explorers. They were also fierce warriors who were infamous for terrorizing much of Europe. The thought of a Viking invasion struck fear into the hearts of people as far west as Ireland, as far south as Spain, and as far east as the Black Sea.

The Viking name comes from the Norse word *vik*, which means "fjord" or "inlet," because the Norwegian fjords provided the ideal conditions for building and testing their ships before taking them out into the open sea. Once confirmed to be seaworthy, the Vikings would sail their sleek dragon-headed vessels on extensive voyages to trade their unique wares, such as furs and amber, along river routes deep into France, Russia, and Turkey. Or they would prepare for even longer voyages and set out across the Atlantic Ocean for Iceland, Greenland, and Canada, which they called Vinland.

These tormentors of the seas were in search of riches of all kinds, but specifically wealth in the form of gold, land, and slaves. If they came across land they wanted but was already settled, the Vikings would kill or enslave the inhabitants so they could take the territory they wanted. The Vikings were led by fierce leaders with names such as Erik Bloodaxe, Sven Forkbeard, and Erik the Red — named both for his red hair and his fiery hot temper. These weren't

Lofoten archipelago in Northern Norway

the types of men you wanted to sit down and bargain with. No, when folks heard that Vikings were coming, they abandoned their homes, ran for the hills, and quietly looked for new places to settle safely out of harm's way.

But the Vikings had a gentle, homey side as well. Many were farmers, fishermen, and skilled artisans who loved their livelihood and quiet lifestyle. Throughout Norway, archaeologists have uncovered sophisticated tools and intricate works of art handcrafted from wood, metal, shell, and stone. However, faced with a limited amount of farmable land and a thriving population, the Vikings traveled south and west, driven by more than a thirst for wealth or warfare; they needed more useable land to support their people.

It was their search for greener pastures that compelled them to descend en masse upon unsuspecting communities in northern England, France, and Ireland. Although their methods were swift and destructive, they came with the sole purpose of taking care of their own by settling in warmer climates that contained more abundant resources.

While the Vikings were fierce, determined, and swift, as an empire they were not structured well enough to function on such a large-scale, spread across multiple continents, separated by oceans and thousands of miles. More organized adversaries and armies rose up to defeat them, and over time, the Vikings assimilated into pockets of European society, particularly in France,

Viking Raids: Remember, the Vikings were pagan and worshiped false gods. Christian churches and wealthy towns were often targeted by them because these places held valuable goods, gold items used in church services, or other items of value that could be sold. While in God's Word Christians are given commandments to not steal and that we are to love one another as Christ loves us, there were no such rules for Vikings when they raided.

England, Ireland, and Iceland. By the late 12th century, the once mighty Vikings had become meek and mild subjects spread throughout foreign kingdoms in a highly Christianized Europe.

But Norwegians never forget their mighty Viking roots. They embrace their vibrant and fierce heritage. Here in the Land of the Midnight Sun, the Viking lives on.

Norway's capital city of Oslo is a short distance beyond the border. It is located at the end of a 60-mile fjord that juts up from the southern end of the country. Oslo is a beautiful and clean city with plenty of sites to see and good food to enjoy.

The city of Oslo dates back nearly 1,000 years to 1049, when Harald Hardrada was king of Norway. This particular Norwegian king attempted to bring both Denmark and England under his control, but in the end was unsuccessful.

Nearly 600 years later, Oslo burned to the ground during the reign of King Christian IV. Now Christian IV was Danish, but at this time in history, he was the ruling monarch over both Denmark and Norway. He ordered a new city built on the site, which included a grand palace for himself, and named the newly built city Christiania after himself. Another 300 years would pass before the people of Norway would reclaim the original name for their capital city, Oslo, thereby disconnecting themselves from their Danish past.

The large brick City Hall building dominates the Oslo waterfront. After World War II, the residents of Oslo agreed to allow their government to tear down an old slum neighborhood that was a disgrace to their pristine downtown and build this massive modern building. While not particularly beautiful on the outside, the interior is an artist's dream, with each wall brilliantly displaying a mural telling some portion of Norway's history.

City Hall is where the Nobel Peace Prize (right) is awarded each December to someone who has changed the world for the better. The award is given out in honor of Alfred Nobel, a 19th century chemist, engineer, inventor, businessman, and philanthropist from Sweden. Nobel is most famous for his invention of dynamite, which he intended for beneficial uses, like boring out tunnels for trains.

However, Nobel received a huge wake-up call in 1888 when he saw his own obituary with the headline that read, *The*

City Hall in Oslo

116 Lesson 6. Day 53

A Child's Geography. Vol. 5: Explore Viking Realms

Merchant of Death is Dead. It was actually Alfred's brother Ludvig who had died, but the obituary caused Alfred to reconsider the purpose of his life. Now even more horrified by how his invention was being used for destruction, Nobel instituted the Peace Prize to reward peaceful scientists and humanitarians who were making a positive difference in the world.

Viking storehouse

From the waterfront, we can take a ferry over to Bygdøy, a peninsula jutting south on the west side of Oslo. There we can wander through three ship museums, displaying ships from various eras of Norwegian history — old Norse Viking longships from the height of the Viking era; the *Fram*, which was the first ship to navigate the northern passage; and the Kon-Tiki, a raft built in 1947 that sailed on a bold and precarious expedition to prove that the Polynesian islands may have been settled by people living in South America thousands of years ago.

The Oseberg Viking ship, Tønsberg, Norway

Two of the Viking ships on display are mostly complete and provide great insight into life on the seas as a Viking warrior. The beautiful oak Oseberg ship built around the year 820 and uncovered in 1903 could be sailed or rowed. Fully manned, it had room for 30 oarsmen. The prow and stern were ornately carved with animal figures, which began below the waterline and led up to the spiraling serpent's head proudly displayed at the very top. Such a decorated ship must have been owned by a wealthy aristocratic family.

Nobel Prize: The first Nobel Peace Prize was awarded in 1901 to Swiss Jean Henri Dunant for his role in founding the International Red Cross. Other notable Peace Prize winners are Mother Teresa for her work with the poorest of the poor in India; Martin Luther King, Jr. for his peaceful opposition to racial discrimination; Nelson Mandela for his work in ending apartheid in South Africa; and Woodrow Wilson for his role in establishing the League of Nations, the forerunner to the United Nations, to initiate world peace after the horrors of the Great War, which later became known as World War I.

Various fields of work are recognized for the Nobel Prize, including physics, chemistry, physiology or medicine, literature, peace, and now economics. A Nobel Prize winner is called a Nobel Laureate. There have been controversies about some of the people selected and questions about the rules for the award process. For example, a scientific discovery in chemistry may be the result of dozens of researchers over a period of time, but Nobel rules limit the award to a smaller number of researchers for a project. Other questions have been raised about the criteria for the guideline selection in the category of literature. And, of course, the category of peace can be another difficult area to agree on.

The word "peace" is spoken throughout the Bible. In the words of Jesus in Matthew 5:9, "Blessed are the peacemakers, for they will be called sons of God." This speaks of blessing and goodness. Later, Jesus talks about how peace cannot be defined by man's terms. In fact, He boldly proclaims that if a person denies Jesus, that person also denies God. Then He says in Matthew 10:34, "Do not think that I came to bring peace on the earth; I did not come to bring peace, but a sword." Here, Jesus reminds us that it is each person's individual choice to follow Him and that a person cannot depend on another family member for the salvation that Jesus offers. When we choose to follow Jesus, we choose to be peacemakers who lovingly invite people into a relationship with Him. We also choose to love Him even more than the deep love we should have for other people.

Only a handful of complete longships have been discovered in Norway over the years. Once a ship was no longer seaworthy, they were used as burial chambers for important kings. When a longship is found underground instead of at the bottom of the ocean, it is usually well stocked with valuables and well-preserved artifacts.

An incredible find was made in a Norwegian farmer's field in the south of Norway in October of 2018. Cutting-edge technology has been invented that uses ground-penetrating radar to locate hidden artifacts without having to dig. One example is a complete 66-foot Viking longship that was discovered less than two feet underground.

But Viking ships and artifacts are not all Bygdøy has to offer — far from it. There are plenty of restaurants and cafeterias nearby. Let's duck into one and try some traditional Norwegian cuisine. A number of the dishes may

Lutefisk

Fårikål

seem very strange and off-putting to your taste buds. Some quirky Norwegian specialties include lutefisk (soaked and salted fish), smalahove (sheep's head), pinnekjøtt (literally "stick meat" made from lamb), and rakefisk (fermented trout). But other specialties on the menu may sound more appealing, such as raspeball (potato dumplings), lefse (flat potato bread used to wrap up meat and vegetables), fårikål (a casserole made with cabbage, potatoes, and lamb), and vaffel (similar to waffles, topped with butter, strawberry jam, and sour cream). What would you like to try?

Fjords and Viking Ships

Norway's Culture and Land:
- ✔ Ny-Ålesund, Norway, is the northernmost community in the world.
- ✔ Norway has breathtaking views of fjords (narrow inlets) and mountains.
- ✔ The capital city of Oslo once burned to the ground and was rebuilt.
- ✔ Alfred Nobel first started the Nobel Prize to award positive difference-makers in the world.
- ✔ Lamb, potatoes, fish, and other fare are Norwegian specialties.

Vikings:
- ✔ Fjords offered the benefit of a place to build and test Viking ships.
- ✔ Vikings eventually spread out across Europe, diminishing their strongholds of power.
- ✔ Viking ship museums preserve artifacts and stories.
- ✔ The Oseberg ship is a reminder of the ornate and wealthy influence of some Vikings.

Design a Viking Ship

Archaeologists' examination of Viking ships, including the Oseberg, Gokstad, and Gjellestad, show us much about how Viking ships were powerful status symbols of the wealthy.

The Oseberg ship at the Viking Ship Museum

Note the following parts of the Oseberg Viking ship:

- The ship is made of oak, a strong wood.
- Ornate wood carvings stretch from the bow at one end to the bow at the other end.
- There are 12 strakes (panels) on each side.
- The deck, or surface for walking or sitting, is made of pine planks.
- With holes for 15 rows on each side, up to 30 oarsmen could row together.

1. Design, draw, and color a Viking ship.
2. Draw and color the water.
3. Color the sky to appear like the aurora borealis that we learned about in our last lesson.

Match the Norwegian Foods

Using the list of words provided, write the correct letter on the line to match each image.

1. _____ vaffel

2. _____ raspeball

3. _____ lefse

4. _____ lutefisk

5. _____ smalahove

6. _____ rakefisk

7. _____ fårikål

8. _____ pinnekjøtt

Therefore, whether you eat or drink, or whatever you do, do all things for the glory of God.

– 1 Corinthians 10:31

Which food(s) would you like to try? _____

If you've been trying the optional recipes (A Tasty Tour) in the lessons so far, what is one you've especially liked? If you haven't been trying them, what is one you would like to try?

_____

Bergen, Norway

→ Our next stop is Bergen, Norway's second-largest city at 250,000 residents (half the size of Oslo) and a popular gateway to the fjords. The city is a collection of islands surrounded by steep mountains. Founded in 1070 by King Olav Kyrre, son of Harald Hardrada, Bergen was originally named Bjørgvin, which means "the green meadow among the mountains." It served as Norway's capital until the 13th century and participated in the trading union known as the Hanseatic League. Bryggen, the row of colorful and historic commercial buildings that line the harbor and were once used for exporting cod and importing foreign valuables, is rich in preserved history.

Bergen's ideal location on the west coast of Norway has brought the city both prosperity and affliction. In 1349, the Black Death was brought to Norway by an infected crew on an English ship arriving at Bergen to deliver goods. Soon after, the city was attacked multiple times by a pirate band known as the Victual Brothers. In 1429, they succeeded in burning down the royal castle and much of the city. In 1665, Bergen's harbor became the ill-fated site of the Battle of Vågen, a skirmish that had nothing to do with the Norwegians. It was a battle between an English naval flotilla that had been attacked by a fleet of Dutch merchant ships just outside their little protected bay.

While Oslo and Bergen, along with many other Norwegian cities, are modern, bright, and friendly, they are not usually what draw people here. Norway is first and foremost a country of unforgettable natural beauty. Bergen is perfectly situated as a starting point for gallivanting

The Battle of Vågen

Sognefjord, Norway

through the majestic fjords of Norway. Trolltunga landmark is a result of the processes and power of the Genesis Flood and the Ice Age that followed. The stark and beautiful landscape is breathtaking.

Fjords are unique geological phenomena that only occur on western coasts of cold northern countries, such as Norway, Iceland, the Faeroe Islands, British Columbia in Canada, and Alaska in the United States. These deep inlets were gouged out by glaciers as they advanced from the mountains and cut their way down to the sea. When the glaciers receded, they left behind towering canyons, misty waterfalls, and deep blue seawater. A few miles north of Bergen is the gateway to the longest, deepest, and most stunning fjord of them all — Sognefjord.

Sognefjord is 120 miles long and a mile deep. It is dotted with quaint harbors, postcard villages, and remote farms. Vessels of all sizes, from cruise ships to tiny fishing boats, **troll** up and down the fjord to enjoy the jaw-dropping scenery and stop in at the brightly painted shiplap hamlets along the shore. And yet, Norway offers even more treasures to behold.

troll: to search in or at

Over 28 medieval stave churches where Vikings worshiped have been preserved or restored in Norway, and several of them are nestled in and amongst the steep mountainsides along the western fjords. Although very old, there is evidence that some of the stave churches were built on the remains of even older churches. Some have very intricate designs.

Christianity came to Norway in several ways. Vikings who had converted during their journeys brought their new religion home. King Harald also led the way when he converted to Christianity, though accounts for why and how it was done differ. And finally, the faith was spreading because of the efforts and travels of early believers. Often, the construction of a church in a community helped to bring a permanent focal point of faith during this transition. Let's stop in to see one up close and personal.

One of the oldest, best preserved, and scenically situated stave churches in Norway is located 15 miles up the Sognefjord in the little town of Vik. Hopperstad Stave Church is rustically beautiful on the outside with its multi-tiered roof punctuated by dragonheads looking out over the rolling hills and dramatic fjord cliffs. But the interior is even more breathtaking — and surprisingly empty. Many other stave churches throughout the region have been subjected to multiple revisions and additions over the centuries. This one has not. It is blissfully uncluttered just as it was when it was built back in the mid-12th century. Its very emptiness is what draws your eyes upward to the light that filters gently down from the high windows far above. And that is when you notice that the underside of the roof looks like an inverted Viking ship.

Artists, poets, and photographers are drawn to Norway's fjords for the beauty they find in the lofty canyons, on the glistening glaciers, beside the cascading waterfalls, within the brightly painted towns, and on the deep crystal bays. It's easy to spend days here, fighting the realization that at some point we will have to leave. The Norwegian people have truly been blessed to be surrounded by such serene beauty.

And on that note, we are off to Stavanger, a city half the size of Bergen at 125,000 residents. The waterfront city on the southwestern corner of Norway is a great place to learn about the oil industry history. Norway struck a goldmine in oil offshore. In fact, it is their possession of this valuable natural resource that prevented the nation from joining the European Union. Joining the EU means sharing resources. Norway became one of the wealthiest countries on the planet, and she would like to keep it that way.

Norwegian citizens have a parliamentary constitutional monarchy, and the government focuses on policies beneficial for its citizens. Norway is a peace-loving neighbor, and Norwegians have been described as the happiest, healthiest, and wealthiest people in the world.

There is another more controversial reason why Norway declined immediately joining the European Union, a union that unifies the majority of European countries, and the reason may surprise you. Joining the EU means discontinuing a profitable whaling industry. Norway has a long history of hunting whale for its commercial products, such as meat, oil, and blubber, the thick fatty skin that covers a whale's entire body. Whalers in Norway have been permitted to hunt and catch the Minke whales, which is a smaller breed of whale that thrives in the cold northern Atlantic Ocean.

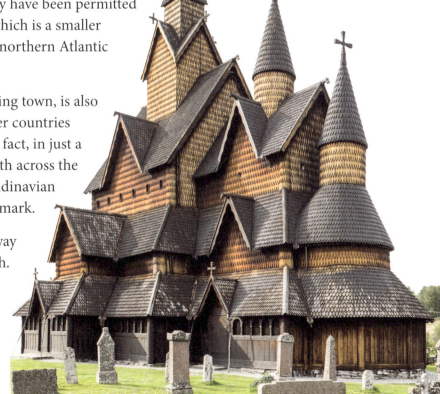
Hoddal Stave Church

Stavanger, besides its history as a whaling town, is also a ferry hub connecting Norway to other countries in Scandinavia and the British Isles. In fact, in just a few short hours, we will be gliding south across the North Sea and arriving in the last Scandinavian country we have yet to explore — Denmark.

And now it's time to say goodbye. Norway is beautiful, vibrant, and historically rich. The scenery and landmarks have been imprinted on our memories forever. Stunning fjords and towering stave churches will visit our dreams in the very best way. Farewell!

Exploring Norway Beyond Oslo

Past and Present:
- ✔ After the Black Death in 1349, the next major threat was the Victual Brothers (pirates).
- ✔ Fjords are inlets gouged by glaciers, which then leave canyons, waterfalls, and blue waters.
- ✔ More than 28 medieval stave churches have been preserved or restored in Norway.
- ✔ Hopperstad Stave Church was built in the 12th century and is beautifully preserved.

Other Cities:
- ✔ The city of Bergen was originally Bjørgvin, meaning "the green meadow among the mountains."
- ✔ Cities in Norway are bright and modern with friendly people.
- ✔ The city of Bergen is a place to begin exploring the beautiful countryside.
- ✔ The city of Stavanger on the coast is a whaling town, ferry hub, and oil industry area.

TIMELINE

820 ▶	The Oseberg ship is built by the Vikings.
1049 ▶	The city of Oslo, Norway, is established.
1070 ▶	Bergen, Norway, is established by King Olav Kyrre, son of Harald Hardrada.
1150 ▶	Hopperstad Stave Church is built along the Sognefjord in Norway.
1349 ▶	The Black Death arrives in Norway.
1429 ▶	Pirates, the Victual Brothers, burn down much of Bergen, Norway.
1500 ▶	Denmark rules all of Norway and much of Sweden.
1665 ▶	The Battle of Vågen is waged between the Dutch and English in Bergen Harbor, Norway.
1888 ▶	Alfred Nobel reads his own (mistaken) obituary in the newspaper.
1901 ▶	The first Nobel Peace Prize is awarded to Jean Henri Dunant for his role in founding the International Red Cross.
1903 ▶	The Oseberg Ship is uncovered in Norway.
2018 ▶	A 66-foot Viking longship is discovered in southern Norway.

124 🌐 Lesson 6. Day 56

A Child's Geography. Vol. 5: Explore Viking Realms

Fill in the Blank

1. Vikings got their name from *vik*, meaning _____ or inlet.

2. Vikings invaded other countries in search of _____.

3. The top of a stave church looks like an upside down _____ _____.

4. Alfred Nobel created the Nobel Prize to recognize someone who changed the world for the _____.

5. Whalers in Norway are known for hunting and catching _____ whales.

Paint a Lily

Stave churches in the Scandinavian countries are known for their unique style. Made from wooden posts and planks, they were fitted together with some of the same woodworking techniques as Viking ships at the time. Likewise, ornamental carving was part of the design.

Materials needed:
- ☐ Paint
- ☐ Paintbrush
- ☐ Surface or paper for painting

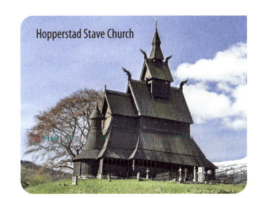
Hopperstad Stave Church

Hopperstad Stave Church has been preserved throughout the centuries. Although some of the carvings resemble styles of the time period, there were also lily-like flowers in the carvings. The lily stands for purity and holds various meanings in Christianity: salvation; resurrection; or Mary, mother of Jesus. Lily flowers grow wild in Scandinavian countries.

Let's paint a lily to remember the Scandinavian countries and heritage we're learning about and also recall the meaning of the lily flower. When you see the lily, you may remember the gift of salvation, the Resurrection of Christ, or Mary.

Using a surface or paper of your choice, paint a lily flower. Consider sharing it or giving it to someone else.

Fjords in Poetry

Fjords capture the attention of artists, photographers, and poets.

The lush landscape of Norway can remind us of the "green pastures" of the 23rd Psalm. God's creation is a reminder of His comfort and eternal presence.

Psalm 23:

Watercolor painting of the fjords of Norway

> The LORD is my shepherd.
>
> I will not be in need.
>
> He lets me lie down in green pastures:
>
> He leads me beside quiet waters.
>
> He restores my soul:
>
> He guides me in the paths of righteousness
>
> For the sake of His name.
>
> Even though I walk through the valley of the shadow of death.
>
> I fear no evil. for You are with me:
>
> Your rod and Your staff. they comfort me.
>
> You prepare a table before me in the presence of my enemies:
>
> You have anointed my head with oil:
>
> My cup overflows.
>
> Certainly goodness and faithfulness will follow me all the days of my life.
>
> And my dwelling *will be* in the house of the LORD forever.

Psalms can be read as poetry or sung.

Write a poem or song describing the amazing landscape of Norway, from fjords, to mountains, to meadows, to waters, and ice. You may also choose to include praise to God for creation.

_____

_____

_____

_____

_____

_____

_____

_____

Mapping It Out!

Complete the map of the country of Norway in the box below. Refer to the map on page 382.

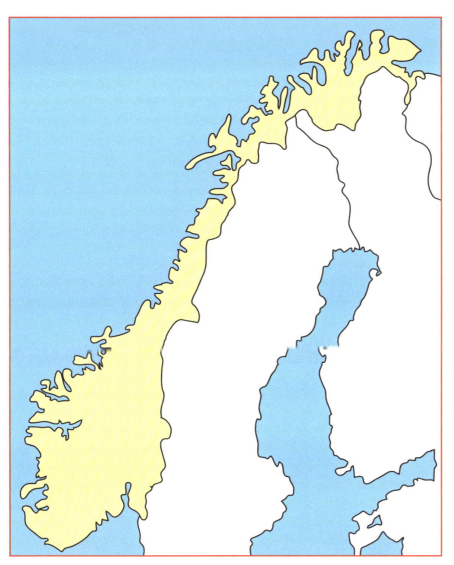

Label the following places on your map. You can use colored pencils to shade areas of land or water, draw rivers and mountains, etc.

☐ Norway

☐ Bergen

☐ Sognefjord

☐ Ny-Ålesund

☐ Add a star ★ for the capital city of Oslo.

Notice how Norway is farther west, farther east, and farther north of Sweden (all three directions).

Flashcards

Make flashcards of the bolded glossary words from this lesson. Then, either add drawings of the terms or act them out in charades. Be creative!

Norwegian buhund

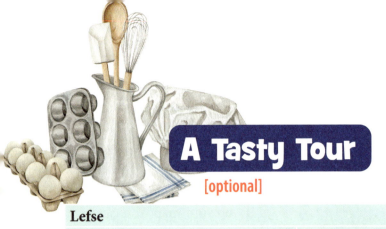

A Tasty Tour

[optional]

Lefse

Ingredients:

10 pounds potatoes, peeled

½ cup butter

⅓ cup heavy cream

1 tablespoon salt

1 tablespoon white sugar

2½ cups all-purpose flour

Special equipment:

Potato ricer

Pastry cloth

NOTE: This recipe requires adult supervision and participation.

Directions:

1. Cover potatoes with water and cook until tender. Run hot potatoes through a potato ricer. Place into a large bowl. Beat butter, cream, salt, and sugar into the hot riced potatoes. Let cool to room temperature.

2. Stir flour into the potato mixture. Pull off pieces of the dough and form into walnut size balls. Lightly flour a pastry cloth and roll out lefse balls to ⅛ inch thickness.

3. Cook on a hot (400° F/200° C) griddle until bubbles form and each side has browned. Place on a damp towel to cool slightly and then cover with damp towel until ready to serve.

Optional: Teacher's Discretion
☐ No   ☐ Yes   Due Date: _____

Learn Geography Terms

Page 342 is a reference page for understanding the terms geographers use to describe landforms.

Love your neighbor

We are thankful for the people who brought Christianity to Norway. When King Harald converted to Christianity, he had the opportunity to use his power and influence to spread the faith. As some Vikings converted to Christianity and traveled, they helped spread the Good News. We thank You, Lord, for the construction of church buildings as a place for people to gather and worship. The beauty of Norway reminds us of Your power, Lord. As Psalm 24:10 says, "Who is this King of glory? The LORD of armies, He is the King of glory." Selah

Denmark: The Danish Islands

After a half-day boat ride, we arrive in our final and most southern Scandinavian country — the beautiful land of Denmark. Denmark is by far the smallest of the Scandinavian countries, but that hasn't always been the case. During the 16th century, Denmark was the largest when it ruled all of Norway and the three southern provinces of Sweden in addition to its modern-day territory. Danes are proud of their mighty heritage as a northern superpower, rulers of the northern seas, and explorers of the vast western frontier. They are also proud of their flag — the oldest flag in the world, unchanged since its inception in the year 1219, with its offset white cross atop a bold red background.

Along with Sweden and Norway, Denmark too was home to the Vikings, the mighty warriors who were known far and wide for their superb strength and superior shipbuilding skills. While the Swedish Vikings ventured primarily east and the Norwegians primarily south, the Danish Vikings journeyed west to Great Britain and Ireland, founding Dublin and

Beech Tree: Beech trees were some of the ancient forests that still seed and grow today. The leaves of the beech tree showcase a unique folding pattern that has inspired mankind to model other beneficial designs, like some heart procedures — and even solar space panels. There are so many ways the beech tree reminds us of the masterwork of God.

other great cities in the British Isles. In fact, it was the Danes that brought Christianity back to Denmark from the devout monks and missionaries they encountered on those islands.

Denmark is composed of a peninsula that juts up from northern Germany along with 443 islands that cluster around it and a handful of islands located much farther away — Greenland and the Faroe Islands. The capital city of Copenhagen is located on the largest island, sandwiched between the jutting peninsula and Sweden.

We are leaving our boat at the port town of Hirtshals, located on the northern tip of the main peninsula known as Jutland. Unlike the landscape of Sweden, which is punctuated by millions of lakes, or of Norway, dotted with jagged mountains, Denmark is flat. This landscape is composed of vast farmland interspersed with ancient beech forests and decorated with whitewashed churches like diamonds in settings of red brick towns.

The Danes who greet us are mostly blond with blue eyes. While many Danish people have moved to other parts of the world, particularly the United States, not many people have **immigrated** here to mix up the gene pool. In fact, two out of every three Danes have last names ending in "-sen," such as Hansen or Andersen. The most famous of all Danes was named Hans Christian Andersen. Andersen, or HC as he is fondly referred to here, was the beloved author of famous children's works such as *The Ugly Duckling* and *The Emperor's New Clothes.*

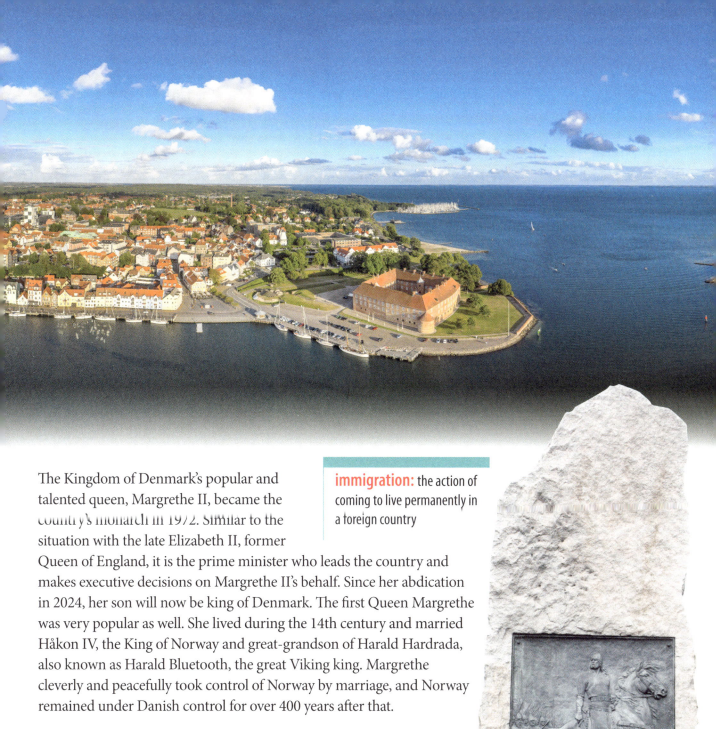

The Kingdom of Denmark's popular and talented queen, Margrethe II, became the country's monarch in 1972. Similar to the situation with the late Elizabeth II, former Queen of England, it is the prime minister who leads the country and makes executive decisions on Margrethe II's behalf. Since her abdication in 2024, her son will now be king of Denmark. The first Queen Margrethe was very popular as well. She lived during the 14th century and married Håkon IV, the King of Norway and great-grandson of Harald Hardrada, also known as Harald Bluetooth, the great Viking king. Margrethe cleverly and peacefully took control of Norway by marriage, and Norway remained under Danish control for over 400 years after that.

> **immigration:** the action of coming to live permanently in a foreign country

We'll drive down through the scenic peninsula and then hop from island to island on the modern Danish bridge system that connects the larger islands in a long consecutive chain. The main attraction on Jutland is LEGO® House. In 1932, LEGO® began here in Denmark when a local carpenter named his wooden toy blocks after the Danish phrase *leg godt*, which means "play well." In 1949, his company started making the iconic interlocking plastic bricks that have become famous the world over. When the company's revenue began to decline in the 1980s, executives decided to create themed sets, which included even smaller and more specialized pieces. Today's kids have grown up assembling kits based on cultural icons and popular movies. And it all began right here!

Monument to Harald Hardrada, Oslo

LEGO® House Denmark is filled with incredible, larger-than-life spaceships, castles, and Wild West towns, but perhaps the highlight for young and old alike is Miniland, where carefully replicated landscapes and cityscapes from the real world have been constructed out of LEGO® bricks. Here, visitors can enjoy world-famous sites such as the Eiffel Tower and Big Ben, situated just around the corner from Dutch windmills, German castles, and even the harbor of Bergen that is so fresh in our memories from our time spent in Norway.

From Jutland, we'll take the bridge from Snoghøj to Staurby on the island of Funen. This is the island home of Hans Christian Andersen. HC was born in Odense, the largest city on the island and third-largest city in Denmark. Odense was founded in A.D. 988, named for the false Viking god Oden, who was also known as Woden, for which our day of the week Wednesday, was named. Andersen was born here in 1805. His childhood home has been converted and expanded into a grand museum.

Just off the coast of Funen is the sleepy and salty island of Ærø. This old fishing and farming village is truly frozen in time from the 1600s because the Danish government will not allow any new buildings to be built on Ærø. Here, the several-hundred-year-old houses practically lean upon one another along the old cobbled lanes. Residents set out baskets of berries on their front porches for passersby to buy using the honor system. To visit here feels like going back to a simpler time when people trusted each other more.

However, the government has agreed to allow the construction of structures that provide renewable energy to its residents. On the island of Ærø, you can see several modern windmills dotting the landscape and one of the world's largest solar power plants. The townspeople have placed a high priority on wind and solar power.

Ærø looks like the type of tiny town you might find assembled in miniature form inside a bottle. In fact, this is where the ships-in-a-bottle were once made, and you can see hundreds of them for yourself in the Bottle Peter Museum.

Land of LEGO® House

Noteworthy:
- ✔ The land is flat with farmland, ancient beech forests, and churches.
- ✔ The prime minister leads the country with the monarchy in the kingdom.
- ✔ The town of Roskilde is home to a large Danish Viking ship museum.

Islands:
- ✔ Jutland includes the famous LEGO® House.
- ✔ Funen is home to playwright and poet Hans Christian Andersen (HC).
- ✔ Baskets of berries to sell dot the porches of Ærø, a fishing and farming village.
- ✔ The capital city of Copenhagen is located on Zealand, Denmark's largest island.

Find the Viking Artifacts

In the maze, start at the Viking museum. Follow the path through the maze to locate all the Viking artifacts. Then, exit the museum.

Playwright and Poet from Denmark

As a child, Danish Author Hans Christian Andersen, who went by HC, was known to say, "Perhaps one day Odense will become famous because of me." Indeed it has, HC.

Hans was an only child who received a basic education. At the age of eleven, after his father's death, he was expected to support himself, so he became an apprentice to a weaver and then a tailor. He had an incredible soprano voice and was encouraged to pursue theater in Copenhagen. Unfortunately, his voice had changed by that time. His new theater friends commented on his talent for poetry and convinced him to pursue a career in writing instead.

Hans Christian Andersen

Andersen's writing style reflected the pain and heartbreak he often felt as a child, and these tales of loneliness, ugliness, and social awkwardness with true happy endings struck a chord in his readers.

Heartbreak was experienced by people long before Andersen. In Isaiah 61:1, we read that the Lord sent Isaiah "to bind up the brokenhearted."

1. What do you think brokenhearted means?

_____

_____

2. How do people experience heartbreak today?

_____

_____

3. What does Isaiah reveal to us about the Lord?

_____

_____

4. What do you think heartbreak means for you and other people today?

_____

_____

Stevns Klint, a white chalk cliff in the Danish island of Zealand.

→ Beyond Ærø, we come to the island of Zealand, where the capital city of Copenhagen is situated on its eastern coast. But before we get there, we have some incredible sights to see. Our first stop is the Viking Ship Museum. I know we already visited one in Norway, but this one tells a deeper story, giving us further insight into how the Vikings were able to discover North America 500 years before Columbus ever set sail for the New World.

The Danish Viking ship museum is in Roskilde, a town strategically located at the far end of a shallow inlet, or *vik*, which is the Norse word for "inlet" and the root for the word Viking, named so because they built their great ships inside these protected coves. This ship museum holds five partially completed Viking ships, not nearly as well-preserved as the three on display in Oslo, Norway, but the experience of seeing them is set up differently here. This is a hands-on museum. As we wander through the museum, we can don Viking clothing, talk with modern-day Vikings who are building replica ships using authentic tools and methods from the Viking age, and even get a chance to row one of the replica ships out of the harbor and set sail around the large bay.

Viking ship at the Roskilde Museum

Denmark: The Danish Islands

Kulusuk, Greenland

Karl, one of the modern shipbuilders, catches our eye, sets down his chisel, and asks us if we'd like to hear more about how the Vikings were able to sail and settle over such a vast territory thousands of miles in diameter.

"Absolutely!"

"The Vikings were an amazingly efficient people group, but not the most content. They were always looking for greener pastures, so to speak." Karl pauses significantly and then continues, "Scandinavia, their homeland, is a harshly frigid region of the world, and there isn't a great amount of farmable land. Denmark has always had the best farmland of the Nordic countries, but size-wise, the amount of land on this collection of islands was not enough to support the growing Viking population. It was time to look for more arable land on distant shores.

"That is precisely the reason why the Danish and Norwegian Vikings sailed mostly south. But they also went west, believing that there was more land to the west that wasn't populated like the countries that they invaded to the south. And they were right! They eventually discovered the Faroe Islands, Iceland, Greenland, and Canada.

"The Vikings were master shipbuilders. They built two types of ships primarily — the warship and the cargo ship. The warship, known as a longboat, was sleek and slender, the perfect shape for gliding through the waters quickly while still carrying upward of a hundred or more warriors. These narrow ships did not have a large capacity for cargo, which meant that they could only remain at sea for about a week before landing somewhere and taking on more supplies, either through raiding or trading.

Viking longboat

136 Lesson 7. Day 65

A Child's Geography. Vol. 5: Explore Viking Realms

"How then did the Vikings sail out and find such distant lands as Iceland and Greenland? Well, they built larger, sturdier cargo vessels that could carry more provisions and people for further explorations. But they didn't have compasses, telescopes, sextants, or other navigational equipment. Yet, living close to the land, they knew how to navigate the seas by observing the sun, stars, and other visible landmarks. They trusted their eyes and their collective wits to determine their location at sea. Once Iceland was discovered, returning Vikings would guide sea captains to the large island by the location of the sun on the horizon, keeping the Faroe Islands to their left, and by their powers of observation of the birds above and the sea life below.

"Iceland was a wonderful place for the Vikings to settle. It was green and farmable, and they settled right in, eager to make themselves at home. However, it wasn't long before it became overpopulated, so adventurous Icelandic Vikings began to venture even farther afield and found Greenland.

"The name Greenland was just a sneaky marketing ploy by the Viking explorers to convince more families to sail west and settle the massive island. Greenland was anything but green. Three quarters of Greenland, the largest island in the world and the least populated territory on the planet, is covered in a solid sheet of ice that never melts.

"Today, Greenland is owned by Denmark, along with the Faroe Islands, but less than 50,000 people live there because of its inhospitable conditions. About the same number of people live on the Faroe Islands, even though the island chain is exceedingly beautiful with stunning fjords and cascading waterfalls, because the cold and unwelcome weather conditions can make life extremely difficult for residents. Only the heartiest of Danish citizens inhabit these outposts today."

We thank Karl for the wealth of information he has shared so generously with us. He thanks us for listening and resumes his work on the hull of the craft he is building.

Viking helmet

Just a short drive north along the Roskilde Fjord, we arrive at the finest castle in Denmark — Frederiksborg Castle. This grand palace sits on an island in the middle of a lake in the small town of Hillerød. Built in the early 1600s by King Christian IV, Frederiksborg is often called the "Danish Versailles." Christian IV, who also built the palace in Oslo, became king of Denmark during the height of its power when it ruled over all of Norway and vast sections of Sweden too. As far as monarchs go, Christian IV, during his 50-year reign, ordered more expansion, reform, and building than any other Scandinavian ruler before or since. You will see his logo, a C encircling the number 4 topped by a crown, adorning many buildings and castles throughout Denmark and Norway.

The castle and gardens are as lovely as they come. We could spend hours here imagining what life must have been like ruling the entire northern capstone of Europe. Spectacular. Dazzling. Magnificent.

Driving back down south, we reach Copenhagen, Denmark's beautiful capital city. Copenhagen is an oasis of scrumptious food, cutting-edge architecture, and the quirkiest counterculture community in Europe.

Copenhagen is home to the five-time winner of "best restaurant in the world." Noma is not a place you can book a reservation on the same day. You would need to plan ahead about three months to get a table reserved. Nor is this a restaurant where you can order prime rib or chicken parmesan. Noma boasts a New Nordic menu, featuring such Scandinavian delicacies as Icelandic seaweed, Faroese deep-sea fish, Greenlandic musk ox, and sorrel from Danish forests. The chefs at 2-Michelin-star Noma do all their own smoking, curing, and pickling to astound their guests with the most memorable culinary experience of their lives.

Painting of Frederiksborg Castle, 1585

Frederiksborg Castle

A single meal may equal a full week's wage or more, so I suggest we fill up on some less expensive fare. Denmark is the land of Danish pastries, and some of my favorites can be ordered just around the corner from Noma in a quaint little cafe and bakery that serves coffee and pastry inside, as well as packing up crisp, white boxes of their specialty treats to go.

A Danish is a multilayered sweet pastry that was brought to Denmark by Austrian bakers but has developed into a Danish specialty named for them. Similar to a croissant, a Danish is made from laminated yeast-leavened dough that creates a layered texture–like puff pastry.

Inside the bakery, we can choose one or two from a list of a dozen varieties. Here are some of your choices:

Michelin Matters: There is a way of designating the very best of the best restaurants in cities and countries around the world by a system of stars or a Michelin Guide. The more stars awarded, the better the food and dining experience. These places are included in a small guidebook so people can know what kinds of food are served and what kind of dining service they will receive.

Surprisingly, this guide was created and remains the work of the Michelin company in France — a producer of tires. Around 1900, the company began developing guides of different places to visit to encourage people to buy cars and travel — and use their tires. As it became more popular, the rating system for the quality of restaurants was included.

laminated: a folding process that creates many thin layers separated by butter

Strawberry Lime Almond Braid

Chocolate, Berry, and Cream Cheese

Cranberry Orange Danish Braid

Raspberry and Cream Cheese

Blueberries and Cream

Danish Kringle

What will you order? I will order the Kringle! This simple almond-flavored puff pastry Danish drizzled with white frosting makes my mouth water just thinking about it. In my family, it is tradition to make Danish Kringle once a year on Christmas morning. It is my favorite.

We have one last stop before we say goodbye to Denmark and the entire region of Scandinavia. This place, Freetown Christiania, on page 145 will surprise you, shock you, delight you, and cause you to contemplate how a community functions and how everyone can contribute to make their neighborhood a better place.

Just across the way to the east, we can see the beautiful bridge that connects Denmark to Sweden. We have come full circle and have experienced Scandinavia almost like a local. What a great adventure we have had so far through the northern realms of Europe. These Nordic nations are friendly, clean, and colorful. But now, we must say farewell to Scandinavia and enter a different part of Europe — the British Isles, located not too far from here. Far enough, though, that we'll take a plane.

And with that, we are off to England!

Vikings, Castles, Danish Pastries, and More in Denmark!

Vikings:
- ✔ The Vikings traveled beyond Denmark to Iceland, which is also green pastureland.
- ✔ Greenland was given its name by Vikings to trick others into traveling to the icy, mostly uninhabitable land.
- ✔ Leif Erikson discovered Newfoundland in North America in the year 1000.

Points of Interest:
- ✔ Greenland and the Faroe Islands are owned by Denmark.
- ✔ Frederiksborg Castle is in the small town of Hillerød on an island.
- ✔ Noma is a restaurant that is the five-time winner of "best restaurant in the world."
- ✔ Austrian bakers brought the Danish, a type of puff pastry, to Denmark.
- ✔ The community of Christiania was named after the 17th-century king, Christian IV.

TIMELINE

980	▶	Erik the Red discovers Greenland.
988	▶	The city of Odense in Denmark is founded.
1000	▶	Leif Erikson discovers Newfoundland in North America.
1219	▶	The oldest flag in the world — Denmark's — is designed.
1500	▶	Denmark rules all of Norway and much of Sweden.
1932	▶	LEGO® company is founded in Denmark.
1971	▶	A large group of homeless people storm a military base, taking possession of it for their new home, now called Christiania.
1972	▶	Margrethe II, Queen of Denmark, begins her reign; abdicates in 2024.

LEGO® House vs. Danish Viking Ship Museum

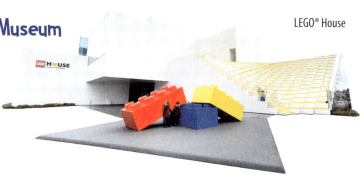
LEGO® House

Answer the questions. As an optional activity, with your parent's permission or guidance, explore books or online sources to learn more about LEGO® House on Jutland and the Danish Viking Ship Museum in Roskilde.

Optional: Teacher's Discretion   ☐ No   ☐ Yes   Due Date: _____

1. What is an interesting feature you learned about LEGO® House?

_____

_____

_____

2. What is an interesting feature you learned about the Danish Viking Ship Museum?

_____

_____

_____

3. Would you rather visit LEGO® House in Denmark or the Danish Viking Ship Museum? Why?

_____

_____

_____

Short Answer

How were Vikings able to travel such long distances without navigational equipment?

_____

_____

_____

Norway vs. Denmark

Remember the fjords and mountains of Norway? The landscape was much different than Denmark with its flat lands and rolling hills. Observe the topographical maps of Norway and Denmark. Notice how different colors and shading are used to show more mountainous regions.

Materials needed:
☐ Colored pencils

1. What color shading on the topographical maps do you think represents the highest or most mountainous point?

_____

Scientists today recognize that the formation of fjords and mountains was caused by a dramatic change, a shift that was not a slow process, but one caused by an abrupt, widespread event.

We learn about the dramatic changes as a result of the global Flood during Noah's time and about God's promise in Psalm 104:5–9:

He established the earth upon its foundations.

So that it will not totter forever and ever.

You covered it with the deep sea as with a garment:

The waters were standing above the mountains.

They fled from Your rebuke.

At the sound of Your thunder they hurried away.

The mountains rose: the valleys sank down

To the place which You established for them.

You set a boundary so *that* they will not pass over.

So *that* they will not return to cover the earth.

2. Choose a colored pencil and underline instances of the word "earth" in the psalm, as well as any parts of the earth or creation.

3. Choose a different colored pencil and underline the words that refer to God.

4. Choose a third colored pencil and underline action words (verbs) that describe what happened.

5. Finally, choose a fourth colored pencil and underline instances of the word "not."

Mapping It Out!

Complete the map of the country of Denmark in the box below. Refer to the map on page 382.

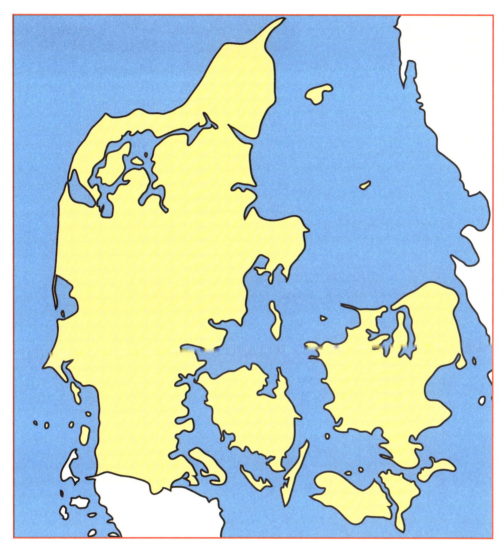

Label the following places on your map. You can use colored pencils to shade areas of land or water, draw rivers and mountains, etc.

- ☐ Denmark
- ☐ Aarhus
- ☐ Esbjerg
- ☐ Odense
- ☐ Add a star ★ for the capital city of Copenhagen.

Flashcards

Make flashcards of the bolded glossary words from this lesson. Then, either add drawings of the terms or act them out in charades. Be creative!

Broholmer

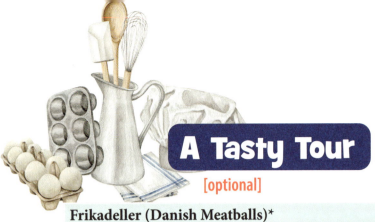

A Tasty Tour

[optional]

Frikadeller (Danish Meatballs)*

Ingredients:

1½ lb ground beef

½ lb ground sausage

1 grated or finely chopped onion

1 egg

½ cup milk

2 tablespoons flour

2 tablespoons breadcrumbs

¼ teaspoon pepper

¼ teaspoon salt

½ teaspoon cloves

NOTE: This recipe requires adult supervision and participation.

Directions:

1. Combine meat with breadcrumbs. Add egg, onion, pepper, and flour. Add milk a little at a time. Mix thoroughly and refrigerate for 3 hours. Before frying, add salt and ground cloves.

2. Heat lard or butter in a pan. Drop meat mixture from large tablespoon into frying pan and brown on all sides. Remove fully cooked meatballs to baking dish and keep warm in low oven. Make gravy from the pan drippings. Arrange the meatballs on a serving dish, pour gravy over them, and serve.

*Compare to Lesson 5's Tasty Tour — Swedish Meatballs.

Optional: Teacher's Discretion
☐ No   ☐ Yes   Due Date: _____

Learn Geography Terms

Page 342 is a reference page for understanding the terms geographers use to describe landforms.

Love your neighbor

What an adventure learning about the Scandinavian countries of Finland, Sweden, Norway, and Denmark! Lord, we give You thanks for the people of each land, from the Finns in Helsinki, to the Swedes in the Icehotel and colorful buildings in Sweden, to the Norwegians in the fjords and mountains of Norway, to the Danes in the rolling hills and flatlands of Denmark. Again, we thank You for Your people and mighty power as recorded in Psalm 104:8: "The mountains rose; the valleys sank down To the place which You established for them."

144 Lesson 7. Day 68

A Child's Geography. Vol. 5: Explore Viking Realms

Talk About It

As tourists throughout this series, we explore beautiful cities and countries. We look at the houses and other scenery and are awed by the beauty. What we do not see is the reality that not everyone has a home or other place to live. Homelessness is an increasing issue everywhere. In a world where so many challenges have been met and solutions found, homelessness remains a lingering problem. In the city of Copenhagen, Denmark, desperate people took a desperate chance.

In 1971, a large group of homeless people chose a closed military base and took possession of it for their new home. The officials of Copenhagen were not sure how to deal with the problem. To drive them out would mean that the homeless individuals and families would be back on the streets. In many ways, it was convenient for Copenhagen to have a secure place for their homeless to live that wasn't being used otherwise. However, it is wrong to assault people and steal property. City officials didn't know what to do, so they ignored the incident and pretended it didn't happen. Yet the issue plagued the leaders of Copenhagen and Denmark because this band of homeless people had broken down the fence, assaulted a guard, and stolen government property, breaking several laws.

Christian IV

The new residents of the former military base officially named their community Freetown Christiania, after the 17th-century king, Christian IV, but also gave it the nickname of Freetown. Everyone is welcome, but strict rules must be followed for the good of the community. No guns. No stealing. No violence. No drugs. And clean up after yourself. If a resident does not follow these rules, he or she is kicked out. It is rather strange and hypocritical to break the law and steal a military base and then create laws for the people who live there. However, as they are building their community, they have come to understand the importance of law and order.

Over time, pre-existing buildings have been renovated into living quarters, but residents of the community are allowed to build their own homes if they prefer. Christiania has become an eclectic mix of unregulated construction. Even businesses have cropped up inside the neighborhood.

After four decades of indecision, the government finally decided what to do about the seized military property. They sold it to the community for one million dollars. Now, residents pay rent to live in Christiania. It is no longer a free town, but the rent is affordable, and the community pays to retain control of their unique living arrangements. About two-thirds of the residents now have jobs in order to pay their rent. Even some of the original invaders, who hadn't worked for decades, are now gainfully employed. While the residents have created rules for their town and most members are productive members of society, this doesn't completely eliminate trouble or crime in the area. It exists here as it does everywhere and this will continue to be the case until Jesus returns, evil is defeated, and the earth is restored.

The townsfolk of Christiania are no longer homeless, nor are they unemployed. They have purpose. They have also converted their strange quirky neighborhood into a major tourist attraction. New restaurants and shops are popping up on every corner, and tourists are coming to witness this strange phenomenon and marvel at the unique town.

Talk with your family or a friend about homelessness.

Conversation starter ideas:

🌐 What could have been done differently, and what does the Bible say?

🌐 How could the mix of unregulated construction in Christiana offer benefits or problems?

🌐 What is something your family or community could do or is already doing for people who are homeless or in need?

One of the main streets in Christiania

146 🌐 Lesson 7. Day 70

A Child's Geography. Vol. 5: Explore Viking Realms

England: Northmen, Royals, and London

Early morning light filtering into the dim candlelit room revealed woolen-clad monks hunched over **vellum** sheets, carefully copying the manuscript set before them. Silence hung heavy in the air, etched only by the scratching of quill on paper. The monks had risen long before the sun, having already committed the previous two hours to prayer.

Shoulders tense, fingers gripping quills tightly, the men of God braced themselves for a storm they felt brewing out at sea. They couldn't see dark clouds, but they could feel a chill in their bones as they worked tirelessly to finish the pages of Scripture assigned to them that day. Glances at the window brought no comfort even as the sun rose gloriously over the horizon. Stay focused, the men reminded themselves. There is no room for error. The Scriptures must be transcribed perfectly. One beautifully scripted letter at a time.

vellum: a smooth material made from animal skin used for making books

Birds screeched overhead. Waves crashed upon the rocks outside the window. A terror was brewing out there. They could feel it, but the holy men could only watch, wait, and write. Keep working. Remain faithful. Trust in Christ, the Lord.

And then the terror manifested itself. Shouts from the sea floated into the quiet room. The men lifted their gaze to the window, and they beheld a horror they couldn't have imagined. Great ships as they had never seen before were crammed with fur-clad warriors storming onto the beach. Ruthlessly, the invaders attacked the defenseless monastery, desecrating the heart of the Northumbrian Kingdom. On June 8, 793, Lindisfarne was plundered of its spiritual and physical riches and then burned to the ground, very few monks escaping with their lives.

Lindisfarne Castle

Survivors spread the message of the Viking raid far and wide, warning everyone they could of the terrors of the northern invaders. News quickly reached Alcuin, the Northumbrian scholar who was working in faraway France as scribe to Charlemagne, the most powerful king in all of Europe. Alcuin was aghast and heartbroken by this news from home when he penned these words, "Never before has such terror appeared in Britain as we have now suffered ..." in a letter to Higbald, the Bishop of Lindisfarne. The Vikings were certainly not the first warring tribe to arrive in Britain. From antiquity, the British Isles had been invaded by legions of armies and barbarians from all directions — the Scots from Ireland, the Picts from Scotland, the Romans from Italy, and the Saxons from Germany, to name a few. But the Vikings changed the face of Britain as their raids increased in both frequency and number around the coasts of England, Scotland, Wales, and Ireland, plunging the Isles into the dark ages on the heels of the prosperous Roman occupation and the age of Christian missions and conversion that followed. Whole libraries filled with books of great literature and Scripture were burned or destroyed. Seemingly indestructible Roman architecture was razed to the ground, entire towns were leveled, and close-knit communities were devastated. Yet a glimmer of light remained for the people of Britain. Despite the ferocity of the attack at Lindisfarne and other unsuspecting locations around the isles, the light of the Gospel continued to burn brightly, and the Christian community flourished through the time we now call the Dark Ages.

Viking Raider Doomsday Stone, Lindisfarne, c. 800

148 Lesson 8. Day 76

A Child's Geography. Vol. 5: Explore Viking Realms

Tales from the Tower

When the Viking raids of Britain began, the **Northmen** did not arrive to find this island a place of chaos, controlled by warring barbarian tribes, as was the case in much of the rest of Europe during the Dark Ages. In fact, in A.D. 793, the people they found in the British Isles were organized, studious, and wealthy compared to other civilizations they had previously conquered. Let's wind the clock back 750 years from the Viking assaults on Britain to find out why.

> **Northmen:** barbaric pirates who were Vikings from Scandinavia

A.D. 43 marks the year that the Roman Empire began their massive invasion of Britain, conquering nearly all of modern-day England and naming their newly claimed land Britannia Province. The Romans brought structure to the formerly tribal society, including roads, architecture, literacy, and centralized government. In fact, as we journey through the British Isles during this portion of our grand adventure, we will drive on highways built atop ancient Roman roads and wander through Roman buildings, baths, and bastions that still stand strong thousands of years later.

However, the mighty Roman Empire and their occupation of Britain didn't last forever. By 410, the empire was in rapid decline as barbarians sacked faraway Rome from every direction. This same year, the Romans withdrew their armies from the British islands to reinforce their borders on the main European continent, leaving Britannia to fend for herself. Wars did ensue as the Scots and Picts descended from the north and the Celts arrived from the west, but a different and more curious movement happened during this turnover of power. The Christian religion flourished as missionaries poured in and out of the country and monasteries like Lindisfarne were built all over Britannia for the study of God's Word and the accurate transcription of Scripture and other great works of literature.

The British people were on a fast track to becoming

the most educated and prosperous people in Europe. Since those early Dark Ages, Britain rose to become one of the world's greatest superpowers during the Middle Ages, Renaissance, and industrial time periods, colonizing regions all over the globe, before shrinking back to her original size within the last 50 years.

Are you ready to explore this island nation that has made such a profound mark on every corner of the world throughout the span of history? I am, but before we go, we need to clear up a little confusion. There are many names that need to be sorted out so we know what we are talking about. Some of the names referring to this area of the world are Great Britain, the UK or United Kingdom, the British Isles, England, Wales, Scotland, etc. Do all these names refer to the same country or region? Good question! Let's get this confusion straightened out once and for all.

Let's work our way from the largest to the smallest grouping. The British Isles encompass several islands and countries, including the Republic of Ireland, Northern Ireland, Isle of Man, the Hebrides, Scotland, Wales, and England. Next down in size is the United Kingdom, which includes only Northern Ireland from the smaller island of Ireland, plus the entire larger island, which includes Scotland, England, and Wales. The United Kingdom also possesses three self-governing entities, known as crown dependencies, which are the Isle of Man, located in the Irish Sea, and the Bailiwicks of Guernsey and Jersey, islands located off the coast of France. The largest island is called Great Britain, and the smaller island to its left is known simply as Ireland, of which only a quarter is included in the UK. Make sense? If you're confused, don't worry, most non-British citizens are.

Royalty on the Throne

The good news is that our plane is coming in for a landing at Heathrow Airport outside London, the capital and largest city in England, which is the largest country in Great Britain, which is the largest island in both the United Kingdom and the British Isles. All in all, London seems like a good place to start our adventure through this stunningly beautiful region of the world.

As we wait for our rental car, we overhear some locals chatting about the royal family. Many British citizens adore "the royals," a fond nickname they use for the royal family of the United Kingdom. Let me bring you up to speed on this highly celebrated and world-famous family.

The late monarch was Elizabeth II, Queen of England. She was the first of two daughters born to her father, King George VI, called Albert or "Bertie" by his family, and her mother, also named Elizabeth. Albert never expected to inherit the throne since he was the second-born son of George V and lived most of his life in the shadow of his older brother, Edward.

When George V died in 1936, Edward became king. Later that year, he announced his decision to marry an American woman, who had previously been married and divorced. The prime minister advised Edward that for political and religious reasons — for the king of England is also head of the Church of England — he could not marry a divorced woman and remain king. Edward chose love over power by marrying the American woman and thus **abdicating** the throne to his brother.

King George VI

Albert, crowned George VI, became king that same year, and his eldest daughter, 10-year-old Elizabeth, became the new heir. She grew up, married Prince Philip, and had four children. Upon the death of her father in 1952, Elizabeth became queen.

abdication: to renounce or give up the right to the throne

Elizabeth's oldest son, Charles, then became king of England. In 1981, he married Lady Diana Spencer, and they had two sons — Prince William and Prince Harry. Princess Diana died in a car accident when the boys were teenagers. Today, they are grown with families of their own.

The succession to the throne goes like this:

When Queen Elizabeth II passed away, Prince Charles became the king in 2023. Next, the throne will go to Prince William, Charles' oldest son. William and his wife, Kate, were married in 2011. Then, the path to the throne continues down the family lineage of their oldest son, George, and his siblings. If a king were to have no children, the lineage passes to the nearest sibling. The Succession to the Crown Act in 2013 changed from males being first in line to the throne ahead of females in the royal family.

But oh! It's getting late. Let's jump into our rental car and drive into London, one of the world's great cities.

The challenge for most people who are new to the United Kingdom, or just visiting like we are, is getting used to the driving. British cars are outfitted with the steering wheel on the right side of the car. And drivers in Britain must remain on the left side of the road so that oncoming traffic passes you on the right. This is opposite of more than 90% of the world's countries, and it takes a little getting used to.

London is an old city. The Romans established it after their invasion in A.D. 43 and named it Londinium. While the official City of London is only one square mile — the same size it was during Roman times — greater London is the largest city in Europe. In fact, it was the largest city in the world until 1925.

There is so much to see and do in London because of its depth of history and strategic location on the globe. London is the official home of King Charles III, who lives most of the year at Clarence House, and perhaps after future renovations, Buckingham Palace. London is also home to many other world-famous landmarks, such as the Tower of London, Westminster Abbey, St. Paul's Cathedral, the Royal Observatory, Trafalgar Square, Piccadilly Circus, and the London Eye. We'd better get busy! We'll start in the oldest quarter of London, where we can almost imagine life as it was during medieval times.

The original City of London covers the one square mile section of town located right in the heart of greater London. Locals refer to this square mile simply as The City. The City lies on the north bank of the Thames (pronounced Tems) River. Its streets are narrow and still retain their names from long ago, such as Fish Street, Milk Street, Bread Street, Wood Street, Candlewick, and Pudding Lane. Streets were named for the products the local merchants sold there. The shops and

restaurants are narrow yet tall, as Londoners built to maximize their space and squeeze as much square footage into their square mile as possible. Dinner theaters host medieval-themed banquets complete with food and knight's costumes. Chophouses (or restaurants that specialize in serving bone-in meats) are also reminders of the feasts from the Middle Ages. Other mixes of historic and ultra-modern food and drink establishments dot the city.

Thames River

Numerous fires have broken out within the old city walls of London over the past 2,000 years. The most notable and devastating fire happened in 1666, leveling 80% of the buildings that used to be there. For this reason, tall, glossy high-rises are sandwiched between old buildings, creating a unique combination of old and new. And yet, The City retains its old-world charm with the Tower of London guarding its rear flank and the rebuilt St. Paul's Cathedral adding a glorious touch of character to the modern-day skyline.

The Great Fire of London, 1666

We'll begin our exploration of this great city at the Tower of London, the castle that served as a fortress, prison, armory, treasury, **menagerie**, and royal residence over the past 1,000 years. Construction of the innermost keep, known as the White Tower, began in 1078 under the command of William the Conqueror, who built it to serve primarily as his royal residence. Later, King Richard the Lionhearted built three additions to encircle the inner keep, known as wards, during his reign from 1189 to 1199. The impressive fortress was finally completed in 1295 under the rule of Edward I when the outer wall was constructed, encircling both the inner keep and the outer wards.

Besides the White Tower that rises prominently from the center of the fortress, 13 additional towers stud the outer curtain wall, their names reflecting the activities that occurred there or the individuals who dwelled within them. For example, the bow maker lived in the Bowyer Tower; the belfry in the

menagerie: unique collection of animals, often exotic

The White Tower within the Tower of London

Bell Tower; and the Lanthorn (Old English for "lantern") Tower was used as a beacon for travelers approaching the castle by night. The Tower of London is a fascinating castle because it has been used for so many different functions over the centuries, but it is known primarily for serving as a prison for royalty and has held captive within its walls some of the most infamous characters of world history, such as Queen Elizabeth I, King James I, Henry VI, Lady Jane Grey, Sir Walter Raleigh, and Anne Boleyn to name just a few.

While the Tower was the most important royal prison in the country, it wasn't very secure. Royal inmates throughout history were known to bribe and cajole the guards to help them escape. While many regal captives were aided in their escape by guards who smashed holes through cell walls and ushered them to boats waiting outside the walls on the Thames River, others were not so favored. Only a handful of prisoners were actually executed within the castle walls, but counted among them were Lady Jane (the Nine Days' Queen), Anne Boleyn (one of the six wives of Henry VIII), and Sir Walter Raleigh (famous explorer to the New World), each of whom were considered to be extremely dangerous to the crown.

Ironically, besides housing royal prisoners, the Tower has also long housed the royal crown jewels — the literal jewel-encrusted crowns and scepters — of the English monarchy. In fact, it was once the custom of kings and queens of England dressed from head to toe in full regalia to begin their

Sir Walter Raleigh

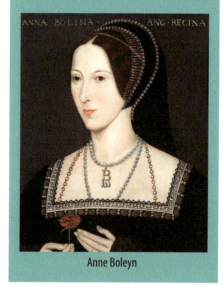

Anne Boleyn

154 Lesson 8. Day 76

A Child's Geography. Vol. 5: Explore Viking Realms

coronation procession from the Tower of London, which held their crowns safe and secure when they weren't wearing them.

The Royal Menagerie, 1820

The Tower of London is the most popular tourist attraction in England, but that is nothing new. The Tower has been a tourist attraction since Elizabethan times in the early 1600s, when travelers to London would visit the imposing fortress to view the crown jewels, spectacular armory, and Royal Menagerie. The animals that lived in the Tower were gifts from other European monarchs to the British crown, intended to promote peace and goodwill. Since as early as the reign of Henry III, the Tower has housed leopards, wolves, bears, elephants, lions, monkeys, and more. At one time, the fee for admission to this royal zoo was three halfpence. However, if you did not have three halfpence to spare, you could still get in to see these magnificent animals with a donation of live food for the ravenous lions.

Traffic on the London Tower Bridge

The King's Guard from Buckingham Palace

To this day, the Tower of London, officially the Royal Palace and Fortress of the Tower of London, is guarded by a unit of the King's Guard from Buckingham Palace, along with the Yeoman Warders who live inside the tower, guarding by night and leading tours by day. Each morning, the Guard and the Yeoman Warders take part in the ceremony of the keys as the Tower of London is opened for the public who swarm in to learn about its fascinating history and gaze upon England's glorious jewels. But beware if you don't leave before closing and find yourself locked up inside the Tower for the night. The king himself is the only one who has the password to let you out.

London: Once the Largest City in the World!

The City of London:

- ✔ It is the largest city in England and its capital.
- ✔ King Edward gave up the throne for his love.
- ✔ Heir or family lineage determines the throne in England.
- ✔ Londinium is the original name for London, a city of only one square mile.
- ✔ Eighty percent of the buildings were destroyed in the fire of 1666.

Stop and Visit:

- ✔ Historic landmarks abound in London, including Westminster Abbey and the Royal Observatory.
- ✔ The city is on the north bank of the Thames River with narrow streets, such as Pudding Lane.
- ✔ The Tower of London is a castle that has been a prison, royal residence, and more.

Who Is Considered Royalty?

A monarchy is a form of ruling a nation that is passed down by heredity or family lineage. Titles frequently used include "king" or "queen" in a royal family, who are associated with having special rights and privileges. They may rule with absolute authority, meaning they are considered sovereign. Other titles for the British monarchy may include Defender of the Faith and Supreme Governor of the Church of England.

Optional: Teacher's Discretion   ☐ No   ☐ Yes   Due Date: _____

With your parent's permission or guidance, use books or online resources to research the present royal family lineage of King Charles III. Draw and label a simple chart.

The True King

The Bible records that the One true God is sovereign and on the throne over all creation. In Revelation 4:2b–3, John tells of his vision from God: "and behold, a throne was standing in heaven, and *someone was* sitting on the throne. And He who was sitting was like a jasper stone and a sardius in appearance; and there *was* a rainbow around the throne, like an emerald in appearance." (Jasper and sardius are precious gemstones.) This level of royalty and brilliance is difficult to comprehend, especially knowing that God is a personal God who also reveals Himself through Jesus the Christ and the Holy Spirit.

For those who have accepted Jesus' gift of salvation, more awestriking information is revealed in 1 Peter 2:9: "But you are A CHOSEN PEOPLE, A ROYAL PRIESTHOOD, A HOLY NATION, A PEOPLE FOR GOD'S OWN POSSESSION, so that you may proclaim the excellencies of Him who has called you out of darkness into His marvelous light." That's an incredible reminder that all who accept Him become royalty in His eternal Kingdom.

Reflect on how the Bible defines royalty and who has access. Write what this means for you.

_____

_____

Word Search

Locate and circle the following words that are names of world-famous landmarks in London.

```
Q S X Q W S A F E R T B R U P O W Q D E T B N
K T S D L K J H G D F Y O I I P Q W X B N J P
A P A P I C C A D I L L Y C I R C U S M G A L
C A C V C M L K P O U W A S M W O U C V C B U
B U C K I N G H A M P A L A C E Q W X W C R E
I L D Q W E R V Y B U N O I M O P P N Q Z A W
L S K K S A L J D F V C B N M Y Y W E R F V C
P C L P Z W E S T M I N S T E R A B B E Y V N
W A S Q P O Q W Z X M N E I U Q Z P M K J H A
I T X O T R A F A L G A R S Q U A R E S S C C
R H V W L A Q Z Q X W C V R V T B Y N P M L S
U E C I M B K D V T N M A Z O P Z M N Q W W W
T D N E N D L M N O P Q T R S T Q V L K S D D
G R B M O E Z T O W E R O F L O N D O N X Z P
J A P B P G H A L Q P W R O R S K K A A C V B
K L U V D L O N D O N E Y E Y E F G J K M L N O P
```

BUCKINGHAM PALACE   ROYAL OBSERVATORY

TOWER OF LONDON   TRAFALGAR SQUARE

WESTMINSTER ABBEY   PICCADILLY CIRCUS

ST. PAUL'S CATHEDRAL   LONDON EYE

➜ Just outside the Tower of London is the majestic Tower Bridge. This bridge looks medieval, but it is one of the newer bridges to span the River Thames. Still, it is worth snapping a photo of the impressive structure before we board the riverboat that will transport us west to the other end of downtown London. Had we boarded the eastbound cruiser instead, we would have been heading in the direction of a little borough, or neighborhood, of London known as Greenwich. Greenwich is pronounced *gren-ich*, and this exact location is referenced all over the world every single second of every single day. You may be wondering why.

This is because the Royal Observatory in Greenwich marks the location of the **prime meridian**, the 0-degree line of longitude. This imaginary geographical line that circumscribes the earth determines the local time here, the time at your house, and the time in every other time zone around the world. The imaginary line that is the prime meridian is displayed physically by a bold yellow line in the pavement that runs right through the observatory building and by a laser beaming from the building. The laser is spectacular at night.

> **prime meridian**: the earth's zero of longitude, which by convention passes through Greenwich, England

However, we are not heading east; instead, we are cruising west to see more of the heart of London town.

On the way, we will glide past the medieval boundary that separates the City of London from the City of Westminster. Keep your cameras handy, as there are many famous landmarks to marvel at on our way up the river.

Royal Observatory prime meridian marker

Notice the houses on the detail of Old London Bridge on the 1632 oil painting *View of London Bridge.*

We pass under several bridges on our journey west to Westminster. The first bridge we pass is the famous London Bridge, which in reality is not very impressive to behold. Historically, there have been three London Bridges that have spanned the Thames River. The first London Bridge was quite spectacular. The old timber bridge of medieval times was a marketplace as well as a roadway. Little shops were built along the sides of the bridge, some several stories tall. But this bridge was falling down, just like the lyrics of the song, so a stone bridge replaced it in 1831.

Like the old bridge, the new London Bridge was the busiest river crossing in the city. With the enormous amount of foot traffic and vehicle congestion, it became apparent that the heavy bridge was sinking! So, in 1967, London Bridge was again replaced — this time with a modern concrete one. Are you wondering what happened to the old stone bridge? An American oil tycoon bought it, disassembled it, and shipped it in pieces to his hometown of Lake Havasu, Arizona, where you can walk or drive across it today. Imagine that! London Bridge in the American Southwest!

We pass under several more bridges on our boat tour, many of them with fascinating names and nicknames too. There's the Blackfriar's Bridge, which is used by the railroad; the Waterloo Bridge, also known as the Ladies' Bridge because it was built primarily by women during World War II; and the Millenium Bridge, fondly nicknamed the Wibbly-Wobbly Bridge by Londoners.

St. Paul's Cathedral

To our right is St. Paul's Cathedral. Although the original cathedral was burnt to the ground during the Great Fire of London in 1666, the Anglican cathedral was rebuilt in all its glory and dominated the skyline for over 300 years until modern London skyscrapers were built on every square inch of real estate. Londoners love nicknames, so all of the skyscrapers in the city have them. There you see the Cheese Grater, the Shard, the Walkie-Talkie, and other fondly named ultra-modern buildings, which have been sandwiched between old medieval structures but stretch way above them, up into the sky.

Off to the left is the Globe Theatre. This is not the exact Globe Theatre where William Shakespeare directed

160 Lesson 8. Day 80

A Child's Geography. Vol. 5: Explore Viking Realms

his plays, as that structure also burned down during the great fire. However, this Globe was rebuilt shortly thereafter and is a perfect replica from bottom to top with its beautifully thick thatched roof. The Globe Theatre is the only building approved by London officials to sport a thatched roof within the city limits.

To our right is Cleopatra's Needle, a 3,500-year-old Egyptian obelisk given to England by Egypt after Admiral Lord Nelson's victory at the Battle of the Nile. Lord Nelson was one of Britain's greatest naval commanders, celebrated for his inspirational leadership, grasp of strategy, unconventional military tactics, and especially the large number of naval victories he won for Great Britain. Nelson's naval strategies were instrumental in stopping Napoleon from conquering much of Europe and northern Africa.

Cleopatra's Needle

The gift of the obelisk cost Egypt over $10,000 to transport in 1819 from Heliopolis, where Pharaoh Thutmose III first erected it in 1450 B.C. Just a block from where the obelisk rises in all her glory is Trafalgar Square, named in honor of Lord Nelson for his hard-fought victories at sea during the Napoleonic Wars. A statue of Admiral Lord Nelson looking out to sea rises high above the square on a column as tall as his ship's main mast.

Finally, you can't miss the London Eye to our left. This giant Ferris wheel is London's biggest tourist attraction and moneymaker for the city. With 32 oval-shaped capsules (one for each of London's 32 neighborhoods) holding 25 passengers each, the London Eye generates more than a million dollars per day. The wheel never stops, but it does move slowly enough that you can easily board from the platform while it is rotating. Once you reach the top, you have one of the best views of London anyone has ever seen.

Finally, we have reached the Westminster Pier where we are getting off the boat. Rising directly above us is Big Ben, the British nickname for the great bell in the clock tower at the north end of the Palace of Westminster. There are five bells in the tower, but Big Ben is the largest of them all, weighing 13½ tons (27,000 pounds). No one knows for sure how it received its nickname, but Big

London Eye

Ben could be named for Sir Benjamin Hall, who installed the bell. A British cultural icon, Big Ben is one of the most prominent structures in London and is recognized all over the world. The tower, officially named the Elizabeth Tower, is part of the Palace of Westminster, the meeting place for the two houses of the British Parliament, the House of Commons and the House of Lords. In other words, this is where the members of Great Britain's government meet to make laws and executive decisions.

On the other side of the Palace — the southwest side — is Westminster Abbey. Once a church for Benedictine monks, this building is no longer considered a church, an abbey, or a cathedral. It is a "Royal Peculiar" of the Church of England. In other words, this is the king's chapel. It is reserved for the sovereign monarch's use only. Since the coronation of William the Conqueror in 1066, all coronations of British monarchs have been held in Westminster Abbey. This is also where those same kings and queens have been buried. The abbey is lined with the tombs of recognized and forgotten monarchs alike.

The history of this cathedral-like chapel stretches back over a thousand years. Meandering through the building is like walking through history. Besides coronations and funerals, the Westminster Abbey is famous for its royal weddings. There have been at least 16 royal weddings at the abbey since the year 1100.

Speaking of royalty, it is time to visit Buckingham Palace. The king is away, which means that the palace is open for visitors. The palace is only a block or two from here, and the walk through St. James's Park is lovely. Let's stroll there on foot. On the way, we'll pass the king's elegant horse stables, known as the Royal Mews, and Winston Churchill's War Rooms. We may spot some lovely horses out for a stroll or find we have time to wander in and see the headquarters for the British army during World War II.

At the far end of the park and at the end of the long driveway, known as the Mall, stands the impressive residence of his majesty, King Charles III. This is one of three residences for the king and where he lives ten months out of the year. Since he is at one of his other two castles this month, we are allowed to go in and see how a modern-day king lives in such a massive home.

The Duke of Buckingham built the house that forms the architectural core of the palace in 1703. King George III purchased the mansion

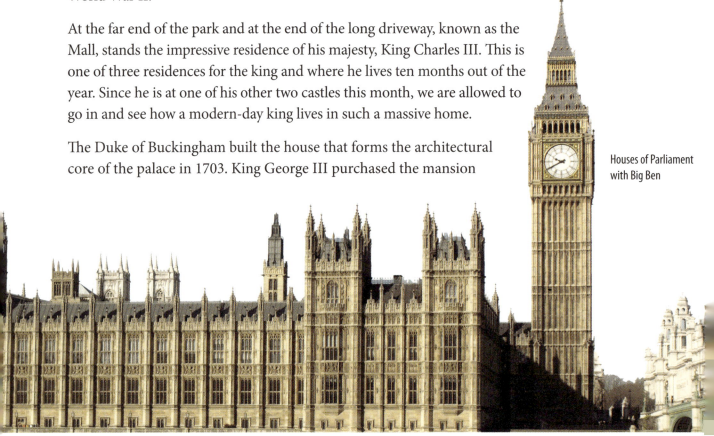

Houses of Parliament with Big Ben

162 Lesson 8. Day 80

A Child's Geography. Vol. 5: Explore Viking Realms

for his wife, Queen Charlotte, and it became known as the Queen's House. After some extensive remodeling, Londoners began referring to the place as Buckingham Palace. However, it didn't become the official royal residence for the British monarch until 1837, when Queen Victoria moved in. Victoria and her husband, Prince Albert, felt the house was too small for court life and their growing family, so they added a new wing, the east wing, which faces the Mall and is now the public face of Buckingham Palace.

The palace has a total of 775 rooms. These include 19 state rooms, 52 royal and guest bedrooms, 188 staff bedrooms, 92 offices, and 78 bathrooms. There is also a post office in the palace, along with a theater, a swimming pool, an operating room, and a jeweler. We won't see most of these rooms today, but when we enter through the Grand Entrance and descend the Grand Staircase to the Marble Hall, we can marvel at the life-size head-to-toe portraits of past kings, queens, princes, and princesses. The lavish gold and cream color scheme lends to the overall impression of extravagant wealth and unapproachable royalty. We tour the stately Music Room, the Blue and White Drawing rooms, and — the pride of the kingdom — the Picture Gallery, which features art masterpieces by Rembrandt, van Dyck, Rubens, and Vermeer. At the end of the gallery is the Throne Room, the destination of the ceremonial route from the Guard Room at the top of the Grand Staircase. The Throne Room is draped from ceiling to floor in red tapestries, and the only furniture in the room are two large red-velvet upholstered thrones.

Our tour of the palace is over, but we have been given permission to wander through the garden before leaving the grounds. The royal garden includes a lake, a tennis court, and a **helipad**. It feels more like a large park than a backyard. In fact, at 40 acres, this is the largest private garden in London. Every summer, the late Queen Elizabeth II would host her annual garden parties here, inviting up to 8,000 guests to a single event. Some wisdom shared by Queen Elizabeth II were the words, "To what greater inspiration and counsel can we turn than to the imperishable truth to be found in this treasure house, the Bible?"

It's getting late. As the sun begins to sink below the western boundary of the garden, we realize that it is time to get some rest. Our quaint

helipad: a landing and takeoff area for helicopters

little hotel is just around the corner from the King's palace, in the borough of Belgravia. In fact, we can walk there! Tomorrow is another big day, but we'll be taking a step back from city life to explore the seaside. British people love the seaside both for the scenery and the therapeutic properties in the salt water.

Here's a tasty place to stop and eat on the way to our hotel. It's called The Bag O' Nails. Let's duck into this 600-year-old historic eatery for England's most iconic dish — fish and **chips**!

With full bellies and a great night's sleep, we'll be ready to enjoy everything we discover along the southern coast of England tomorrow. Night-night!

chips: French fries

Places to See by the Sea in London

More Sightseeing:
- ✔ The old London Bridge was rebuilt because it was falling down.
- ✔ Cleopatra's Needle is a 3,500-year-old Egyptian obelisk given to England by Egypt.
- ✔ The Ferris wheel called the London Eye never stops spinning.
- ✔ The Elizabeth Tower has five bells in its tower, with Big Ben being the largest.
- ✔ The Westminster Abbey has been the prized location for coronations and funerals.
- ✔ The seaside is a popular place for the scenery and the salt water.

The Royal Palace:
- ✔ The Duke of Buckingham first built the main part that became the core structure.
- ✔ With a total of 775 rooms, the Royal Palace even includes a jeweler.
- ✔ The Picture Gallery features art masterpieces by Rembrandt, van Dyck, Rubens, and Vermeer.
- ✔ The Royal Garden includes recreational activities and a helipad.
- ✔ A statue of Admiral Lord Nelson is in Trafalgar Square to commemorate his strategies against Napoleon.

 **TIMELINE**

1450 B.C. ►	Cleopatra's Needle is erected in Egypt by Thutmose III.
1295 ►	The Tower of London is completed under the rule of Edward.
1666 ►	The Great Fire of London devastates the City of London.
1819 ►	Cleopatra's Needle is given as a gift from the King of Egypt.
1831 ►	Like the song, London Bridge is falling down; so it is replaced by a stone bridge.
1837 ►	Buckingham Palace becomes the official residence of the British monarchy.
1936 ►	George VI becomes king of England after his brother, Edward, abdicates the throne.
1952 ►	Elizabeth II is crowned Queen of England.
1967 ►	The second London Bridge is sinking, so it too is replaced.
1981 ►	Charles, Prince of Wales, and Lady Diana Spencer are married.
2011 ►	Prince William and Catherine Middleton are married at Westminster Abbey.
2013 ►	Succession to the Crown Act came into effect.
2022 ►	King Charles III took over the British throne after the death of Queen Elizabeth II.

Rank the Choices

You read about the Tower of London, Big Ben, and the London Eye. Place the three landmarks in the order you would like to visit them, starting with the one that sounds the most interesting to you. Why did you choose the order of each?

1. _____   Why? _____

2. _____   Why? _____

3. _____   Why? _____

Design a Palace

Buckingham Palace, the royal residence in London, is made of stone, brick, and stucco. It has a total of 775 rooms, which include (fill in the blanks):

    19   state rooms

1. _____   royal and guest bedrooms

2. _____   staff bedrooms

    92   offices

3. _____   bathrooms

    post office, theater, swimming pool, operating room, and jeweler

Design and sketch a palace. Label the rooms.

Nicknames

In London, nicknames have been given to some bridges and ultra-modern skyscrapers. Remember a few of the examples? Some skyscraper nicknames are the Cheese Grater, the Shard, and the Walkie-Talkie.

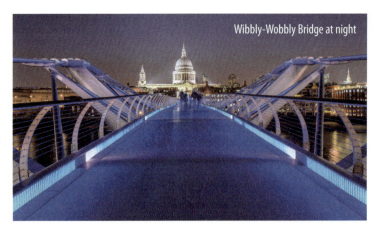

Wibbly-Wobbly Bridge at night

The Wibbly-Wobbly Bridge was originally named the Millennium Bridge, but on opening day in 2000, pedestrians felt a swaying motion on the footbridge. The study of physics has helped to understand that the rhythm of people naturally walking in the same gait or foot pattern is what creates the swaying motion, called oscillation. How do we sometimes fall into the same step or pattern of those around us? When do we conform or simply follow the world's ways?

And do not be conformed to this world. but be transformed by the renewing of your mind. so that you may prove what the will of God is. that which is good and acceptable and perfect.

— Romans 12:2

Create some nicknames for some buildings or locations around your community and region. Have fun by using your creative and even humorous abilities!

Building or Location Name	Nickname You Created

Mapping It Out!

Complete the map of the country of England in the box below. Refer to the map on page 383.

NOTE: Keep this map for use on Days 91, 100, and 108 of your schedule.

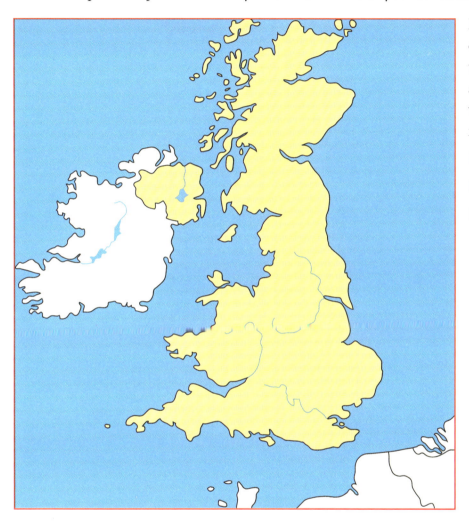

Label the following places on your map. You can use colored pencils to shade areas of land or water, draw rivers and mountains, etc.

☐ England

☐ Thames River

☐ Add a star ★ for the capital city of London.

Flashcards

Make flashcards of the bolded glossary words from this lesson. Then, either add drawings of the terms or act them out in charades. Be creative!

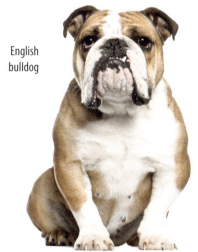

English bulldog

A Tasty Tour

[optional]

Fish and Chips

Ingredients for the fish:

4 (7-ounce) white fish fillets (usually cod or haddock)

½ cup of all-purpose flour

½ cup of cornstarch

1 teaspoon baking soda

Salt and ground pepper (to taste)

Ingredients for the chips:

2 pounds potatoes, peeled

1 quart (1 liter) vegetable oil

NOTE: This recipe requires adult supervision and participation.

Optional: Teacher's Discretion

☐ No   ☐ Yes

Due Date: _____

Directions:

1. Mix the flour, cornstarch, and baking powder in a bowl with water until thick consistency. Season lightly with a tiny pinch of salt and pepper. (Save 2 tablespoons of flour reserved from the batter mix.)

2. Cut the potatoes into chip wedges and rinse.

3. Place the fish fillets on a paper towel and pat dry. Season lightly with a little sea salt. Cover fillets in 2 tablespoons of flour reserved from the batter mix.

4. Dip fillets into the batter, coating the entire fillet.

5. Heat the oil to 350°F in a deep-fat fryer or large saucepan. Cook the chips until brown then remove and dry on paper towel.

6. Fry fillets for approximately 8 minutes, or until the batter is crisp and golden then remove and dry on paper towel.

7. Serve while hot, accompanied by your favorite condiment.

Learn Geography Terms

Page 342 is a reference page for understanding the terms geographers use to describe landforms.

Love your neighbor

London is a city of contrast, from old to new. Lord, we thank You for the light of the Gospel in this city throughout the centuries in spite of attacks. Today, we ask for a brightening of Your Spirit in the hearts of people in London, across the world, and in our community. Your Word says in John 8:12, "Then Jesus again spoke to them, saying, 'I am the Light of the world; the one who follows Me will not walk in the darkness, but will have the Light of life.'"

Southern England: The Seaside Cure

Now that we have explored the great city of London, it's time to head south to England's southern shore. When you think about the coast, you may imagine sandy beaches, noisy boardwalks, and flocks of seagulls boldly snatching food scraps from complaisant children. While England's south coast has a smattering of those things, it boasts so much more. Surprises await you, my young explorer! Dramatic landscapes, underground passageways, and heart-stopping stories of events that occurred on England's southern shore are soon to be revealed.

But first, we need to make a quick stop in famous Canterbury before continuing to the seaside. It takes about an hour to drive from London to the famous medieval town of Canterbury, as we travel along the road.

Canterbury is located in the center of the county of Kent, once the Kingdom of Kent. This town dates back to the 1st century, when the Romans still occupied England. Not far from the center of town is St. Augustine's Abbey, which symbolizes the return of Christianity to this corner of England. After the Roman troops were ordered to retreat from England after the fall of Rome, barbarian tribes poured into this region of Kent from the north and west.

Gate of St. Augustine's Abbey

After the initial chaos, a barbarian king came to power, and his name was King Æthelberht. When Æthelberht married a Christian princess from France, Pope Gregory the Great saw an opportunity to re-Christianize England. He sent Augustine from Rome to Kent in A.D. 597 to share the message of Christ's love and sacrifice with the new king. Æthelberht immediately converted to Christianity along with 600 of his subjects. The pope was so pleased with the success of the mission that he appointed Augustine as Archbishop of Canterbury. St. Augustine's Abbey was soon built in the center of town. This church is the third abbey to exist on this site; Danish Vikings burned the first one to the ground in the year 842 and the second one in 1011.

Just around the corner from the abbey is the most dominant structure in this old town, the towering Gothic cathedral rising from the center of Canterbury. This glorious church — the Canterbury Cathedral — is the setting of one of the most infamous and tragic deaths in world history: the murder of Thomas Becket. Thomas was born in 1118 in Cheapside, a merchant quarter of London, to middle-class parents. He had the opportunity of becoming acquainted with Theobald, the Archbishop of Bec, who essentially made him a member of the family when he was in his early 20s, following the death of his parents. Theobald sent him to study civil and religious law in Italy, then France. The Archbishop, who loved and respected Thomas greatly, appointed him to the position of archdeacon of Canterbury and, less than three months later, recommended him to King Henry II as chancellor, an important government position.

True Faith: Throughout history, we see examples of wars, political marriages, and revolutions that led to huge changes. Sometimes that change was focused on enforcing a new religion or eliminating a religion completely. This has even been done by Christian leaders in the past. For example, once a king or other leader of a group of people accepted Christianity as their faith, those in the rest of the group would also become Christians. This was often done because the king commanded them to, or they did it in fear of displeasing the king if they didn't. It wasn't always because they believed in the God of the Bible.

However, that is not true faith. Christ died on the Cross, and we each have the choice to recognize our sins and seek salvation through Him. It has to be a decision after awareness of our sins and our desire to change and live as God tells us to for it to be authentic and true. Ephesians 3:17–19 records, [S]o that Christ may dwell in your hearts through faith; and that you, being rooted and grounded in love, may be able to comprehend with all the saints what is the breadth and length and height and depth, and to know the love of Christ which surpasses knowledge, that you may be filled up to all the fullness of God.

King Henry and Thomas worked well together, and the people of England regarded Thomas as a brilliant chancellor. Trusted completely by the king, many historians have compared their relationship to Joseph and the pharaoh of Egypt. However, when Theobald died, it made sense to the king to appoint Thomas Becket as the

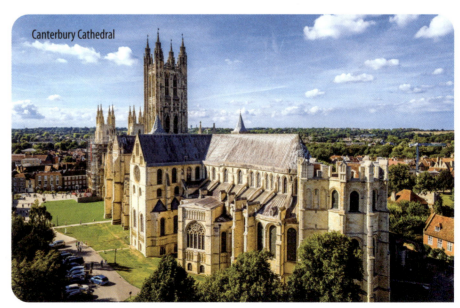
Canterbury Cathedral

French depiction of Becket's assassination

new archbishop. Thomas assumed his new role with fervor and quit his job as chancellor, much to the dismay of the king.

No longer a civil leader but a religious leader, Thomas began to make decisions that were contrary to the king's wishes. Henry became furious. Thomas was no longer his right-hand man, but his adversary. They began to fight against one another on issues of church versus state. Who had more say in the matters of the Church — Henry II or Archbishop Thomas Becket? Over the next decade, Henry and Thomas' close friendship disintegrated, and they became mortal enemies.

Their disagreements over church politics became heated, and Henry spat out violent words against Thomas in the presence of his four head knights of the court, who unfortunately took his words literally. They galloped swiftly to Canterbury on December 29, 1170, and forced themselves into the cathedral to resolve the most pressing argument between King Henry and Thomas. Unwilling to set aside his religious views and condescend to the king's wishes, Thomas turned to walk away from the furious knights. There, upon the altar, with the last rays of twilight filtering through the stained glass, the knights walked up behind Thomas, each striking him with their sword, killing him.

The people of England, along with the king, were shocked and angered by the murder of Thomas Becket. The king appeared to be so horrified at the murder of his former friend that he refused to leave his room for three days. Some accounts note he refused food, wearing sackcloth and ashes and rejecting any kind of comfort during that time. The four knights were banished and eventually sent to join the Crusades in the Holy Land as their punishment. Three years after Thomas was murdered, the Catholic Church declared

Saint: The pope in Rome later canonized Thomas Becket as a saint. Thomas had stood for the issues of the Church against opposition. He lost his life for his faith, which is why he was called a martyr. The pope's declaration of Thomas as a saint of the Catholic Church was because of his unwavering devotion to God.

The word "saint" is used by many people in the context of faith.

In the Catholic Church, there is a tradition of saints — people who lived extraordinary lives of faith that are now in heaven, have performed a miracle, and are **canonized**.

In the Protestant tradition, the word "saint" can describe someone who is a follower of Christ, as they are set aside from the world to be holy because they received Christ as their Savior (Ephesians 3:17–19).

Both definitions agree that a saint is holy or set apart for God.

canonized: officially declared a saint by the Catholic Church

A broken ivory carving of St. Thomas Becket's assassination

him a saint. His tomb became a site for Christians from all over Europe to visit and pay their respects to this brave martyr and saint.

Now that we have made our visit to St. Thomas' tomb and honored his memory, let's continue our journey southward to the White Cliffs of Dover. The 350-foot White Cliffs face the southeast coast of England and can be seen from France across the English Channel on a clear day, making them a national landmark. The sight of these cliffs from the air or sea is like a comforting embrace felt by returning soldiers and any wandering English man or woman coming home.

The White Cliffs stretch for eight miles in this location, but over 260 miles in total across the whole southern shoreline. Centrally located along these cliffs is Dover Castle, whose curtain walls extend to the very edge of the majestic cliff face. William the Conqueror founded Dover, the largest castle in England, in 1066. It is fondly referred to as the "Key to England" because it has stood as England's first line of defense for nearly a millennium.

The pinnacle of Dover's landscape is the Great Tower of Dover, which rises from the center of the formidable castle. While the tower is certainly a site to behold with its thick walls and imposing height, it is the network of secret wartime tunnels underground that make this castle so unique. The passageways hewn from the chalky earth were first excavated in order to surprise attack invaders from the sea when Napoleon threatened to invade England. Later, these chalky claustrophobic corridors were converted into a command post during World War II and even housed a hospital for wounded soldiers evacuated from Dunkirk, France, across the English Channel. Imagine the stories these honored halls would tell if these walls could speak.

Besides their historical significance, these unusual cliffs have been designated as an ecological conservation site and an Area of Outstanding Natural Beauty (AONB). The United Kingdom's (U.K.'s) AONB designation is for areas of exceptional natural beauty and ecological importance that need to be carefully conserved and protected. In and among the chalky cliffs and the grassland that stands like hair atop them live a wide variety of wildflowers, butterflies, birds — and ponies! **Exmoor ponies** graze on the grasses above the cliffs and peregrine falcons swoop and dive along the chalky white faces, preying on rodents and fish along the shore. There is also an edible plant here that grows along the cliffs, called rock samphire, that was collected by foragers who hung from ropes down the side of the cliff.

> **Exmoor ponies:** a horse breed that has roamed the bleak, open moors of southwestern England, known as Exmoor, for centuries

The White Cliffs of Dover

172 Lesson 9. Day 85

A Child's Geography. Vol. 5: Explore Viking Realms

However, the abundance of wildflowers provides a perfect home for more than 30 species of butterfly. The butterfly that truly stands out is the Chalk Hill Blue as it flutters about the samphire and other flowers growing along the cliffs.

A large herd of wild Exmoor ponies

There, at the foot of Shakespeare Cliff, named after the famous playwright, is a cave-like shelter built into the earth mound that was left behind when the Channel Tunnel was dug out under the English Channel, connecting England to the mainland by train. Inside this great dirt mound is a classroom and exhibition area where students such as us can learn all about the flora and fauna of this amazing region of the world.

Lighthouse on top of Beachy Head

About 75 miles east is the cliff face known as Beachy Head. Like the White Cliffs of Dover, the sight of Beachy Head is breathtaking. In fact, it may be even more spectacular because Beachy Head is the highest chalk sea cliff in Britain, rising to 531 feet above sea level. You may be wondering why this beautiful cliff wall is named Beachy Head. That was not always its name! During the Middle Ages, it was called *Beauchef*, which means "beautiful headland" in French. But over time, the sound of the name was distorted by British accents and replaced by a more English-sounding name, even if there is no beach to be seen for miles. Twenty miles to be precise!

So, let's continue 20 miles east to visit the popular seaside resort town of Brighton. Here we see a classic Georgian (1714–1830) pier with rickety rides, carnival games, and sticky sweet candy.

Modern-day beachgoers flock to Brighton for their seaside holidays every summer, but it wasn't the carnival atmosphere that originally drew tourists to Brighton.

A young doctor became famous when he began to encourage his patients to "take the cure" in the sea at Brighton. In the 1730s, Dr. Richard Russell enthusiastically prescribed seawater both for drinking and for bathing as a cure for a variety of illnesses. Suddenly, Brighton found itself on the map as royalty and wealthy nobles flocked to the Brighton beach like starving seagulls on their way to a picnic. Seawater has not been proven to cure illness of any kind, and while bathing in seawater may be relaxing, it can be very dangerous to drink it. Travelers enjoy time at the sea because of the warm sunshine, the calming rhythm of waves upon the sand, and the salty water on the skin. What amazing sensory beauty God created!

Salt Water: The British people soak in the seaside for day trips or even for vacations — called holidays by Brits. Historically and culturally, salt water — or saline water — has been said to have healing properties or therapeutic benefits. Science is revealing a variety of advantages, from improved breathing to relaxed muscles, to reduced inflammation, and more. Reasons point to the magnesium in salt combined with the rhythmic sounds of water. The refreshment of the salt water combined with the scenery together create a holiday feel.

A new addition to the Brighton Beach is the i360 Tower. Shall we go up? The i360, the tallest observation tower in England at 531 feet, was designed by British Airways™ to be a "vertical pier" for visitors to enjoy. While it is certainly impressive in stature with its sleek modern design, the glass observation bulb rises to the exact same height as the cliff at Beachy Head. What do you think of that? Does this fun fact make the i360 seem a little shorter now or Beachy Head taller?

About halfway between Brighton and our next stop is a curious geological gem — a door to the sea. It is called Durdle Door. Eroded over time by nature's forces, Durdle Door is one of the most photographed landmarks on England's southern coast. The magnificent limestone arch was formed by the power of waves, eroding the rock and forging a hole through the middle. The name Durdle is derived from the Old English word *thirl*, which means to pierce, bore, or drill, which is exactly what happened here.

The Royal Pavilion in Brighton

About 200 miles west of Brighton is another seaside resort town named Torquay, which has been nicknamed the English Riviera because the weather can get so warm here. In fact, it is so warm and balmy that palm trees flourish in this little corner of England. The reason why palm trees flourish and people flock to Torquay is because of something mysterious happening out at sea in the big, wide-open Atlantic Ocean. Let's find out what is causing this curious weather phenomenon!

An oceanographer who lives here in Torquay has agreed to give us a quick little science lesson to help us understand the unusual weather pattern. We meet Robert out on the pier and find that it is warm here indeed. We remove our sweaters that certainly came in handy a couple hours ago when we stood on the precipice of the wind-whipped chalk cliffs

Durdle Door

Torquay City

"Hello, young travelers!" greets Robert. "Isn't it a beautiful day to learn about ocean currents, particularly the Gulf Stream?"

We nod our heads enthusiastically and Robert continues. "People who visit the southern coast of England think it is warm because we are at the southern end of the country. That is not true. Even at its most southern point, England is still very far north. The southern coast of England is located at the latitude of 50 degrees north, which is the same latitude as British Columbia in Canada and northern Mongolia in Asia. These are pretty chilly places on our globe. But it's not chilly here! The reason why this region is so warm is because of huge swirling currents out in the ocean.

"You see, out in the dark depths of the ocean are wide currents, like enormous rivers, that carry cold water from the frigid north down south, and warm water from the tropics back up north. It's almost like a mighty conveyor belt moving water, oxygen, and marine life around the vast oceans of the earth. These currents have names that usually indicate where they are located, such as the North Atlantic Current (NAC) or the East Australian Current (EAC). Ocean currents act as a convenient super highway for sea turtles and other migrating sea creatures. Some currents are wider than others, but today, I'm going to tell you about one of the grandest of all, the Gulf Stream. The Gulf Stream is anything but a small stream or trickle; it is an immense current that moves 100 times more water than all the rivers in the whole world combined. And this stream is hurrying along at 60 miles per hour!

"The Gulf Stream moves food and oxygen around the ocean, which keeps marine animals alive and well — but it also carries temperature change. When the ocean water warms, so does the air. The

Gulf Stream current originates in the Gulf of Mexico and brings warm water up to Iceland and the British Isles. The rush of warm water in the ocean translates into mild weather in the winter and warm weather in the summer. And that is why palm trees flourish in Torquay!"

Drake's Island in Plymouth, England

Now, isn't that fascinating! Who knew that water deep in the ocean could make such an impact on the temperature of the air?

We have one final stop before we call it a night. Tonight, we'll arrive in Plymouth, England, the port town where the Pilgrims set sail to find religious freedom in the New World. When their boat landed on the other side of the Atlantic Ocean in the state of Massachusetts, miles and worlds away from their homeland, the Pilgrims named their new colony Plymouth to remind them of home.

In the 17th century, England's city of Plymouth was an important shipping center, shipping goods and people all over the world. In fact, Sir Francis Drake, the famous explorer, set sail from this port city when he circumnavigated the globe. But when Plymouth shoved the Pilgrims out to sea in the cramped *Mayflower*, she played a small but crucial role in the birth of a new nation, forever changing the course of world history.

And on that note, let's turn in for the night. Tomorrow, we will discover ruins that may help us separate fact from fiction. We'll visit an ancient Roman bath town and gaze upon one of the oldest and most mysterious manmade megaliths on the face of the earth. Maybe we'll be able to uncover some ancient mysteries while we are there. Have a good rest! I'll see you bright and early tomorrow morning.

Coastlines and Stories

Stories of Events:
- ✔ After marrying a Christian princess, King Æthelberht converted to Christianity.
- ✔ Years after Danish Vikings burnt the first two abbeys to the ground, St. Augustine's Abbey was built.
- ✔ The murder of Thomas Becket took place at Canterbury Cathedral.
- ✔ Pilgrims set sail on the Mayflower from Plymouth in search of religious freedom in the New World.

Dramatic Landscapes:
- ✔ The 350-foot White Cliffs of Dover can be seen from France across the English Channel.
- ✔ Beachy Head is 531 feet above sea level and stands as the highest chalk sea cliff in Britain.
- ✔ The town of Brighton drew patients looking for a salt water "cure."
- ✔ The i360 Tower at Brighton Beach is a "vertical pier" at 531 feet.
- ✔ The English Riviera is the nickname for the town of Torquay with warm weather from the Gulf Stream.

Fill in the Blank

Complete the missing information by filling in the blanks.

1. The White Cliffs of Dover can be seen across the English Channel in the country of

   _____ on a clear day.

2. _____ _____ _____ built Dover Castle, and below the

   castle is a series of _____.

3. The famous ship the _____ set sail from Plymouth, England.

Dover Castle

Latitude and Longitude Layout

In Lesson 4 when we visited Finland, we traced the Trans-Atlantic Gulf Stream, which also creates a warm environment for Southern England. Let's identify the latitude and longitude of the Trans-Atlantic Gulf Stream and then follow its path. Using the map on the next page as a guide, prepare to create latitude and longitude markings in an open space, such as room in your house or outside.

Materials needed:
- ☐ Chalk or 48 feet of yarn or thick string
- ☐ Pen or pencil
- ☐ Tape
- ☐ Ruler, yardstick, or tape measure

Latitude (horizontal mapping lines) = parallels

Longitude (vertical mapping lines) = meridians

Coordinate = location identified with latitude and longitude

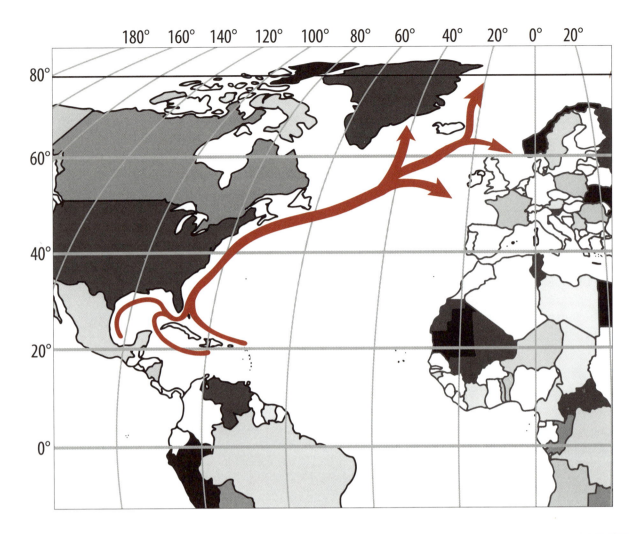

1. With your parent's permission or guidance, select an open space that is at least 7 feet by 10 feet.

2. With a pen or pencil, label each index card with one of these identifiers: equator, 20°N, 40°N, 60°N, 80°N, 120°W, 100°W, 80°W, 60°W, 40°W, 20°W, and 0°W.

3. Determine if you will use chalk, yarn, or thick string as your medium to mark latitude (parallels) and longitude (meridians). Refer to the latitude and longitude markings on the map of the Trans-Atlantic Gulf Stream. For every twenty degrees, measure one foot apart. With your selected medium, draw or place lines for latitude and longitude to look like a grid. Place the labeled index cards along the left side and bottom in the areas to match the map. Tape if necessary to secure.

4. Using your map as a guide, follow the path of the Trans-Atlantic Gulf Stream on the grid you created. (Take caution with your steps.)

Hints:
a. Begin where the stream starts in the Gulf of Mexico.

b. Follow it as it splits three directions: south, east (Canary Current), and north (releases warmth).

c. Remember that in addition to temperature change, the Gulf Stream moves at 60 miles per hour to transport food, oxygen, and sea turtles along with other animals.

Penzance fishing port in Cornwall, England

➡ It's a glorious morning! The sun is peeking its head over the eastern hills and bathing the port town of Plymouth in swaths of golden light. Today, we will drive along the rugged southwestern coast to Land's End, the westernmost point on the whole island of Great Britain.

As soon as we leave Plymouth, which is located in the county of Devon, we enter Cornwall, a jutting peninsula of wild moorland laced with hundreds of sandy beaches. Cornwall, home to the Cornish people, is recognized as one of the six Celtic nations of Europe, along with Brittany, Ireland, the Isle of Man, Scotland, and Wales. Their native language, Cornish, is more closely related to Welsh (spoken in Wales) and Breton (spoken in Brittany, across the English Channel in France) than it is to English.

The southern coast of the Cornwall peninsula is fairly well sheltered from Atlantic storms. We drive past several natural, secluded harbors that offer safe anchorage for ships and boats. Alongside these harbors are quaint old maritime villages, such as Fowey and Falmouth. Let's stop and take some photos to send home.

Before we reach the end of the long peninsula, we arrive at Lizard Point. The geology, or makeup, of the land at Lizard Point is very unusual. It is the only place in Britain where you can see oceanic crust pushed up from the earth's **mantle**, which has now been exposed on land. It is called ophiolite, which means "snake stone" in Greek. It likely received its exotic name because of the highly prized green and red serpentine stone found within the cliff. Chunks of the stone that fall away from the cliffs are collected by local artisans, carved and polished into ornaments and figurines, and then sold in gift shops along the Cornish coast.

> **mantle:** a layer of rock between the crust of the earth and the outer core

As we continue around a few more bends in the road, we skirt around Penzance, which overlooks Mount's Bay, and soon arrive at Land's End. You can't go any further west in Great Britain than this spot right here. This point, along with most of the Cornish coastline, has been designated an Area of Outstanding Natural Beauty by the nation of Great Britain. In fact, Cornwall has been the backdrop for many great books and plays because of its dramatic and rugged windswept beauty. As you inhale the salty sea air and feel the wind whip about you, perhaps you can imagine the pirates and smugglers who often used the waters off this rocky coastline to ply their trade. Or think about the miners who made their living from the granite cliffs.

China clay mine in Cornwall

This area has long been known for mining. As far back as Roman times, the Cornish people made their living by mining for tin. Soon copper was discovered on the cliffs, and the metal became the lifeblood for miners here during the Middle Ages. Over time, the mines shut down as the prices of tin and copper dropped, and the Cornish people focused on farming and fishing for their livelihood.

Eventually, China clay was uncovered in pockets alongside the granite, and this substance is still mined on the peninsula today. China clay is the substance used to create exquisite and delicate porcelain teacups, saucers, and plates. The best China clay is found in China and Cornwall.

China Clay: Kaolinite clay or kaolinite is another name for China clay. Named after the hill called Kao-ling in China, its composition is $Al_2Si_2O_5(OH)_4$. Cornwall, England, is another place where the clay is mined. In addition to porcelain pottery, kaolinite can also be used in the manufacturing of paper, rubber, paint, ink, and other products.

It's time to set out for our next destination … Bath!

No, we are not going to take a bath — Bath is the name of the town where we'll stay tonight. It's a curious name for a town, isn't it? I'll show you why the town has such an unusual name, but before we get there, let's stop in Newquay, a popular beach town on the northern coast of the Cornwall peninsula.

Cornwall is the sunniest place in all of England. The wilder northern coast of the peninsula is battered by mighty waves from the Celtic Sea, a branch of the Atlantic Ocean. These two things — sun and waves — mean just one thing here … surfing! Many visitors to Newquay like to try their hand at surfing. Or maybe I should say foot! Would you like to give it a try?

180 Lesson 9. Day 88

A Child's Geography. Vol. 5: Explore Viking Realms

Newquay Beach

The other popular pastime here in Newquay, along with all the towns in Cornwall and neighboring Devon, is the enjoyment of cream tea in the mid-afternoon. Cream tea, also known as Devonshire tea or Cornish cream tea, is a light afternoon meal that includes hot tea served with scones, jam, and clotted cream. Clotted cream — cream thickened by steam or water bath, then cooled to a soft buttery-like consistency — was first made here in Cornwall. It is a beloved local delicacy served all over England.

Remember, when you have the chance to travel, don't forget to try some of the local dishes or treats. All around the world, people every day enjoy regional recipes that highlight the special plants, meats, and ingredients only found in their area. God created an amazing array of edible plants and vegetables — many of which are unique to specific areas of the world!

Cornish pasties

Let's pop into this teahouse situated along the cliff's edge and have cream tea while we watch the surfers catch the waves below. While **Cornish pasties** are not typically included in a traditional cream tea, let's break with tradition and order some of those as well. The warm meat pies wrapped in flaky pastry are a local specialty. It would be a shame to leave Cornwall without tasting one!

Cornish pasties: British pastries that are meat pies and are common in Cornwall

Legendary Tintagel Castle ruins on Tintagel Island

Next stop, the city of Bath. Let's go!

As we begin our journey east to Bath, we pass by another fascinating town called Tintagel. The town was named for the tin mines that operated here over the centuries, yet it is most famous for its castle ruins. There, situated on a peninsula connected to the mainland by a narrow land bridge, are the ruins of Tintagel Castle, which have stood here for nearly a thousand years.

The **legend** of the castle is that this was once the home of Igraine, the mother of King Arthur, and the place of Arthur's birth. There is a cliff wall opposite the castle with related carvings. No one knows for sure whether King Arthur actually existed, let alone was born here, but the legend of the great king and his round table and band of knights is a great story celebrated especially in this region of Cornwall.

legend: a popular or traditional story that is unproven

We have quite a drive before we reach Bath, so go ahead and rest your eyes for a while if you are tired. I'll let you know when we arrive.

Three hours later, we arrive in the beautiful town of Bath. Let me tell you how Bath got its name.

This city was built long ago atop thermal hot springs, which are springs of warm, sometimes even boiling hot, water that has been heated by the earth's piping hot mantle and then pushed up through the earth's crust. The ancient Romans loved hot springs and built public bathhouses around them so that people could bathe in warm water. Remember, warm bath water was a luxury for ancient civilizations because water heated by electricity wasn't invented for a couple thousand years.

When the Romans occupied Britain nearly 2,000 years ago, around A.D. 60, they built bathhouses in this region to take advantage of the hot springs, and later built the town around them. At that time, they named the city *Aquae Sulis*, which in Latin means "The Waters of Sulis," named for a false goddess of water. (Any goddess or god that is not the One true God, is false.) After the Romans left, the Christians arrived. The new townspeople didn't like the pagan name for the town, so they changed it to Bath. There is one Roman bathhouse still standing here in Bath. Shall we take a look?

The original Roman bath is sandwiched between structures that were built much later. In fact, the only parts of this bathhouse that have been here since Roman times are the columns, the tile floor, and the water itself. Yes, the water is green, and no one bathes in it anymore. Apparently, there are parasites in the water that can make you very sick, so we'll just observe from the poolside portico.

The ancient Romans had an unusual tradition of etching metal tablets, hoping the many false gods they worshiped would punish the person who had offended or wronged them. Most of the tablets found here were written by people whose clothes were stolen while bathing in the spa. No wonder they were mad! That is an awkward situation for sure, but their false gods didn't exist, nor did they have any power to make anything happen to anyone.

The thermal spring water was believed to be good for you in more ways than one. The minerals in the water were supposed to be good for your skin, but also good for your overall well-being. The Romans, along with all the other people who have arrived here since, strongly believed that "taking the waters" internally would keep you healthy. There is great health value to having clean, fresh water for drinking and bathing. Knowing the source of water is important.

Old Roman baths at Bath, England

Next door to the Roman bath is the Grand Pump Room, where thermal mineral water is served by the glass. Or you can take a drink straight from the indoor fountain. That water is pumped up through a borehole, which provides a clean and safe supply of spa water for drinking.

Later, during medieval times, bathing was discouraged, Bath was abandoned, and it became a ghost town for a few hundred years. Later still, in the 18th century, when it became fashionable once again to "take the waters" at the seaside or at a thermal hot spring, Bath bubbled back to life.

False Gods: The Roman Empire contained numerous conquered countries and provinces. They, and many of those in these regions of the empire, worshiped false gods, which was popular at the time.

It's fitting that Jesus Christ would be born near this time in the empire and grow up to share the truth of the One true God and sacrifice Himself on the Cross, surrounded by Roman soldiers, to give us the opportunity for salvation.

Even though Christ died on the Cross, He was resurrected, defeating death, and His disciples would use the vast roads of the Roman Empire to share God's truth far and wide about love and forgiveness.

During the Georgian period, Bath became a boomtown, and buildings began popping up everywhere. The Georgian period was named for the succession of kings from George I through George IV. Georgian architecture is symmetrical yet whimsical, as you can see in the housing developments known as the Circus and the Royal Crescent, separated by only a couple of city blocks.

Bath is once again a popular spa town. While you cannot dip your toe into the green waters of the original Roman bath, you can stroll a block down the street to the Thermae Bath Spa, a pricey public bath house that boasts crystal clear, blue, mineral-rich water, naturally warmed by the earth's mantle, perfect for a swim or a soak any time of year. Shall we go? Relaxing in an ultra-warm and super-clean pool sounds like a great way to finish our busy day of driving and exploring.

We are up before the sun and ready for a quick day trip out of Bath before we head north into central England. Today, we are visiting the most curious of all monuments in the entire world … Stonehenge!

The abbey in Bath and the Roman baths building

On our way out of Bath, we cross the beautiful, historic Pulteney Bridge before the sun even reaches the horizon. The Pulteney Bridge, built in 1774, crosses over the River Avon, once connecting the city of Bath to the land owned by the Pulteney family. What makes this bridge exceptional is that it is one of the only bridges in the world with shops built atop it, spanning both sides of the bridge. It is one of the most photographed bridges in the whole world. Go ahead and snap some pictures!

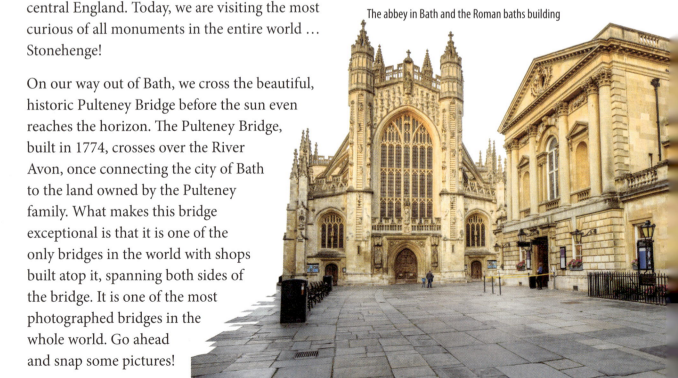

Pulteney Bridge

With our favorite photos of the bridge saved to share with friends, we continue our drive to Stonehenge. Once we park, there is a bit of a hike over the hill before the ancient stone circle comes into full view. Ah ... there it is with the sun shining through the stones, casting long shadows on the grassy plain. Come closer. Let's take a moment to marvel along with scholars and everyone else in the world as to why an ancient people would transport such large stone pillars weighing an average of 25 tons all the way from faraway Wales to a virtually rockless landscape in southern England. Why would any group of people do such a thing, and how exactly did they pull it off?

What could possibly motivate a group of people to push, drag, pull, or carry such massive stone pillars more than 100 miles and erect this large circle we see here? No one knows for sure, but archaeologists speculate that Stonehenge could have been used as a burial site, or for pagan religious ceremonies, or as an astronomical timepiece to help predict the occurrences of lunar and solar eclipses.

Just as their motivations are unclear to us, so are their methods, because Stonehenge was constructed leaving no written records to provide us with this insight. Its construction may have occurred before the invention of the wheel in this region, which further complicates how these 13-foot stone towers were transported across such a great distance.

And that is why people come here — to marvel and wonder how a remote community in ancient England accomplished such a remarkable task, and how they used the stone circle once it was completed. Stonehenge is an incredible accomplishment that modern-day engineers estimate could have required more than a million man-hours to complete.

Stonehenge Timeline: According to a secular-dated timeline, 5,000 years ago around the year 3000 B.C. is when Stonehenge was constructed. There are no written records about how it was made or when, but according to a biblical timeline, it would have to be after the Great Flood and after the dispersal of people at the Tower of Babel, over 4,000 years ago.

Stonehenge

Let's snap some photos for our friends back home. The best shots of this massive stone circle are when the sun is low on the horizon and filtering through the spaces between the pillars. There are other possible connections between the design of Stonehenge and the heavenly bodies of the sun and the moon. It is just one of many mysteries of this place.

But, oh! I'm starting to get hungry. How about you? I've got some pastries waiting for us back in the car. It's time to drive north to one of the most picturesque regions of the world. We are bound for sheep country and a quaint little region of England known as the Cotswolds. Let's go!

Visit a Spa in Bath as Part of Southern England

Land and Legend:
- ✔ Cornwall is one of the six Celtic nations of Europe.
- ✔ Ophiolite, or oceanic crust now exposed to land, is found at Lizard Point.
- ✔ Mining in Cornwall through the eras has included tin, copper, metal, and even China clay.
- ✔ A maritime area, villages like Fowey and Falmouth depend on fishing and farming.
- ✔ Legend holds that King Arthur was born at Tintagel Castle.
- ✔ Pillars for Stonehenge were brought all the way from Wales.

Bath:
- ✔ Newquay is a popular place for surfing along the Celtic Sea, a branch of the Atlantic Ocean.
- ✔ The Romans built ancient bathhouses in Bath because of its thermal hot springs.
- ✔ The Grand Pump Room serves thermal mineral water by the glass.

3000 B.C. ▶	Stonehenge is built in England.
60 ▶	The Romans build a bathhouse in Bath.
1066 ▶	William the Conqueror builds Dover Castle.
1170 ▶	Thomas Becket is murdered in Canterbury Cathedral.

Fill in the Blank

Complete the missing information by filling in the blanks.

1. The six Celtic nations are:

    a. _____

    b. _____

    c. _____

    d. _____

    e. _____

    f. _____

2. Local artisans in Cornwall carve jewelry, ornaments, and figurines from the prized stone

    _____, which is _____ in color.

3. The city of _____ was built above thermal hot springs.

4. Thermal hot springs provide warm or even boiling water that is heated by the earth's mantle and

    pushed up through the earth's _____.

5. Create your own fill-in-the blank question about the history, geography, or culture you read

    about in this chapter and write the answer.

    _____

    _____

    _____

    _____

    _____

    _____

Archaeoastronomy

Stonehenge reveals much about ancient humans. The smaller stones (bluestones) were moved from Wales and weigh two to five tons. The larger stones (sarsens) weigh an average of 25 tons. Fill in the blanks on the questions below by calculating the weight in pounds of each type of stone.

1 ton = 2,000 pounds

1. Bluestones weigh _____ to _____ pounds.

2. Sarsens weigh an average of _____ pounds.

3. There is a mystery about how the stones were moved. How do you think the stones were moved?

_____

_____

A Mystery

The arrangement of the stones helped determine the length of days at different times in the year along with solar and lunar eclipses. The accomplishment of moving the stones and arranging them in a manner to measure the length of days reveals intelligence.

4. If "archeo-" means architecture in ancient times, what does "archaeoastronomy" mean?

_____

_____

5. Stonehenge was constructed with a design that used archaeoastronomy and engineering to move massively large stones. What does this reveal about humans during ancient times?

_____

_____

Optional: Teacher's Discretion   ☐ No   ☐ Yes Due Date: _____

To learn more about **archaeoastronomy**, with parent permission or guidance, you may explore the Answers in Genesis website.

From the rising of the sun to its setting,

The name of the LORD is to be praised.

−Psalm 113:3

Mapping It Out!

Refer to the map on page 383. Label the map from page 167 with the following places:

☐ English Channel

☐ Plymouth

☐ Newquay

☐ Celtic Sea

Flashcards

Make flashcards of the bolded glossary words from this lesson. Then, either add drawings of the terms or act them out in charades. Be creative!

Regional British Accents Map

Optional: Teacher's Discretion   ☐ No   ☐ Yes   Due Date: _____

With your parent's permission or guidance, explore books or online resources about regional British accents. Practice taking turns with British accents.

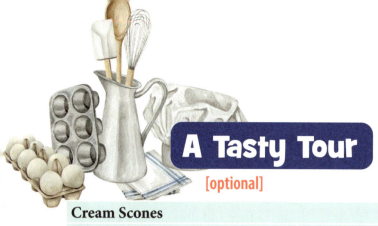

A Tasty Tour

[optional]

Cream Scones

Ingredients:

1¾ cup flour

¼ cup sugar

2 teaspoons baking powder

⅛ teaspoon salt

½ cup dried cranberries or chocolate chips

⅓ cup butter, chilled

½ cup whipping cream

1 large egg

1½ teaspoons vanilla or almond extract

Directions:

1. Stir together the flour, sugar, baking powder, and salt. Add the chilled butter to the mixture and blend in with a pastry blender. In a separate bowl, lightly beat the whipping cream, egg, and flavoring with a fork, then stir gently into the flour mixture.

2. Flour the counter and roll dough to ¾ inch in thickness. Cut with a round cookie cutter or cut into triangles. Bake scones at 350 degrees for about 15 minutes (until golden).

3. Serve with jam and clotted cream (optional).

NOTE: This recipe requires adult supervision and participation.

Optional: Teacher's Discretion

☐ No   ☐ Yes   Due Date: _____

Learn Geography Terms

Page 342 is a reference page for understanding the terms geographers use to describe landforms.

Love your neighbor

From the warm, salty beaches of Brighton to the sunny beauty of Cornwall and the spas at Bath, Southern England is a captivating landscape for relaxation. Just like soaking in the sea or at a spa, we can be in the presence of the Lord. The words of Jesus in John 7:38 are: "The one who believes in Me, as the Scripture said, 'From his innermost being will flow rivers of living water.'"

Central England: The Ancient Universities

10

Cotswold sheep near Chipping Campden

Today, we are meeting up with a tour guide in the region known as the Cotswolds. The word "cotswold" is generally understood to mean "sheep enclosure on rolling hillsides." *Wold* is an Old English word that can be translated to mean either "hill" or "forest." However, modern linguists are questioning the interpretation of the word and believe that it could come from an even older language still, and could refer to someone's property boundaries, such as "Cod's woods" or "Cod's property." Well, if a person named Cod owned the area now referred to as the Cotswolds, he owned a very large piece of property indeed. This Area of Outstanding Natural Beauty encompasses 800 square miles of beautiful rolling hills. These special places remind us of the power of our Creator and His wondrous creation, as well as the importance of careful stewardship of it lest we destroy it. We get to appreciate it by foot, thanks to a footpath crossing right through it from Bath to Chipping Camden for a total of 102 miles. Don't worry; we won't walk the whole distance! That would take days!

Broadway Tower in the Cotswolds

Look! There's Jane, our rambler guide to the Cotswold Way. She is dressed like an everyday hiker. She makes her living by giving tours of this countryside, by foot on dry days and by van on rainy days. Today is a beautiful day with lots of billowy clouds and the sun shining brightly between them. It's the perfect day for an easy hike.

"Hello, young explorers!" Jane calls out. "Are you ready for an adventure?"

"Yes!" we respond with anticipation of what the day will bring.

"Then let's get started here at Bourton-on-the-Water. We'll pass through the public garden, then cross the highway before we reach the access point to the trail. The best part about this hike is that the landowners along the Cotswold Way are obligated to give us 'right of access' through their property. That means that we'll be going through many private gates to stay on the trail, like this one.

"Always make sure you close the gate tightly behind you. We wouldn't want to let the cows or sheep out of their enclosures. That's right! We will be walking right through herds of cattle and sheep during our walk today!"

The trail we're walking feels like a private path as we pass through field upon field of sheep pasture, dotted with humble barns, storybook cottages, and grand mansions. This area is outstanding in its natural beauty — rolling hills, quaint farms, and picture-perfect fields of English sheep. We can even see a rock quarry from the trail.

Bourton-on-the-Water

"Local quarries are harvesting the limestone that runs throughout and beneath the Cotswold region," says Jane. "All of the houses and buildings in the Cotswolds are built from blocks of this honey-colored stone that is chipped from the quarry."

The path begins to widen, and we find ourselves walking on what appears to be a cobblestone road.

"We are walking on Fosse Way," Jane tells us. "Fosse Way is an old Roman road that runs all the way through the Cotswolds. It is incredible to me that we can walk along a road that has existed for nearly 2,000 years, dating back to the same time period when the Lord Jesus walked on the earth. Fosse

Limestone: If you look up the stone, it is considered to be Jurassic limestone, dated by secular science as the period between the Triassic and Cretaceous periods as a period lasting 55 million years, and featured the dinosaurs among other creatures.

The Bible tells us that this would have been formed during the catastrophic effects of the Great Flood, when deposits were rapidly laid down due to Flood waters through the movement of currents and waves.

192 Lesson 10. Day 93

A Child's Geography. Vol. 5: Explore Viking Realms

Lower Slaughter

Way will take us through the tiny towns of Lower Slaughter and Upper Slaughter." Jane explains that this area has historically been sheep country. The people here made their living from sheep's wool and the products that they made from it, such as blankets, scarves, and sweaters. Wool made the people and towns in the Cotswolds wealthy. That is, until cotton came along and was cheaper to buy than wool. At that point, this area sank into a financial depression, and the residents moved away. The towns became frozen in time, and now they look very much like they did hundreds of years ago. While you might guess that these towns were the places where animals were processed, the word "slaughter" actually comes from the word "slough" or "wet land," because Upper and Lower Slaughter are built along both banks of the River Eye. In fact, we'll walk over an old stone bridge to cross the river and continue our hike.

Our destination is Stow-on-the-Wold, a quaint little town where we can enjoy some lunch in one of the cafes on the green. These towns no longer make their money from wool. Tourism is what brings in the cash flow these days. From our window seat, we can watch couples and families meander through the town and pose for photos around the medieval stocks in the town square.

English meat pie

Many traditional English specialties are listed on the menu, such as fish and chips, bangers (sausage) and mash, roast beef with Yorkshire pudding, and an assortment of meat pies. What will you try? Personally, I love a flaky English meat pie!

A panoramic view of Blenheim Palace

Jane has arranged a ride for us back to our car so that we can continue our journey through the beautiful central portion of England to the famous old college towns of Oxford and Cambridge. On our way there, we must stop at Blenheim Palace, one of the largest private homes in England and the only non-royal residence to bear the title "palace."

The palace belongs to the Churchill family, also known as the Duke and Duchess of Marlborough. It came into the family's possession in 1702 as a gift from the king to John Churchill, a military general who fought and won many battles during a war with Spain and France, including the Battle of Blenheim. Churchill was also granted the title of duke when he was given the land, along with a large budget to build his home on said

John Churchill

land. Curiously, the crown asked for rent to be paid for the land that the palace sits on — but only a **peppercorn rent**. A peppercorn rent is a rent so small that it is hardly worth mentioning. But still, the rent must be paid once a year, even now 300 years later. And what is the rent? A flag! Each year, the Duke of Marlborough would deliver a French royal flag to Windsor Castle. The flag remains a reminder of how and why the Dukes of Marlborough were given their lands.

peppercorn rent: very small payment or nominal rent used to satisfy the requirements for the creation of a legal contract

Twelve dukes have lived in this palace, some better stewards than others, but none you have probably heard of before, except one — Sir Winston Churchill. Winston was born and raised here in his family's immense estate before serving as Prime Minister of the United Kingdom during the dark days of World War II, leading Britain to victory.

Over the course of his long life as a soldier, journalist, author, politician, and statesmen during the 20th century, Winston Churchill used his wit, wisdom, and dramatic way with language to inspire and influence world events. To this day, he is one of the most quotable people of all time.

"It is not enough that we do our best; sometimes we must do what is required."

– Winston Churchill

Today, the Churchills graciously open their home to the public for many months of the year, giving tours, displaying their vast collection of rare and antique automobiles, and entertaining the crowd with sword duels, music concerts, nature studies, good food, and a hedge maze. They even have a playground for the kids. Doesn't that sound like a fun afternoon?

Next stop, Oxford! Remember how the word "Cotswold" means "sheep enclosure on rolling hillsides"? Well, Oxford means "ford for the oxen." The ox part makes sense, but what is a ford? A ford is a place in the river that is ideal for crossing, at least most of the time. It is a shallow area where the current is not too strong. In medieval times, it was much more common to cross the river with your herd of oxen at a ford than over a bridge. From as far back as A.D. 900, Oxford was an ideal place to ford the River Thames with oxen.

Nowadays, Oxford is a university town, home to the oldest university in the English-speaking world. The University of Oxford was founded nearly a thousand years ago, but the actual date of its beginning is unknown. We do know that there were classes taught in 1096, but it was a small and scrappy establishment in those years. In 1167, when King Henry II decreed that English students could no longer study abroad at the University of Paris, the college grew rapidly. Oxford is now one of the most prestigious universities on the planet. It has the largest academic library system in the world along with the oldest university museum, and the largest printing press in the world. Its motto is *Dominus Illuminatio Mea*, which means, "The Lord is my Light."

Radcliffe Camera at Oxford University

Oxford is one of seven "ancient universities" established in the British Isles before the year 1600. Four of these are located in Scotland, one is in Ireland, and two are in England — Oxford and Cambridge. These two English medieval universities are frequently referred to jointly as "Oxbridge."

Just down the street from Oxford University is a little ramshackle establishment hardly worth a second glance, but it's a place where some of the best stories were born. The place is called The Eagle and Child, but it is

fondly nicknamed The Bird and Baby by its most
frequent customers. Some of those customers called
themselves The Inklings and were all members
of a literary club which met regularly on Tuesday
afternoons in the Rabbit Room between 1933 and
1950 to share their imaginative stories. Among
the writers in this club were C.S. Lewis and J.R.R.
Tolkien, along with other famous authors who joined
in on the lively discussions, such as Roger Lancelyn
Green, author of *The Legend of Robin Hood*.

Imagine that you are part of this literary club
and you get a chance to listen to the author read
portions from a book before it was ever a movie
or even a published book for that matter. Oh boy,
what stories!

Let's order dinner and soak in the atmosphere of
this quaint old location. Sitting on the rough-hewn
benches and seeing the medieval history of this place
in every detail, you can almost imagine hearing
words read by the author himself!

Time to finish up that scrumptious pie and drive north to Cambridge, Oxford's sister university town.

Cambridge is a bit newer than Oxford, as it was established in 1209. It is the second-oldest university in the English-speaking world, second only to Oxford. Strangely, Cambridge grew out of a dispute and eventually a battle that happened in the town of Oxford. It was not uncommon in medieval university towns for arguments to erupt between scholars and townspeople as they shared the same space but expected different treatment. Students wanted stimulating discussions, deep discounts, and high

The Rabbit Room

esteem. Townsfolk wanted peaceful public places, fair prices, and common courtesy. Arguments would often occur in public establishments over policies, privileges, and professions. Some of these quarrels became so violent that, in 1209, many scholars from Oxford had to flee to the nearby town of Cambridge where they set up their new college.

Oxford shut down for a short time to seek protection from the king, but even though it re-established itself a few years later, enough scholars had become attached to their new location in Cambridge that they didn't want to return. So the new college began to thrive and develop its own campus and culture.

However, the town didn't form around the university. It was already there. In fact, the remains of a 3,000-year-old farm have been discovered beneath the university. Later, the Romans occupied this

Aerial view of Cambridge

University of Cambridge

town for a time and so did a tribe of Belgae people who sailed across the English Channel from what is now the country of Belgium. Later still, the Vikings came through, and Cambridge became an important trading center for the Vikings due to its central location. Cambridge was granted township status in the 12th century, prior to the opening of the university, but it didn't officially become a city until 1951.

In its early history, these universities were influenced by the Christian faith, resulting in many graduates who became priests. As time passed, the secular teachings became more influential. History, literature, and philosophy are the focus of Oxford, while Cambridge specializes in science and technology. Cambridge is the heartbeat of England's high-tech industry. Many modern software and science start-up companies are born out of this ancient university every year.

If you would prefer to set the books aside, you can try your hand at punting down the Cam River, a popular pastime in Cambridge. A punt is a long boat with a flat bottom that is moved along by pushing against the bottom of the river with a long pole.

Rolling Hills and Ancient Universities

Across Hills and Roads:
- ✔ Cotswold is a region of rolling hills with herds of sheep and cattle.
- ✔ Limestone is quarried to build houses and other structures in Cotswold.
- ✔ Fosse Way is an ancient Roman road that runs through Cotswold.
- ✔ English menu specialties include fish and chips, bangers (sausage) and mash, and roast beef with Yorkshire pudding.
- ✔ Sir William Churchill was raised at Blenheim Palace, which is now open to the public for tours.

Oxbridge:
- ✔ The University of Oxford and the University of Cambridge are referred to jointly as "Oxbridge."
- ✔ Oxford University is known for specializing in the study of history, literature, and philosophy.
- ✔ The high-tech industry benefits from Cambridge University with its emphasis on science and technology.

Crossword Puzzle

Complete the crossword puzzle using the hints below.

ACROSS

1. Rent so small that is hardly worth mentioning

3. Literary club which met regularly on Tuesday afternoons in the Rabbit Room

4. "Sheep enclosure on rolling hillsides"

6. Grew out of a dispute between students and townsfolk

8. Oxford is one of seven "_____ universities"

DOWN

2. "Right of access" gates and paths are actually not public, but _____

5. "Ford for the oxen"

7. The last Latin word in Oxford's motto, "The Lord is my Light"

Cambridge Comic Sketch

Using the list of event details that are in chronological order, illustrate and color a comic sketch about the events related to Cambridge. (Illustrate one event in each space.) Add a title.

Materials needed:
☐ Colored pencils

1. Cambridge was originally a farm 3,000 years ago.

2. Romans once occupied the town.

3. The tribe of Belgae people sailed to Cambridge across the English Channel from what is now Belgium.

4. Cambridge was then a trading center for Vikings (central location).

5. Cambridge was granted township status in the 12th century.

6. Oxford students wanted something different than the townsfolk, so the scholars fled to the town of Cambridge.

7. The University of Cambridge was established in 1209.

8. Cambridge became an official city in 1951.

1	2
3	4
5	6
7	8

Caves at Nottingham Castle

→ As we drive north away from Southern England and into the heart of the country, this is a good time to get the lay of the land. England shares the island of Great Britain with Wales to the east and Scotland to the north. England covers five-eighths of Great Britain, and because it is shaped somewhat like a triangle, it becomes narrower the farther north we go. England's terrain is mostly low hills and plains, especially in the south and central regions. However, there are uplands in the north and in the west. We'll see some of those higher mountains when we get to the Lake District in the next lesson. For now, we can enjoy the beautiful green rolling hills by gazing outside our car windows.

We are driving along A1 Great North Road, which is one of the largest freeways in England. A1 was built atop an old Roman road, which connected London with the outlying Roman fortifications in the north all the way up to Hadrian's Wall at the Scottish border. We won't be driving that far today, though. In a couple hours, we'll arrive at Nottingham Castle, and just beyond that, Sherwood Forest, the home of Robin Hood and his band of merry men.

Side view of Nottingham Castle

England receives a great deal of rain nine months out of the year, but today it is beautiful outside with a sapphire sky and billowy clouds floating lazily overhead. It is a perfect day to wander through a drafty medieval castle and an old-growth forest, imagining what life must have been like during those tumultuous years when King Richard was out of the country and his brother, Prince John, was at the helm.

Central England: The Ancient Universities

Nottingham Castle was constructed in the year 1068 on a massive outcropping that looms over the River Leen. The Normans of France built the castle on the orders of William the Conqueror after the Norman Conquest of England. For centuries, this was one of the most important castles in the country, visited often by nobles and royalty alike. Not only was this castle centrally located in a strategic position along the river, but it was also a perfect place for some royal rest and relaxation. The castle is situated very close to several royal hunting grounds, which were known as the "King's Larder." Only the king and the people whom the king approved were allowed to hunt for deer or hare in the royal forests.

Robin Hood: The legend of Robin Hood is a story of stealing from the rich to give to the poor. The tale of Robin Hood is said to have been based on Robert of Loxley, who lived in Sherwood Forest. This was during a time when Prince John was forcing high taxes and fees. Stealing, no matter the reason, is as bad as what Prince John did. It is biblically wrong to steal, even if it is to give to the poor. It is always right to be generous with what we have been blessed with. You may talk to your parent about the legend of the Robin Hood character. Even if with good intent, stealing is harmful to others, including the person who steals. Truth, honesty, and generosity are traits to pursue.

During the 12th century, Prince John seized Nottingham Castle along with his **sycophants**, including the Sheriff of Nottingham, while King Richard I of England — also known as Richard the Lionhearted — was away on the Third Crusade. In the legend of Robin Hood, this castle was the scene of many a showdown between the sheriff and the outlaw hero.

Historically speaking, a significant battle took place here at Nottingham Castle in March 1194 after King Richard returned and squashed the rebellion of his evil brother, Prince John. Using siege machines that he had used on the crusade, King Richard besieged the castle. The castle and its inhabitants surrendered a few days into the attack.

sycophants: people who act obedient or loyal toward someone important in order to gain advantage

A quick drive in the car brings us to the edge of Sherwood Forest, steeped in legend and imagination. You may be wondering why Robin Hood would choose to live in this forest instead of an actual home. Well, the story goes that a nobleman named Robert of Loxley, indignant over the amount of taxes and fees that Prince John was extracting from the people of Nottingham, became an outlaw by stealing from the rich and giving that money to the poor. Taking on a new name and a new camouflaged suit of Lincoln green, Robert, or Robin as he was known to his friends, had to hide his whereabouts, otherwise he would be arrested by the

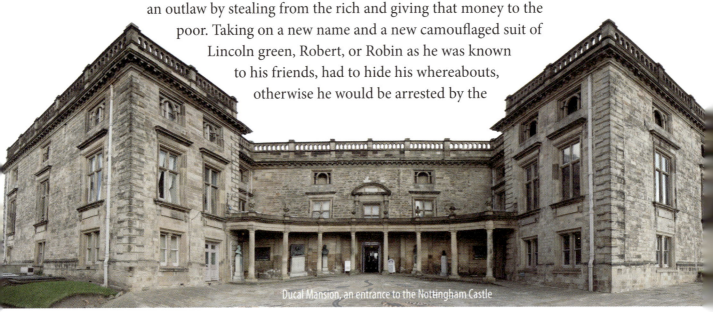
Ducal Mansion, an entrance to the Nottingham Castle

sheriff and possibly executed for being a thief and an enemy to the prince. So, this beautiful old-growth forest became his home, along with his merry band of men who joined him. In the heart of Sherwood Forest stands a huge oak tree, known as Major Oak, which is believed to be over 800 years old. This massive oak has long been thought to be the actual hideout of Robin Hood and his men. If the dating of the tree is correct, it would have been a mere sapling during the years when Prince John set himself up to rule in King Richard's absence. However, there were certainly older trees than this one here at those times that are no longer living. I'm sure if he did hide in a tree, it was as big and glorious as this one is now.

Major Oak

Sherwood Forest in autumn

The legend of Robin Hood has been told for more than 600 years, but historians still debate whether Robin Hood actually existed. While the story may have changed over the years, most history scholars do believe that there was a man, excellent with the bow, who lived in these woods and robbed wealthy travelers passing through. There is a grave not far from here that is agreed to be his, for the stone reads: ⟶

HERE UNDERNEATH THIS LITTLE STONE
LIES ROBERT, EARL OF HUNTINGDON
NO OTHER ARCHER WAS AS GOOD
AND PEOPLE CALLED HIM ROBIN HOOD
SUCH OUTLAWS AS HE AND HIS MEN
WILL ENGLAND NEVER SEE AGAIN.
DECEMBER 24, 1247 (KIRKLEES)

Whether Robin Hood lived among these trees or not, Sherwood Forest was and is a royal forest that has been here for thousands of years and encompasses over 1,000 acres. Every August, a week-long Robin Hood festival is held at Sherwood Forest, and these woods are transformed to another time when jousting and jesting were the entertainment of the day. The forest comes alive with music, games, and legendary characters dressed in period clothing. A complete medieval encampment is set up, and knights, jesters, and rat-catchers entertain visitors.

Thynghowe: an important Viking era open-air assembly place or thing, located at Sherwood Forest, in Nottinghamshire, England

However, long before King Richard, Prince John, or Robin Hood ever lived, this forest was the location of another, still older, historical event. Sherwood was once the site of a **Thynghowe**, an official open-air meeting place for Viking tribes who lived in this region. A "thing" was where Vikings came to resolve their arguments and settle their disputes, similar to a courtroom today.

No matter how you think of it, this forest is as fascinating as it is beautiful, and there have been many stories told of it. If you listen carefully, you can almost hear them told in the whispering of the majestic trees overhead and in the soft crunch of the leaves underfoot.

A little more than an hour's drive north of Sherwood Forest is an old English town that has made a significant impact on our world. The Roman Emperor Constantine was crowned here. Later, Alcuin, Charlemagne the Great's leading advisor, studied at its university. Much later, one of the largest cities on earth was named after it. It is sung about in a popular nursery rhyme, and it was here that the Kit Kat® chocolate bar was concocted. What is the name of this remarkable town? Can you guess?

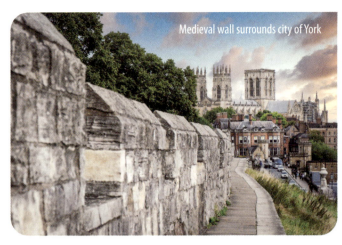
Medieval wall surrounds city of York

You've got it! We are bound for the beautiful old town of York on the eastern side of Central England. We have much to see and learn about in York. Make sure your camera's batteries are charged, because there are some amazing sights to see in this old town.

York Minster

The first thing we notice about York are the thick walls set on high ramparts surrounding the city. This city's outer wall is the most complete medieval defense enclosure in England and retains all its original gateways. Portions of the wall date back to the Roman fortress that was built on this site in the year A.D. 71, but most of the stone wall that we see here was erected between the 12th and 14th centuries. The walls were built thick enough to allow watchmen to walk along its parapet. Today, it is a popular walk about the city for tourists.

Dominating the skyline of York is the great York Minster cathedral. In the year 627, the first wooden **minster** church was hurriedly built in York for the purpose of baptizing Edwin, the King of Northumbria. The name "minster" was reserved for churches built during the Dark Ages that were to be used for teaching and preparing missionaries for the field. A stone church replaced the original wooden structure a few years later. Over the years, decades, and centuries, the humble minster church was built upon and refined into a great cathedral, complete with lofty **transepts**, a glorious nave, and the largest expanse of medieval stained glass found anywhere in the world. More than 850 years later, the great cathedral was declared complete. York Minster, officially named the Cathedral and Metropolitan Church of Saint Peter in York, is considered one of the most beautiful churches on earth. It is glorious!

minster: church structure built in the Dark Ages that was later replaced with a large church structure, typically a cathedral, in Northern England

transepts: cross-shaped spaces to the side of the nave in some cathedrals

Our destination this afternoon is The Shambles, a narrow, crooked street in the heart of York that dates back nearly 1,000 years. What makes this cobbled lane so unique is that it has remained virtually unchanged, architecturally speaking, since the 14th century. Its winding way is punctuated by low, overhanging, half-timbered buildings, which used to house butcher shops at street level, displaying their meats proudly for passersby, and apartments above for the shop owners to live.

We are meeting up with a tour guide on one of the **snickelways**, a term used for the narrow pedestrian tangle of lanes that branch off from The Shambles, the main boulevard through the old marketplace. Get ready for some gripping and slightly grim tales about old York!

"Welcome, young explorers," calls the tour guide as we approach him. "Are you ready to explore my great city of York? Let's get cracking!"

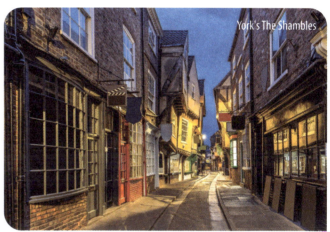

York's The Shambles

"York is a very old city, as you can see from the medieval buildings leaning over the cobblestone lanes about us. However, what you may not know, and what you cannot see, is that under the very streets we are walking now, there is a network of even older streets, dating back to the Roman fortress that once stood on this site. York — then known as Eboracum — was a central trading hub for the Romans and then later, the Vikings.

Ouse River

"You see, once the Romans pulled out of Britain after the Fall of Rome in A.D. 476, the Saxons swooped in for a while and then a few hundred years after that, the Vikings captured York in 866. Because of its perfect location on the Great North Road, now our modern A1 freeway, where it crosses the River Ouse, this city became a major river port, part of the extensive Viking trading network that crisscrossed Northern Europe during their heyday.

snickelways: collection of small streets and footpaths in the city of York, England

"The Vikings renamed their newly conquered city Jórvik, which means 'the place of the yew trees.' The name York comes from this Scandinavian word. Eventually, the Vikings were driven out, but York continued to be a central trading port for England well into the Middle Ages. York merchants exported grain and wool to the mainland in exchange for wine from France, cloth and wax from Belgium, and fur and timber from countries farther north, such as Denmark and Sweden.

"This road is known as The Shambles, which is short for The Fleshammels, or the Great Flesh Shambles. *Shambles* is an Old English word for 'shelves,' so this road was named for the shelves that the local butchers used to display their meat. In fact, you can see outside many of the shop doors large meat hooks where the meat would hang to entice passersby to step in and make a purchase. There are no longer any butcher shops located on this street, but back in medieval times, there were at least 25 butchers here

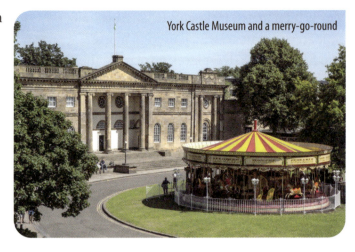

York Castle Museum and a merry-go-round

competing for local sales. It was a butcher's pride to serve his loyal customers well, and a sale to a traveler wandering through The Shambles would make him feel mighty **chuffed** indeed.

"Let's wander through and then make our way up to York Castle there ahead. We are passing the **cufflinks** shop at the address of No. 10 Shambles. This was once the home of Saint Margaret Clitherow, wife to a humble butcher and later saint to the Catholic Church. She lived in the 16th century during the Protestant Reformation, when Catholicism was forbidden in England, Catholics were persecuted, and Roman Catholic priests were ordered to leave the country. Risking her life, Margaret hid priests in her home through a 'priest hole' — literally a trapdoor constructed from an old fireplace, which then opened into a secret hideout. Her home became one of the most important hideouts for fugitive priests in Northern England. When a frightened boy under interrogation revealed the location of the priest hole, Margaret was imprisoned in York Castle and then sentenced to death. To this very day she is fondly referred to as 'the pearl of York.' She was a pearl, indeed."

chuffed: very pleased

cufflinks: decorative fasteners for men's dress sleeves made popular in the 19th century

A hike up the steep hillside brings us to Clifford's Tower, the best-preserved portion of York Castle. From up here, high in the keep, we can see portions of the old castle wall below, which now surrounds newer buildings. Andrew, our tour guide, continues to regale us with fascinating stories from the past.

"The first castle built on this site was a hasty wooden affair, supposedly built in just eight days by William the Conqueror. It didn't last long. The original structure, as well as the next couple attempts, were burned down. When King Henry III came for a visit in 1244 to find the keep burnt to the ground, he ordered this tower built from white limestone, a longer-lasting material assuredly, for here it still stands.

Clifford's Tower

206 Lesson 10. Day 96

A Child's Geography. Vol. 5: Explore Viking Realms

"This castle has been used for multiple purposes, including a military base, a debtor's prison, and a refuge for those needing protection. But King Henry III used it for diplomatic purposes, as a place to meet with the neighboring king of Scotland and as a venue for their children's upcoming wedding. Alexander and Margaret were still babies when the two kings met to arrange their future marriage to one another. When Alexander's father died unexpectedly, Alexander became the new king of Scots at the tender age of seven. Determined to ensure his daughter's position as queen of Scotland, Henry moved up the wedding. It was held two years later when Margaret was eleven and Alexander was nine.

Henry III

"The National Archives holds all sorts of documents from the reign of Henry III, and several of them detail the huge amount of planning that went into that royal wedding, which took place nearly 800 years ago. King Henry placed over 130 orders to supply the royal wedding. Game was hunted in the king's forests, and ponds were dug so that fish could be caught but kept alive to serve fresh at the wedding feast. His order from the sheriff of York alone included 1,000 hens, 300 partridges, 30 swans, 20 cranes, 25 peacocks, 50 rabbits, and 300 hares.

"Then, there was the vast quantity of bread that needed to be baked. Drinks for the event cost £200, well over 100,000 pounds in today's money, and had to be imported from French estates and shipped to London. Despite the careful planning there were still hitches. Because so many invited guests were arriving for the wedding, along with thousands more uninvited but curious onlookers, the town lacked the space to hold them all, and the narrow streets became dangerously crowded. Fights broke out while English and Scottish marshals alike worked hard to maintain peace and find suitable accommodation for the invited lords and ladies.

"What the official documents do not reveal is how young Margaret felt about her grand wedding or even about the prospect of becoming the queen of Scotland at so young an age. What we do know is that Henry III kept a close eye on his oldest daughter by visiting her and her husband regularly in Scotland while they grew up together as a royal couple."

Our tour of York has come to an end. Let's grab a bite to eat and call it a night. I'll bet you are a bit **knackered** after our long walk around York. We passed an old inn back in the Shambles that has roast beef with Yorkshire pudding on the menu and comfy rooms for rent upstairs. Sounds like a perfect end to a wonderful day!

Oh, that's right — I have left some mysteries unresolved. Let's clear those up now….

knackered: extremely tired

A small town on the east coast of America was built back in the 17th century, and the residents decided to name their new city after this great city of York. The colonists named it New York. Meanwhile, back in York, a chocolate factory was built and had become one of the main employers in town. By the 1800s, most of the townsfolk worked either for the railroad or Terry's Chocolate Factory, which produced the Kit Kat® and other delectable treats. Let's have a chocolate wafer bar after dinner with our **cuppa tea**! And here are the words to an old nursery rhyme about the Duke of York:

The grand old Duke of York

He had ten thousand men

He marched them up to the top of the hill (possibly referring to Clifford's Tower)

And he marched them down again.

When you're up. you're up

And when you're down. you're down

And when you're only halfway up

You're neither up nor down.

Have you heard that song before? Perhaps the Duke of York was the original "Captain Obvious." Goodnight, friends. Tomorrow, we explore the charming Lake District in Northern England.

The Famous Sherwood Forest in Central England

Land and Geography:
- ✔ England, Wales, and Scotland share the island of Great Britain.
- ✔ Nine months of the year, England receives a great amount of rain.
- ✔ William the Conqueror ordered the construction of Nottingham Castle.
- ✔ In the "King's Larder," or royal hunting grounds, only the king and those he approved could hunt.

Sherwood Forest:
- ✔ Sherwood Forest is the setting for the legend of Robin Hood, an archer.
- ✔ Robin Hood refers to a story of Robert of Loxley stealing from the rich to give to the poor because of high taxes.
- ✔ Major Oak — a large oak tree older than 800 years — is at the center of Sherwood Forest.
- ✔ A Thynghowe — an official open-air meeting for Viking tribes — was held in Sherwood Forest.

TIMELINE

71 ▶	The wall around York is built by the Romans.
627 ▶	The first version of York Minster is built; the final version is completed 850 years later.
1068 ▶	William the Conqueror orders the construction of Nottingham Castle.
1096 ▶	University of Oxford is established.
1194 ▶	Battle between King Richard and Prince John occurs at Nottingham Castle.
1209 ▶	University of Cambridge is established.
1244 ▶	King Henry III orders the construction of Clifford's Tower with limestone.

208 Lesson 10. Day 96

A Child's Geography. Vol. 5: Explore Viking Realms

Vikings and the Balance of Justice

On the western edge of the Sherwood Forest, Vikings once gathered at the top of Hangar Hill, or "hill of assembly," for something called a Thynghowe, an official open-air meeting. At set times, a "Thyng" was held where disputes were settled, arguments were resolved, and punishment for crimes took place.

Thynghowe was like a courtroom; however, there are differences from what a justice proceeding looks like today. While some of the proceedings or order of events at a Thyng were structured and civil, others were not. Known for violence and barbaric traits, the Vikings displayed the same style when ordering punishment that included torture, depending on the crime. The Viking tribes made an occasion of it, drawing crowds, setting up tents for selling and trading wares, and staying for several days.

A definition of justice is equal weight between a person and the good or bad. The image of a scale and seeking even balance can be used to visualize the meaning of justice. When a person commits a more severe crime, that person has a weightier punishment to even out the scale.

Let's create a balance scale. Choose either a basic design or an advanced design.

Basic Design:

1. With a hole punch, create two holes across from each other near the top of the empty containers or cups.

2. Fold the yarn or string in half and cut in the middle.

3. Loop one piece of yarn or string through the shoulder groove. Tie each end to the holes in the container or cup. Repeat with the second string. Make sure both sides are even.

4. Place the hook of the hanger on a doorknob or horizontal rail.

5. With your parent's permission or guidance, select items to determine which weighs more. (The container or cup that dips lower is heavier.)

Basic Design materials needed:

☐ Two empty applesauce containers or two paper cups

☐ Hole punch

☐ Three feet of yarn or thick string

☐ Ruler

☐ Hanger with shoulder grooves

☐ Small household or outdoor items* (parent's permission or guidance)

*Ideas for items are coins, batteries, rocks, etc.

Advanced Design:

Design type ☐ Basic Design ☐ Advanced Design

1. With your parent's permission or guidance, gather various household items. Design and create your own balance scale. Decorate with extra art supplies available.

2. With your parent's permission or guidance, select items to determine which weighs more. (The container or cup that dips lower is heavier.) Note which scale you made by checking the appropriate box below and write down what objects you chose to weigh with your scale.

_____

_____

_____

_____

_____

_____

Which items weigh more? _____

The One true God is just and teaches justice. That means there is loving discipline for not following His truths and ways. Without discipline, justice is incomplete. He is also a God of love and mercy.

Righteousness and justice are the foundation of Your throne:
Mercy and truth go before You.
– Psalm 89:14

Mapping It Out!

Refer to the map on page 383. Label the map from page 167 with the following places:

☐ Oxford

☐ Cambridge

☐ Nottingham

Flashcards

Make flashcards of the bolded glossary words from this lesson. Then, either add drawings of the terms or act them out in charades. Be creative!

Draw the Triangle

1. England shares the island of Great Britain with Wales to the west and Scotland to the north. Label Wales and Scotland.

   a. _____

   b. _____

England covers five-eighths of Great Britain and resembles a triangle shape. Draw a triangle on the map over England's borders.

Old English sheepdog

a

b   *England*

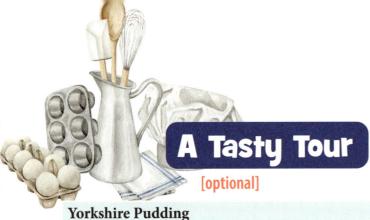

A Tasty Tour

[optional]

Yorkshire Pudding

Ingredients:

¼ cup beef drippings or butter

½ cup milk

⅞ cup flour

½ cup water

½ teaspoon salt

2 eggs

NOTE: This recipe requires adult supervision and participation.

Optional: Teacher's Discretion

☐ No ☐ Yes

Due Date: _____

Directions:

1. Begin with all ingredients at room temperature. Preheat oven to 400°. Heat a 9x13 oven-proof dish with ¼ cup of beef drippings or melted butter.

2. While the dish is heating in the oven, add the flour and salt to a bowl. Make a well in the center into which you will pour the milk and water. Stir the liquid into the flour mixture. Beat the eggs in a separate bowl and then add. Beat the mixture until fluffy and bubbles begin to rise to the surface.

3. Open the oven and pour the batter into the dish with the hot drippings. Bake the pudding for 20 minutes. Then reduce the heat to 350° and bake for 10 minutes longer. Serve immediately.

Learn Geography Terms

Page 342 is a reference page for understanding the terms geographers use to describe landforms.

Love your neighbor

Major Oak, the massive oak tree that stands in Sherwood Forest, is believed to be more than 800 years old. Oak trees begin as small saplings or young growths and grow into large, strong trees that stand for centuries. Lord, we pray to grow in you as "oaks of righteousness" written about in Isaiah 61:3.

Northern England: Tales from Miss Potter's Farm

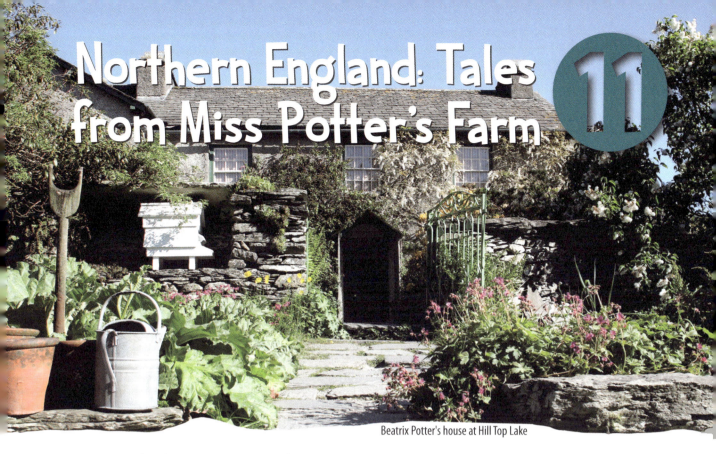

11

Beatrix Potter's house at Hill Top Lake

Crisscrossing England once again, we are driving northwest to the Cumbrian Lake District. The distance isn't far, but we'll be winding our way around gently curving mountain roads through a purple-infused, heather-soaked countryside. People have been flocking to the Lake District for hundreds of years as a peaceful getaway from the hustle and bustle of city life. The Lake District gets its name from the more than 200 lakes nestled among the green and mulberry mountains in this region.

We'll enter from the south side of the national park. Our first stop is Hill Top Farm, the home of writer and illustrator Beatrix Potter. You have probably heard of her. Her most famous book, about a rabbit named Peter, was self-published in 1901 after it had been rejected by multiple book publishers. The tale follows the antics of the mischievous and disobedient Peter as he is chased around the garden by a farmer. The book with her illustrations was a smashing success. With over 45 million copies sold, it is one of the best-selling books of all time.

Beatrix went on to write dozens more stories all featuring charming farm and woodland creatures. Publishers who initially rejected her now **clawed** for the rights to print her captivating tales. Miss Potter was more than a famous author and illustrator. She was a farmer, a prize-winning sheep breeder, a natural scientist, and a botanical illustrator. She was also a conservationist who not only lived in the Lake District but worked tirelessly her whole life to preserve it for future generations.

Stockley Bridge in Cumbria

clawed: fought

When we drive through these verdant hills and valleys, appearing almost untouched by human hands, we have Beatrix Potter to thank for this. Our greater thanks is to God, the Creator of it all. Yet, people have been living in this region for thousands of years. We'll see proof of that when we finish our tour of the Cumbrian Lake District and drive back out the northern side. But that adventure will come later.

Right now, we are pulling up to Hill Top Farm. The first thing we notice is the iconic Herdwick sheep grazing on the property, marked by low, slate stone walls. Sheep meander everywhere in this part of England, and a person can instantly be recognized as a tourist when he or she stops to photograph the sheep. I don't mind being recognized as a tourist. Let's snap some shots to send home! There is nothing more tranquil to behold than sheep grazing through lush green grass on a billowy cloudy day.

While wandering around the perfectly preserved Hill Top Farm, one can imagine where Beatrix got many of her ideas for her books. Imagine ducks aimlessly waddling along the drive, frogs hopping from lily pad to lily pad on the pond, or rabbits scurrying around the slate wall in front of the old stone house. Inside, it is just as easy to picture mice scurrying into the little mouse hole in the corner or kittens strutting around the farmhouse.

It's not too hard to imagine what life must have been like here at the turn of the 20th century, thanks to the National Trust, who inherited Potter's country home and preserved it for thousands of visitors to wander through each year.

It is time to be off! We are meeting up with the son and daughter-in-law of some dear friends a little later today. They run a bed and breakfast in the charming town of Keswick, a short drive to the north. On the way, we'll drive along the shores of the largest lake in the Lake District, Windermere. However, the locals don't refer to this body of water as Lake Windermere. Since "mere" means "lake," that would be redundant — like saying, "Lake Winder Lake."

Thanks to the Norse Vikings who lived here well over a thousand years ago and left their mark on the English language of this region, you will hear many unusual words spoken in this corner of Great Britain. You may hear the words "tarn" and "mere" used instead of lake; "beck" instead of stream; "gill" instead of gorge; "fell" instead of mountain; "dale" instead of valley; "force" instead of waterfall; and "thwaite" to refer to a clearing in the woods. All these words refer to outdoor terrain because the people who live here love the outdoors.

The Lake District is made for hiking and biking. The highest mountain in England is located here, but Scafell Pike, at less than one thousand meters (3,209 ft), is not much more than a large rolling hill and is fairly easy to climb. The mountains, or fells, in these northern parts often look more purple than green. That is not because they are massive or distant, but because they are covered in heather, a low-growing perennial shrub covered in lavender-colored blooms.

Viking raids: The question of why Vikings would go on raids is a complex one, with no singular answer. As a culture, they worshiped false gods that had warred for dominance, and violence was a way of life to avenge a wrong, settle disputes, or defend one's honor or reputation. They also believed that when they would die was already predetermined. Combine this with a sense of adventure, lack of fear, experience in navigating the sea, and a need for wealth and slaves for status and alliances, it was a perfect recipe for the devastation they would visit upon their victims.

Often Christian sites such as churches and monasteries were chosen because of their wealth of gold, silver, and other precious metals, books, jewels, and more. These isolated sites had little protection and were easy targets. But in the future, despite fierce resistance, Christianity would eventually conquer the hearts of these bold warriors.

As you take in the magnificent scenery, it is not hard to believe that other creative geniuses often sought refuge here among the colorful fells and serene tarns. One of the most famous poets of all time, William Wordsworth, often came to the Lake District to reignite his creative juices and draw more poetry out of his mind and onto the page. Wordsworth was known for wandering through these mountains and valleys "as lonely as a cloud" but preferring it that way.

Scafell Pike

Charlotte Mason, a 19th-century thought leader on education, also enjoyed this place. So much so, that she settled down in Ambleside, the small town we are driving through now. In fact, it was this countryside that spurred her belief that all students should carry a nature journal with them. Thus equipped, they can record or illustrate what they observe in nature and appreciate the lavish creation of the Almighty God to gain wisdom from it.

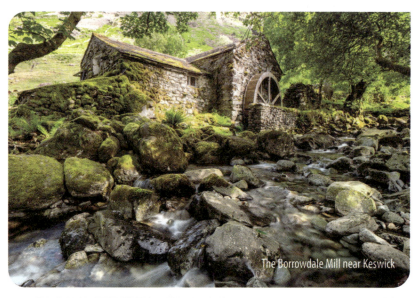
The Borrowdale Mill near Keswick

While the primary industry in this region since Roman times has been sheep farming, there have been other industries that provided a living for the families who settled here throughout the years. Long ago, the Lake District was a major source of stone axes, sometimes nicknamed the "stone axe factory," as many ancient axes have been found along the **fellsides**.

The Bridge House, Ambleside

Later, during medieval times, mining became the major source of income for lake residents. Mines were dug deep into the earth to retrieve copper, silver, lead, graphite, and slate. While many of these mines have been abandoned, some mines

fellsides: hillsides or mountainsides

still operate today, mostly for slate and graphite. This locally mined graphite led to the development of the pencil industry, with more pencils coming out of Keswick than any other place on earth. In other words, we are on our way to the pencil capital of the world!

Another industry that has thrived here and kept the local economy going is the bobbin industry. Yes, the little metal thread holders that are inserted into sewing machines are called bobbins and were manufactured here. During the 19th century, over half of the world's bobbin supply came from the Lake District. Now, in the 21st century, bobbins are all but forgotten, and tourism is the main industry in the district and the primary source of income for the region.

Here we are in Keswick, a quaint tourist town located on the north shore of Derwent Water — oh yes, "water" is yet another word used here to refer to lakes. Steven and Ruby have taken over the family home and business, a world-renowned bed and breakfast located on the emerald-green hillside above

216 Lesson 11. Day 101

A Child's Geography. Vol. 5: Explore Viking Realms

the lake. Steven's family has been hosting guests in their grand Victorian home for nearly a hundred years.

Old jetty on Isthmus Bay, Keswick

As we motor up to the four-star bed and breakfast, we are surprised by the stately mansion we'll be staying in. The slate-built Victorian home is enormous, with high peaked turrets, grand bay windows, graceful gables, and a meticulously manicured garden out front. The oversized front door is open wide on this mostly sunny day, and we gratefully step inside. Ruby calls for Steven to park our car for us around the back of the house, then rushes down the stairs to greet us.

"Welcome, friends! Welcome to our home and the northern lakes!" Ruby beams.

Steven, pink cheeked from parking the car and hauling our entire collection of luggage up to our rooms, returns briskly to further welcome us to his home.

"I am so thrilled that you are here! My folks send their love and greetings to you and your families. I have planned our day; I hope that is alright with you. If we head out to the **jetty** just there, we can board one of the lake steamers that will carry us around the lake. Should we board the clockwise vessel, we can stop halfway to hike up the highest fell on our lake and enjoy the incredible view. On our way back down the fell, we can stop in for tea and scones at the Lingholm Estate, a favorite destination of Beatrix Potter when she stayed at the northern lakes. Then we'll board the boat back here to Keswick."

jetty: stones or other structure that extends into the sea to protect a harbor

Keswick on the shores of Derwentwater

Northern England: Tales from Miss Potter's Farm

Steven's thick northern accent can be initially hard to understand, but his smiles and gestures certainly are not.

"We're game! Let's go!" we cry.

"Excellent! Then tomorrow, we will rustle up a fine English breakfast of local Cumbrian sausage, black pudding, tomatoes, baked beans, and soft-boiled eggs before we head out to take in the wonder of Castlerigg."

"Castlerigg? What is Castlerigg?" we ask.

"Oh yes, Castlerigg! I won't spoil it for you by trying to describe it. You'll just have to see it for yourself," Steven says as Ruby smiles knowingly. "Well, let's snap to it then and make haste! We have quite a bit of adventuring to do before the sun goes down this evening. Grab your cameras and coats and let's be off!"

With rain jackets and umbrellas in hand, just in case, we step back into the afternoon sun and scurry down to the pier to board the next boat circling the lake, full of happy, wide-eyed passengers.

Nature Inspiration for Writers

Resources:
- ✔ The Cumbrian Lake District was named for the 200 lakes in the region.
- ✔ Mining started in medieval times to retrieve copper, silver, lead, graphite, and slate.
- ✔ The bobbin industry is no longer booming and has been replaced by tourism.
- ✔ Herdwick sheep graze in the area of Hill Top Farm.

Writing Influence:
- ✔ Beatrix Potter wrote and illustrated at Hill Top Farm.
- ✔ Norse Vikings influenced language with words like "tarn" for lake and "dale" for valley.
- ✔ Some of William Wordsworth's poetry was inspired by the Lake District.
- ✔ Charlotte Mason was a 19th-century thought leader who believed all students should carry a nature journal.

Economy of Northern England

The geography and natural resources of a region impact the economy. Next to the economic industries, write what you learned from the lesson about each of them. Write complete sentences.

Industry in Northern England	What I Learned
1. Sheep	
2. Stone axe factory	
3. Mines: copper, silver, lead, graphite, and slate	
4. Bobbin	
5. Tourism	

Optional: Teacher's Discretion   ☐ No   ☐ Yes   Due Date: _____

With your parent's permission or guidance, explore books or online resources to learn more about one of the following. Then write five or more sentences about what you learned.

The impact of one of these industries on the people and economy of Northern England.

OR

The conversion of the currency in England to the currency in your own country.

_____

_____

_____

_____

_____

Nature Journal

Charlotte Mason was a 19th-century thought leader from Northern England who believed everyone should carry a nature journal to record and illustrate observations in nature and appreciate the lavish creation of the Almighty God to gain wisdom from it. Instead of the false worship of nature, there is a call to worship the Triune God, Jesus, and Holy Spirit who created all of the heavens and earth.

Grab a bag of some sort for your nature walk. Collect interesting specimens of leaves, moss, lichen, bark, and small stones. Make note of the animals and plants that you see.

Animal Observations	Plant Observations

"But just ask the animals, and have them teach you;

And the birds of the sky, and have them tell you.

Or speak to the earth, and have it teach you;

And have the fish of the sea tell you.

Who among all these does not know

That the hand of the Lord has done this."

—Job 12:7-9

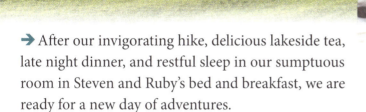

English breakfast

Kissing gate

→ After our invigorating hike, delicious lakeside tea, late night dinner, and restful sleep in our sumptuous room in Steven and Ruby's bed and breakfast, we are ready for a new day of adventures.

Down in the cozy dining room, Steven and Ruby are busy serving their guests a scrumptious breakfast spread. The menu consists of two appealing choices — the traditional English breakfast or a hearty bowl of Scottish oatmeal, served with honey and thick cream. A traditional English breakfast is quite different from a typical American breakfast. A large plate is filled with items we don't generally associate with breakfast, such as tomatoes and baked beans. Black pudding for breakfast has a long history in England and Ireland. It can be found in recipe books dating as far back as 1450 when it was spelled "blak podyngs." This traditional dish is made with pork or beef fat, some type of grain — usually oatmeal or barley — water, and one part beef or pork blood to four parts water. It sounds terrible, but some people like it. I'm choosing the hearty bowl of Scottish oatmeal instead!

With our stomachs pleasantly full and the dishes cleaned and drying on the rack, it is time to drive out to nearby Castlerigg. Steven and Ruby have insisted that they want to surprise us with what we will discover there. So, on our winding drive up the hill to our destination, we talk of other things, such as why heather grows everywhere here and why the cows are quite large with unusually thick and curly hair. Ruby explains that both heather and highland cows thrive exceedingly well in the north. Each is a hearty breed of their species that can gracefully withstand the wet and cold temperatures of this highland climate.

We have arrived at Castlerigg! Time to discover what mystery awaits us here.

Just across the road, we see a small **kissing gate**, which we can only pass through one at a time. Let's see what is on the other side. Will it be a castle? Or a pile of ruins? I cannot imagine what else it might be.

kissing gate: gate hung in a U- or V-shaped enclosure, letting one person through at a time

From this distance, it looks like an ordinary sheep pasture with an extraordinary view.

As we draw near, we can see large stones erected on end, forming a large circle. Castlerigg is an ancient stone circle! It is slightly reminiscent of Stonehenge — though not quite as colossal in shape and size. Its backdrop of lilac-hued fells above and cascading chartreuse valley below sets this stone circle apart as perhaps one of the most dramatic ancient megaliths in the United Kingdom — so vast, so wild, and so strikingly beautiful.

Castlerigg stone circle

While there are over 1,300 ancient stone megaliths located in the British Isles, none are as breathtaking, and few are as ancient, as this one. Archaeologists believe this circle of stones was erected around 3,000 B.C. Several ancient stone axes have been found within and around the stones. Scientists speculate that this circle on the plateau with the astounding view was formerly used for one or more of these purposes: 1) a trading center for axes and other objects of value; 2) a calendar to mark the days and seasons of the year; or 3) an astronomical instrument to track and predict events in the night sky.

There is an obvious entrance into the circle on the north end and a smaller inner circle located on the eastern side. Whatever its previous use, this place appears to have been forgotten in time. Grazing sheep wander through and take shelter in the shadow of the upright rocks.

Whatever the reason this stone circle was constructed initially, it is clear the ancient people who lived in the northern Cumbrian Lake District chose to go about their business in this jaw-dropping setting, conducting their most important meetings here among the circle of stones.

Leaving Castlerigg and the scenic Lake District behind, it's time to drive north to our final stop in England. We are heading to Hadrian's Wall, the farthest outpost of the Roman Empire, which was built all the way back in the year A.D. 122. This landmark is less than a mile from the border with Scotland here on England's western coast. But the wall stretches from the western coast over 70 miles to the eastern coast, and as it does, it veers away from the modern boundary line the farther east you go.

Hadrian's Wall was built by and for the Emperor Hadrian shortly after he rose to power. The wall, which stretched across England's northern territory from coast to coast, complete with **milecastles**, or mini-forts, spaced at every Roman mile, was meant to intimidate the barbarians to the north and send a strong message that England was a force to be reckoned with. It took six years to complete. Besides the 75 milecastles, each including a lookout tower and accommodations for a small armed troop, the Romans also built full-sized fortresses every five miles or so that could house between 500 and 1,000 soldiers.

milecastles: small forts or rectangular fortifications built during the period of the Roman Empire, placed at intervals of approximately one Roman mile along several major frontiers, such as Hadrian's Wall

Hadrian's Wall

Hadrian's Wall is the largest Roman artifact in the world. It was declared a UNESCO World Heritage Site in 1987, which means that it is intended to be preserved and protected for generations to come by the United Nations Educational, Scientific, and Cultural Organization. However, as of this writing, it is still legal to walk on top of the ancient stone wall. In fact, a pathway — Hadrian's Wall Path — has been created so that hikers can walk beside the wall along its full length from coast to coast.

We drive east a short distance and then get out of the car to walk a while beside the incredibly old historical wall to see the remains of the ancient fortifications. Most of the wall was built along a ridge with a ditch, either natural or man-made, swooping down on its northern side. The Romans always preferred to hold the higher ground. This gave them the advantage of time, preparedness, and position, should the warring barbarian tribes of the north attempt to storm the wall.

A couple miles to the east, we arrive at Vercovicium, one of the oldest and largest fortifications built along the wall. Vercovicium was the Roman name for the fortress, but today it is known as Housesteads, the name of the 16th-century farm whose lands included the ruins of the fort. The Armstrong family, who were famously known to be Border Reivers — thieves who lived along the English-Scottish border between the 13th and 17th centuries — owned the farm. Their band of

Ruins of a Roman fort along Hadrian's Wall

Reenactment of Roman garrison

thieves included both English and Scottish people, who pillaged and stole from one end of the entire frontier to the other, caring little whether the victims were of their own nationality or not.

Housesteads, or Vercovicium, gives us a very distinct glimpse into the lifestyle of the ancient Roman soldiers stationed in this most remote outpost of the Roman Empire. Large rooms were built for the soldiers over crawlspaces used for storing their provisions and supplies. Smaller rooms with private entrances were reserved for the officers and their families. The Romans dug wells to access fresh, clean drinking water, and kitchens were built to provide the soldiers with hot meals.

"An army marches on its stomach" was a common motto of the Romans. For this reason, Roman soldiers were well-supplied with rations — both prepared meals and basic ingredients to cook their own hearty dishes. When a soldier was on the march, he would often be supplied with **hardtack**, hard cheeses, and beef jerky. But for the soldiers stationed along Hadrian's Wall, the food was often much better. The **garrisons** were supplied with grain, beef, beans, root vegetables, soft cheese, oil, and salt.

hardtack: dry bread

garrisons: troops stationed in a fortress to defend it. The term also refers to the building occupied by the troops stationed in a town to defend it.

The fortress at Housesteads, along with the other 15 fortifications along the wall, was outfitted with brick ovens for baking loaves of bread and roasting root vegetables. However, a popular dish among the soldiers was puls, which did not require an oven.

Hardtack

Puls was a dish that could be cooked fairly quickly over an open fire. Grain (usually wheat or barley) would be mixed with water and boiled in a large kettle along with some salt for seasoning. Chopped meat could be added to the mixture, along with garlic, vegetables, milk, oil, and spices. This porridge was a quick, easy, and satisfying meal when there wasn't enough time to bake bread or roast their supply of vegetables and meat.

Puls

After the death of Hadrian, a new emperor came to power who wanted to construct a new wall approximately 100 miles to the north. The Antonine Wall, named for Emperor Antoninus Pius, was about half the length of Hadrian's at 40 Roman miles in length but equipped with just as many fortifications. However, Antoninus was unable to conquer the northern tribes after several attempts and eventually abandoned the new wall, pulled back his troops, and reoccupied Hadrian's Wall as the main defense barrier of the northern frontier.

This Roman ruin from antiquity tells its story at every mile post and inside every **bulwark**, but we are still left to imagine what daily life must have been like here in the rugged wilds of the northern empire. However, in March of 2010, on the 1,600th anniversary of the end of Roman rule in Britain, a public event took place here to help modern visitors envision what a highly fortified Roman presence along the English-Scottish border was really like back in its heyday. To celebrate, the wall was lit with 500 fiery beacons along its full length, illuminating the wall and its place in both British and world history.

bulwark: wall or other structure for self-defense

Statue of Emperor Hadrian

Ruin of a Roman fort on Hadrian's Wall

England, both rugged and refined, tells a complex story of deep roots and a constantly developing civilization. Wild England, graceful England, burly England, noble England, it has been a pleasure exploring the varied landscape and riveting history. We shall miss the land that is a significant part of our past and a beautiful part of our present. Thank you for this delightful tour of your country, from shore to stunning shore.

Next up, we hop over the wall and within a few miles enter the spectacular land of the Scots. Scotland, here we come!

Hadrian's Wall in Northern England

Ancient Structures:

✔ *Castlerigg is an ancient stone circle, which is accessed through a kissing gate.*

✔ *Hadrian's Wall was the furthest outpost of the Roman Empire and is the largest Roman artifact.*

✔ *Vercovicium, known as Housesteads, was one of the oldest fortifications.*

✔ *After Emperor Hadrian rose to power, Hadrian's Wall was built by and for him.*

✔ *After Hadrian's death, Emperor Antoninus Pius came to power and built the Antonine Wall.*

Interesting Foods:

✔ *Black pudding is made from pork blood, pork or beef fat, and a grain like oatmeal or barley.*

✔ *Marching Roman soldiers carried hardtack (dry bread), hard cheeses, and beef jerky.*

✔ *Roman garrisons by Hadrian's Wall were well supplied with grain, beef, beans, root vegetables, and more.*

✔ *A common porridge for Roman soldiers was puls, which includes grains, meats, and vegetables.*

TIMELINE

122	▶	Hadrian's Wall is built by the Romans.
793	▶	Viking attack occurs on Lindisfarne in Northern England.

226 Lesson 11. Day 105

A Child's Geography. Vol. 5: Explore Viking Realms

Short Answer

Answer the following questions.

1. What do you remember about Northern England?

_____

_____

_____

2. How is Castlerigg similar to Stonehenge?

_____

_____

_____

3. How is Castlerigg different than Stonehenge?

_____

_____

_____

4. Why was Hadrian's Wall built?

_____

_____

_____

5. What did a typical Roman soldier stationed out on the frontier eat?

_____

_____

_____

Visit Hadrian's Wall

Write a travel feature about Hadrian's Wall, the farthest outpost of the Roman Empire. Also include an illustration or illustrations. Your purpose is to persuade potential visitors to plan a trip to Hadrian's Wall and to educate them.

Materials needed:
☐ Colored pencils

In your writing, include details about five key topics.

history	preservation	features
appearance	modes of transportation to visit	

_____

_____

_____

_____

_____

_____

_____

_____

_____

Milecastles and Viking Raids

Mini-forts, or milecastles, spaced approximately a mile apart were designed to protect against Viking raids along Hadrian's Wall and other locations. The Antonine Wall was also constructed.

With your parent's permission, build a fort. For an indoor fort, use pillows, cardboard or plastic storage boxes, or other materials. For an outdoor fort, use branches, rocks, or other materials.

Political division, battles over who would become leaders, worship of false gods, plots over wealth from greed, and lifestyles filled with sin helped to lead to the destruction of the once-mighty Roman Empire. While the empire may have been engineered to last forever, the works of many never do. There is only One true God who controls eternity.

I will say to the Lord,

"My refuge and my fortress,

My God, in whom I trust!"

—Psalm 91:2

Mapping It Out!

Refer to the map on page 383. Label the map from page 167 with the following places:

☐ Cumbrian Lake District

☐ Lake Windermere

England's Topography

Topography is the physical features of the land. This may include hills, flatlands, mountains, waters, valleys, and other differences. Contoured lines show areas of changes in elevation. Color or shade the topography of England (Southern, Central, and Northern) on the map to match the colored map.

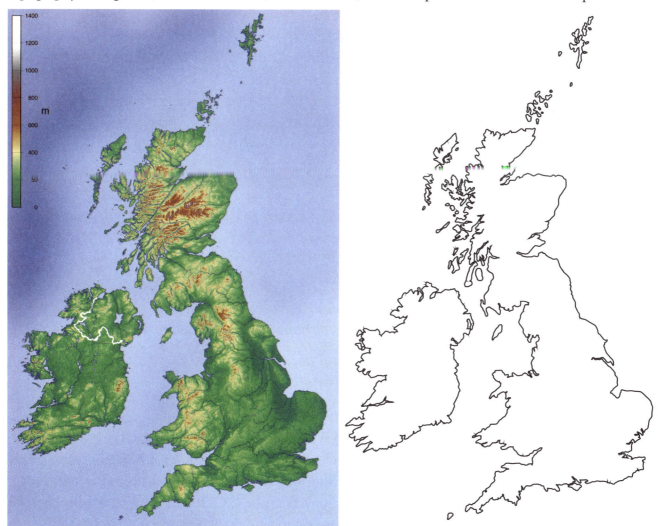

What observations can you make about the topography of Southern England, Central England, and Northern England?

_____

_____

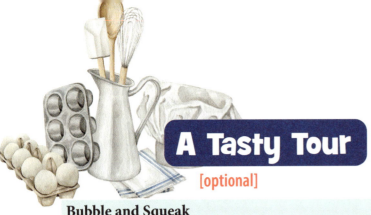

A Tasty Tour

[optional]

Bubble and Squeak

Ingredients:

6 tablespoons unsalted butter

4 strips of bacon (chopped)

1 onion (finely sliced)

1 garlic clove (chopped)

1 whole cabbage (boiled, shredded)

1 pound mashed potato

Salt and pepper (to taste)

NOTE: Requires adult supervision and participation.

Optional: Teacher's Discretion

☐ No ☐ Yes

Due Date: _____

Directions:

1. In a large frying pan, melt the butter over medium heat. Add the finely chopped onion and fry for about 3 minutes or until soft.

2. Add the mashed potato and all of the chopped-up vegetables and bacon. Fry for 10 minutes. Brown the outside edges of the vegetables.

3. When the mixture is heated right through, give the vegetables one long final press onto the base of the pan with a spatula and leave to cook for 1 minute. Flip over and repeat. Season with salt and pepper.

4. Serve.

Learn Geography Terms

Page 342 is a reference page for understanding the terms geographers use to describe landforms.

Love your neighbor

We are thankful for learning about the people and land of Northern England. "I thank God, whom I serve with a clear conscience the way my forefathers did, as I constantly remember you in my prayers night and day," are the words from 2 Timothy 1:3. Although our time with England has come to a close, we continue to thank you, Lord.

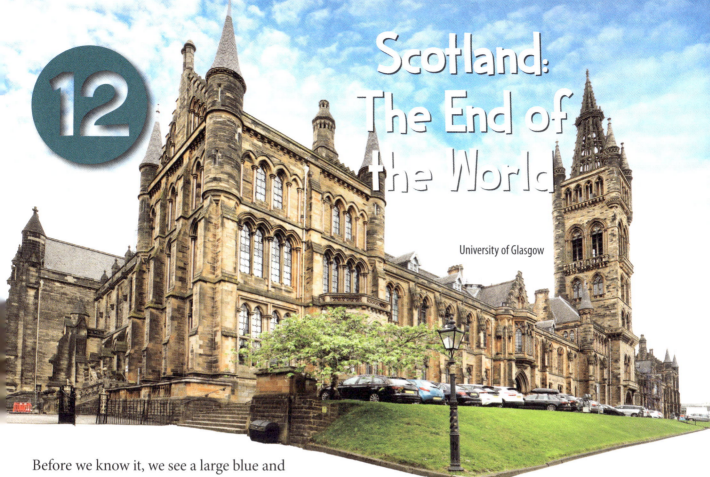

12

Scotland: The End of the World

University of Glasgow

Before we know it, we see a large blue and white flag waving proudly on a high hill, welcoming us to Scotland, the second country on our tour of the United Kingdom and the ninth since we began this journey. Scotland is located on the northern third of the island of Great Britain and is home to over five million people. In addition to the mainland, Scotland includes more than 790 islands! Most of the islands belong to four large **archipelagos,** or island chains, known as the Inner and Outer Hebrides to the west and Orkney and Shetland to the north.

archipelagos: groups of islands

You may know quite a few people of Scottish descent back home. In truth, more Scots live outside of Scotland than live here in the homeland of their ancestors. We'll learn why very soon.

We are driving north to Edinburgh, the capital of Scotland. If you don't want to draw undue attention to yourself as a foreign visitor, it's a good idea to learn how to pronounce the name of the capital city. It's not pronounced the way you probably think. The "g" sound is replaced by an "a" sound, like this: "*ed-in-burr-a*." Say that a few times out loud so you can get used to the pronunciation.

Before we get to Edinburgh, we'll ramble through the southern uplands, then through the sparsely inhabited lowlands before we reach the capital city. Later, after we have spent some time in Edinburgh and have passed through to the other side of the city, the landscape will get even more striking as we cross over two major fault lines and head into the famous Scottish Highlands. In fact, you can see the coast-to-coast fault lines from space.

It's almost as if Scotland were scored like a delicate Scottish shortbread cookie and ready to split into three equal thirds to share with friends. But don't worry; while Scotland does experience occasional earthquakes, the tremors are usually quite mild and unfelt by most residents. The largest recorded earthquake in Scotland occurred just north of the Great Glen Fault in 1880 and registered a 5.2 on the Richter scale.

Edinburgh is a fascinating city with its Old Town in the center, the New Town right next to it on the north side, and still newer parts of town radiating out from both of these.

We are meeting up with an old childhood friend outside Edinburgh Castle, the imposing fortress that dominates the city's skyline, built atop a dormant volcano known as Castle Rock. I see her! She's waiting in the courtyard just outside the large front entrance.

"Stephanie!" I call to her as we come within hearing distance.

She hastens toward us with arms outstretched. "Oh, my dear old friend! How good it is to see you! Please introduce me to your other friends." We share introductions all around, and Stephanie hugs us all, so glad to see faces from home.

"Let me be the first to welcome you to Scotland, and especially to her capital city of Edinburgh, my new home," Stephanie beams. "I can't wait to show you around. This is Edinburgh Castle, which was built in the 12th century. Over the past 850 years, this castle has been used as a royal residence and a military prison. Today, the castle continues to function as an army base and is where the nation's crown jewels are kept safe and secure. Shall we go inside and see them? They are the oldest crown jewels in all of Great Britain!"

Inside, we see the great hall, the weapons room, the dungeon, the new barracks, and so much more. We hear stories of past kings and queens, of battles and mutinies, of loyalty, patriotism, and devotion to God and country. The Scottish people are fiercely patriotic and work hard to preserve their culture and tell their history — the good, the bad, and even the ugly sides of it.

Back outside, Stephanie points to the road running downhill away from the castle through the old medieval part of town, ending at the king's house — his home away from home here in Scotland — the Palace at Holyroodhouse.

"That's where we are going next. This road is called the Royal Mile because it is a full mile from the castle to the palace, and this used to be all there was to the city of Edinburgh,

232 Lesson 12. Day 110

A Child's Geography. Vol. 5: Explore Viking Realms

back in the Middle Ages. In fact, most people who lived within the city's medieval walls never left them, or at least didn't leave them too far behind. This was the only place they knew. They didn't travel to other parts of the world or even the country like we do today. There is an old restaurant where the original city gate once stood, which we'll pass by on our way to the palace.

Holyrood Palace

It is named 'The World's End.' They named it so because that is what the medieval city dwellers thought it was — the end of the world, as they knew it. Can world travelers such as yourselves even imagine such a thing?"

Together, we've wandered through several well-preserved medieval streets on this exploration, but there's something about this particular street with its Scottish charm that makes us want to slow down and enjoy the old-world feel of the tall, narrow buildings with the low doorways and curious names. At the far end of the Royal Mile stands the Holyrood Palace in all her grandeur. Before their deaths, Queen Elizabeth II and sometimes her husband Philip, the Duke of Edinburgh, would travel to the palace one week each year, hosting garden parties and other events. Their son King Charles III and his wife, Queen Camilla, continued this tradition. As generations continue, some traditions remain while others change with time. Let's go inside and have a look around.

You may be wondering why the English monarch is also the reigning king here. First of all, in 1707 under the Treaty of Union, England and Scotland were "United into One Kingdom by the Name of Great Britain" and are still united to this day. For this reason, they share the same kings and

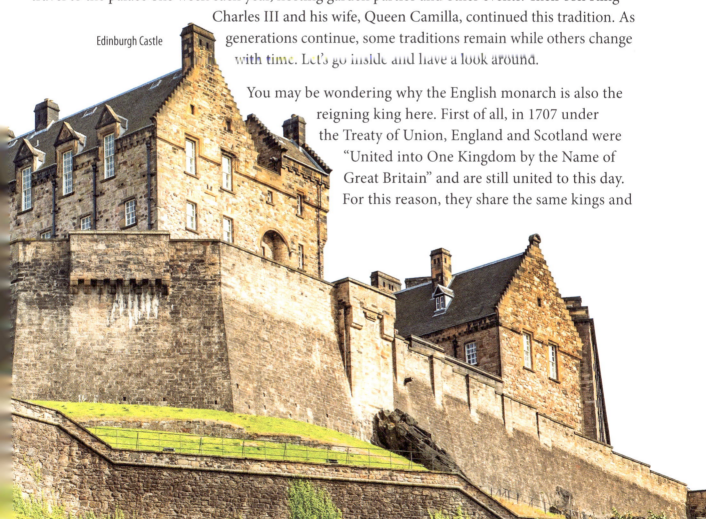
Edinburgh Castle

Scotland: The End of the World

The ruins of Kilchurn Castle

queens of Great Britain, but they also run their own limited self-government within Scotland, as well as participate in the leadership of the larger government of the United Kingdom.

Now, about the late queen and her husband, Philip … Queen Elizabeth inherited the throne from her father, King George VI, when he died because she was his next of kin — in other words, his closest blood relative. In 1947, Elizabeth became engaged to Philip, Prince of both Denmark and Greece. While Philip was born a prince to both the Greek and Danish royal families, he gave up his right to those thrones and titles to marry Elizabeth. In exchange, he was given the title of His Royal Highness, the Duke of Edinburgh, on the evening before the wedding, even though he wasn't from Scotland or of Scottish heritage. Their oldest child, King Charles III, became the next reigning monarch. As the family story carries on, the throne continues to be a topic of public interest. The title of Duke of Edinburgh has been given to another of Prince Philip's sons.

The Palace of Holyrood dates back to the 16th century and has been the royal residence of the kings and queens of Scotland since that time. The palace sits adjacent to the abbey that shares her name — Holyrood — which means "holy wood," as it was believed that a splinter from Jesus' Cross was salvaged and kept here as a **relic**.

Visitors can wander through the grand banquet hall, the throne room, and other chambers that are still used to this day, as well as peek into the historic apartments of past monarchs, including the very ones that were used by Mary, Queen of Scots, the youngest child to become the ruler of Scotland when she was but one week of age.

relic: revered historic object with a religious connection

Stephanie is happy to show us around other parts of Edinburgh that are of great historical importance, such as the sophisticated New Town, the University of Edinburgh, and the Grassmarket. She tells us about many of the famous men and women who have lived and died in this city and who have made a significant mark on our world.

"You'd probably be surprised by how many world-famous Scots there have been over the years, many of whom were educated at the secular University of Edinburgh, one of the oldest universities in the world, founded in 1583. Like many early places of higher learning, the University of Edinburgh started with an emphasis on preparing students for church leadership. It has become a more secular institution that is much different from its original roots. By the way, there is no full-time tuition cost for residents of Scotland who meet requirements.

"First of all, you need to know about Bonnie Prince Charlie. That was Prince Edward Charles' nickname. Believing he had a right to the throne, he incited a rebellion among the Highlanders, which was called the Jacobite Uprising of '45 — that is, 1745 — in an effort to reclaim Scotland for his family, the House of Stuart. He's a very popular legendary figure here, as he represents everything that is true and right and noble about Scotland to this day. He was not a perfect man by any means, but he is remembered as much nobler than he probably was.

"I'll bet you've also heard of James Watt, the scientist who was fascinated by his mother's kettle and the power of steam to push the lid right off the top. He invented the steam engine in 1781, which was soon used to power steamboats, trains, and factories, essentially powering the Industrial Revolution that began in Great Britain. However, Watt didn't study at this university, but rather the University of Glasgow, about 45 miles west of here.

Street view of Edinburgh, Scotland,

"Other notable Scots include John Knox, the leader of the Scottish Reformation and founder of the Presbyterian church; John Witherspoon, his great-grandson, who became an American pastor and signer of the Declaration of Independence; and of course, Alexander Graham Bell, the inventor of the telephone.

Haggis

"And if that isn't enough, we have many literary giants who hail from our beloved Scotland. There is even a monument in honor of our Sir Walter Scott.

"Enough talk of history and famous Scots," says Stephanie. "Let's duck into my favorite restaurant and grab a bite to eat. I think you'll love the atmosphere in this old 16th-century establishment — but even more importantly, you'll love the food!"

Passing by more modern buildings, Stephanie chooses the old-world option. We squeeze through the smaller-than-average front door, where little has changed, including the old worn door and stone facade. Stephanie says we should order the "haggis, neeps, and tatties," which is short for haggis, turnips, and potatoes. **Haggis** is a savory pudding made from sheep *pluck* (or organs, meaning the heart, liver, and lung) minced and combined with onion, oats, spices, salt, fat, and stock; cooked down; and served encased in the sheep's stomach lining. It may seem a wonder that anyone would eat such a concoction, but it is Scotland's national dish and is well loved by locals and visitors alike. They say it tastes better than it sounds.

If you aren't feeling that adventurous, there are some other wonderful dishes on the menu that you might want to try. How about fish and chips or a pie filled with steak? Or, if you are in the mood for something lighter, I understand the goat cheese salad with fresh greens, apple, and beetroot is delicious.

haggis: a Scottish dish consisting of a sheep's or calf's organs mixed with suet, oatmeal, and seasoning, then boiled in a bag, traditionally one made from the animal's stomach

Whatever you choose, I'm sure you'll enjoy it. We'll chase our dinner down with some Scottish ice cream and then drive 20 minutes west of town to sleep at Stephanie's house tonight. We've got a big day tomorrow, exploring the Scottish Highlands and some of the nearby islands. I can't wait! How about you?

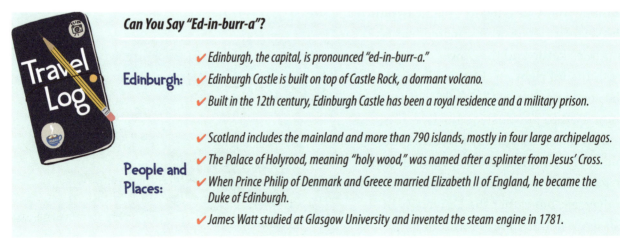

Can You Say "Ed-in-burr-a"?

Travel Log

Edinburgh:
- ✔ Edinburgh, the capital, is pronounced "ed-in-burr-a."
- ✔ Edinburgh Castle is built on top of Castle Rock, a dormant volcano.
- ✔ Built in the 12th century, Edinburgh Castle has been a royal residence and a military prison.

People and Places:
- ✔ Scotland includes the mainland and more than 790 islands, mostly in four large archipelagos.
- ✔ The Palace of Holyrood, meaning "holy wood," was named after a splinter from Jesus' Cross.
- ✔ When Prince Philip of Denmark and Greece married Elizabeth II of England, he became the Duke of Edinburgh.
- ✔ James Watt studied at Glasgow University and invented the steam engine in 1781.

236 Lesson 12. Day 110

A Child's Geography. Vol. 5: Explore Viking Realms

Archipelagos

Of the more than 790 islands of Scotland, most are part of four large island chains, or archipelagos — pronounced *aar·kuh·**peh**·luh·gowz.*

Materials needed:
☐ Ruler or index card

Using the scale on the map and a ruler or index card, measure and calculate the approximate distance from selected cities on the Outer Hebrides.

1. Stornoway to Leverburgh

2. Daliburgh to Lochboisdale

3. Balivanich to Lochmaddy

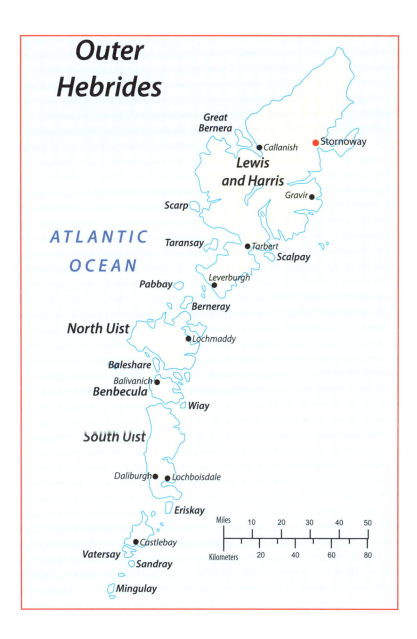

Short Answer

Answer the following questions.

1. What is located along the Great Glen Fault?

_____

2. What are the four large archipelagos that belong to Scotland?

_____

_____

_____

Faults Exploration

The Great Glen Fault runs through Scotland into Ireland. Why are there fault lines or long cracks in the earth's surface? As a result of the Flood during Noah's time, tectonic plates, or large slabs of rock, dramatically shifted to adjust the continents. Because of the mightiness of the Flood, cracks also resulted. One side of the Great Glen Fault is the hanging wall that is higher, and the other side is the foot wall that is lower.

1. Genesis 7 records that the water rose 15 cubits above the mountains. If a cubit is approximately 20.4 inches, approximately how high above the mountains did the water rise?

_____

Genesis 7:24 tells us, "The water prevailed upon the earth one hundred and fifty days." Remember that it had already rained for forty days and nights. After this major event and after the earth dried, the earth's crust was stressed, leading to fault lines.

There are other fault lines that have also led to earthquakes: the San Andreas Fault in California along the West in the United States, the New Madrid Fault through the Midwest and South in the United States, and the Great Sumatran Fault in the entire island of Sumatra in Indonesia. Throughout the world, there are many fault lines that lead to earthquakes caused by the shifting and stress on the tectonic plates.

Find More
Optional: Teacher's Discretion ☐ No ☐ Yes Due Date: _____

2. Discover more about fault lines through books or online resources. Explore the Great Glen Fault and two more fault lines.

Fault Line	Location	Earthquake History
Great Glen Fault		

What is additional information you learned from your exploration of faults and earthquakes?

_____

_____

The Cairngorms

→ Time to lace up our hiking boots again! Today, we are heading north into the Cairngorms, the mountain range located in the middle third of Scotland. About 45 miles west is Glasgow (pronounced *glass-go*), the largest city in Scotland and the third largest in the United Kingdom.

Glasgow was once a small rural settlement on the River Clyde, but since medieval times, it has grown to become the largest seaport in Great Britain. With the establishment of the University of Glasgow, and later, the onset of the Industrial Revolution, the people of Glasgow refined their knowledge of modern shipbuilding and engineering to become the world's preeminent hub for the marine engineering industry. Since the 18th century and onward, the city is one of the main ports for transatlantic trade between the UK, Europe, and North America.

But today, we are leaving Scotland's big cities behind and plunging into her glorious natural landscape. The Cairngorms are the highest, coldest, and snowiest plateaus in Great Britain and experience the most extreme temperature fluctuations. Domed summits dot the high plateaus, many of them with *tors*, free-standing rock outcroppings that rise abruptly from the surrounding smooth granite slopes. While there are no glaciers in the Cairngorms, snow can fall any month of the year, and snow patches may remain frozen all summer long.

This alpine-arctic environment with tundra-like groundcover is home to some rare animal species, such as the pine marten, capercaillie, mountain hare, and Britain's only herd of reindeer. The steep granite cliffs draw out the outdoorsy types who enjoy winter sports such as extreme skiing, mountaineering, and ice climbing.

The Cairngorms boast five of the six highest mountains in Scotland. However, the tallest mountain in Scotland is not here. We'll visit that peak a little later today.

Red deer stag walking in the Cairngorms

Just north of the Cairngorms is the Great Glen Fault, the fracture in the earth's crust that you can see from space. Loch Ness, world-famous for its legendary monster that supposedly dwells in

Ruins of Urquhart Castle along Loch Ness

the dark depths of the lake, is located right along this fault line. Loch Ness is neither the largest nor the deepest lake in Scotland. It comes in second in both categories. The network of lakes, locks, and canals along the fault line make it possible for boats to cross from the east coast to the west coast of Scotland without having to navigate the open sea.

The legend of the Loch Ness Monster — fondly nicknamed Nessie by the locals — began long ago. The first recorded sighting of the beast was by Columba, the first missionary to Scotland from Ireland across the Irish Sea. He founded an abbey on the island of Iona in 563. His life and work as a missionary was recorded in a book by Adomnán, who included the tale about his encounter with a "water beast" in Loch Ness.

The story goes that Columba was visiting the land of the Picts when he learned of a man attacked by a monster living in the depths of the great lake. Columba, with one of his followers, crossed to the other side of the lake when they spotted the beast. The sea monster advanced toward his companion, but Columba made the sign of the cross and shouted, "Come no closer; go back! Do not touch this man." The creature pulled up abruptly as if reined back by a harness, then disappeared into the deep blackness of the lake. Columba's men and the Picts gave thanks to God for miraculously saving their lives.

Columba was not the only one to report a sighting of the Loch Ness Monster. Within the last hundred years or so, several individuals have captured strange images on film that they believe to be the **"prehistoric"** water creature. Most have been proven to be elaborate hoaxes. The locals don't believe the monster exists, but they do enjoy telling tales and teasing tourists who come to catch a glimpse of the storied water beast for themselves. The true history of the world is found in God's Word, that He wrote from the beginning.

Beyond Loch Ness, we scramble up into the northern and more rugged half of the Scottish Highlands. This windswept landscape is breathtaking and yet bare, almost forlorn. Old stone **crofts**, abandoned and crumbling with age, stand humbly at the foot of each farm, a testament

prehistoric: secular label for time before written records

crofts: small agricultural land units in Scotland that are often associated with stone homes on the property

240 Lesson 12. Day 113

A Child's Geography. Vol. 5: Explore Viking Realms

to the heartbreaking reality that locals abandoned these mountains in droves a couple hundred years ago. After the 1707 treaty, merging England and Scotland into one country, the British government feared uprisings by the Scottish people and began to consolidate smaller properties into larger farms to be run by wealthy aristocrats. The land was converted from crop farming to sheep herding, which required fewer people to maintain. This resulted in mass evacuations of tenants who lost the only homes they ever knew and had nowhere else to go.

Some farmers moved south into the lowlands, but many fled Scotland entirely and arrived on the shores of North America and Australia during the 18th and 19th centuries. This tragic event is known as the Highland Clearances and is the reason why more people of Scottish heritage live outside of Scotland than inside her borders. And it is clear to see that more sheep live in the highlands than do people.

When we think about the Scottish Highlands, several images may pop into mind, such as bagpipes, **kilts**, sporran (fur pockets), tartan (plaid fabric), and clan **brooches**. Traditional Scottish dress and highland music compose an arrangement that is both beautiful and deeply cultural. Each Scottish clan, or extended family group, had their own custom tartan fabric woven to be worn exclusively by them to proudly display their heritage. Yards and yards of this warm woolen fabric would be used to create wraps, cloaks, knee-length kilts for men, and ankle-length skirts for women.

Scottish music has long been and still is a significant aspect of the nation's culture. The great highland bagpipe, a wind instrument with three pipes and an airbag, is symbolic of the beautiful highland culture it represents as it warbles out its heart-wrenching tune carried aloft by the wind.

kilts: pleated garments traditionally worn by Highlanders in Scotland

brooches: decoratively designed pins attached to clothing

Scottish Highlands

Medieval castles, tower houses, and ancestral estates dot the Scottish countryside. Many were once the ancestral homes of powerful clan chiefs, heads of the kinship groups known as Scottish clans, and were sometimes used for clan gatherings, giving members a sense of shared familial identity.

Macrae: In Gaelic, this means "son of grace," which some believe to be related in some way to the Christian Church. The clans appear to be connected historically due to three brothers. They were also involved in the royal and faith upheavals with some siding with the Jacobites, who focused on restoring the throne to the descendants of the Stuarts, beginning with King James II, who had been exiled.

We are passing one of the most photographed castles in all of Scotland —Eilean Donan —which rises from a small tidal island where three sea lochs meet in the western highlands. This well-preserved ancestral stronghold was built in the 13th century and belonged jointly to the allied clans of MacKenzie and Macrae.

Just past Eilean Donan, we cross over a bridge and leave the mainland altogether. We have reached the Isle of Skye, famed for its dramatic windswept natural beauty. Skye is the largest and most northern island of the Inner Hebrides archipelago. Humans have dwelled on the island for thousands of years, including a season of Viking rule and then a long period of domination by the clans MacLeod and MacDonald. Both of their beautiful ancestral castles are open for the public to visit.

The Isle of Skye is rugged with rocky crags, steep cliffs, barren plateaus, and heather-covered hills. In fact, the lush heather and spiny thistle — the national emblem of Scotland — give the island countryside a lilac hue. This is a photographer's paradise; sometimes the landscape looks green, other times blue, purple, or even fiery orange, depending on the light and the flora that thrive on the hills and dales. Skye is also covered in peat, a dark brown soil-like material found in bogs, mires, moors, and peatlands. Peat forms when plant or vegetable matter does not fully decay. Over long periods of time, when this partially decayed substance is exposed to very wet conditions, it compresses into a dense soil-like material that can be cut like bricks from the earth and dried for use as fuel.

Thatched stone cottage, Isle of Skye

Farmers in Scotland, both on the mainland and throughout the islands, used peat fires for cooking and for heating their stone houses, called crofts, all winter long. Although it would seem otherwise, peat is not considered a renewable resource. The peat that is chunked out of the ground today has been slowly forming over thousands of years. Peat accumulates slowly at a rate of between one and three millimeters per year.

Peat: Creationist scientists have calculated that 4,000 years is enough time to have created even 40-foot peat bogs and that's at 3 mm of peat developed per year on average. Secular scientists date the old peat to around 10,000 years based on their theory that the peat only develops 1 mm per year.

Peat covers 20% of Scotland. Its use for heating fuel is not being encouraged due to concerns of wildfires, considered by some to be a major source of greenhouse gases, so it is mostly used in horticulture.

Skye is as far north as we'll travel on this exploration of Scotland. However, should you ever return here in person, you may want to go farther north still. Up at the tippy top of Scotland, on the Orkney Islands, is an archaeological dig site known as Skara Brae. Eight stone houses have been uncovered after having been buried for millennia that give us a peek into what life in the Scottish Northern Isles may have been like as far back as around 2000 B.C., after the dispersal at the Tower of Babel in 2246 B.C.

But for now, we travel back south past the Great Glen Fault to Ben Nevis, the highest peak in not only Scotland but all of the United Kingdom, reaching an altitude of 4,410 feet. The collapsed dome of an ancient volcano, Ben Nevis means "venomous mountain" in Gaelic, one of the languages still spoken by many Scots today. However, the name doesn't scare away the mountaineers who refer to the peak simply as "Ben." An estimated 100,000

Peat fire

Ben Nevis from Corpach Sea Port

people make the climb to the top every year. An abandoned observatory awaits those who reach the summit, its ruins attesting to the fact that it hasn't been used since 1904.

What a time in Scotland we've had! And yet I have saved one of the best corners of the country for last. Our final stop on land in Scotland is Oban, a quaint Victorian sea town situated on a protected bay on the Firth of Lorne. A **firth** in Scottish English is a long estuary, where the river meets the ocean tide, similar to a **fjord** in Norway. The modern town of Oban was founded around the year 1794. Oban is also a great site to visit the lower islands of the Inner Hebrides archipelago.

> **firth:** narrow inlet of the sea; an estuary
>
> **fjord:** narrow channel of the sea between high cliffs or hills
>
> **trawler boat:** seacraft designed for long voyages
>
> **basalt:** dark, fine-grained volcanic rock that sometimes displays a columnar structure

Let's board the Caledonian MacBrayne ferry that is leaving now for the Isle of Mull. At the port of Fionnphort, we will transfer to a **trawler boat** that will whisk us out to a very small island just beyond. A surprise lies in wait for us there.

We are passing the island of Iona, which is where Columba, the first missionary to Scotland, built his abbey and set up his base for ministry. Our final destination in Scotland is Staffa, an island located north of Iona and west of Mull. The name comes from the Old Norse language and means "stave or pillar." The Vikings gave Staffa this name because the columnar structure reminded them of their houses, which were built from vertically stacked tree logs.

There it is now! As we approach, I think you will be amazed by what you see. The island consists of **basalt**, an igneous rock structure that forms in prismatic columns due to the rapid cooling of mineral-rich lava. When the thick lava cools quickly, it forms an extraordinary pattern of typically hexagonal columns, though others may have anywhere from three to eight sides. There are three layers of basalt on this amazing little island. First, there is a basement of **tuff**, which is volcanic ash that has been compressed into rock. Then, you see the crystalline basalt structure, topped by a layer of flood basalt, which is runnier in nature and cools into a more random pattern or no pattern at all and sits like a crust atop the other two layers. The island of Staffa is like a house after all, having a foundation, columnar walls, and a roof.

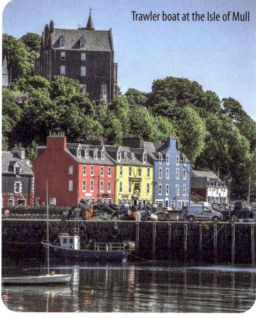
Trawler boat at the Isle of Mull

One of the most incredible aspects of this surprising island is the caves. Our trawler boat has rafts, which we will use to explore the inside of some of these caves. There's the Goat Cave, the Clamshell Cave, the Boat Cave, Mackinnon's Cave, and the Cormorant Cave. But Staffa's most famous feature is Fingal's Cave, a large sea cave located near the southern tip of the island formed by long hexagonal basalt columns.

tuff: light, porous rock formed by consolidation of volcanic ash

magnum opus: large and important work of art, music, or literature, especially one regarded as the most important work of an artist or writer

The cliff face at the entrance to the cave is called the Colonnade, and it was this great cliff face along with Fingal's Cave that inspired Felix Mendelssohn to write his **magnum opus**, *Hebrides Overture*. The original Gaelic name for this cave is *An Uamh Bhin*, which means "the melodious cave." You'll understand why as soon as we enter its mouth. The crystalline columns provide great acoustics. This is a singer's cave!

Fingal's Cave, Island of Staffa

Cloisters of Glasgow University

Go ahead and sing a few lines of your favorite song. You will love the way you sound in here. It's better than the shower.

And on that glorious melodious note, it is time to say goodbye to the dear people of Scotland. It was a delight to explore and discover the land. The people are ambitious, brilliant, and kind. Our minds are expanded, and our hearts are softened by our visit to this nation. May God continue to bless you through your amazing contributions to the world.

"*Tioraidh an dràsta, Scotland!*" we shout, which in Scottish Gaelic means "Goodbye for now, until we meet again!"

Where Would You Explore in Scotland?

People:

✔ *The great highland bagpipe, kilts for men, and skirts for women are associated with Scottish culture.*

✔ *Eilean Donan, built in the 13th century, belonged jointly to the clans of MacKenzie and Macrae.*

✔ *Vikings once dwelled on the Isle of Skye, the largest and most northern island of the Inner Hebrides.*

✔ *Columba, the first missionary to Scotland, built a ministry from the island of Iona in A.D. 563.*

Environment:

✔ *The Cairngorms mountain range is an alpine-arctic environment with tundra-like groundcover.*

✔ *Tales of the Loch Ness Monster abound from Loch Ness.*

✔ *A non-renewable resource, peat was used for peat fires for cooking and for heating stone houses.*

✔ *Ben Nevis means "venomous mountain" and is the highest peak in the United Kingdom at 4,410 feet.*

✔ *Fingal's Cave means "the melodious cave" and is formed by long hexagonal basalt columns.*

TIMELINE

563	▶	Columba establishes an abbey on the island of Iona in Scotland.
1707	▶	The Treaty of Union — England and Scotland are united.
1745	▶	Prince Charlie incites a rebellion among the Highlanders to reclaim the Scottish throne.
1880	▶	The largest recorded earthquake in Scotland occurred along the Great Glen Fault.

Multiple Choice

Circle the letter of the correct answer.

1. What is a croft?
    a. Scottish hairstyle
    b. The opposite of a loft
    c. Building made of stone on agricultural land
    d. Cave dwelling

2. Why did the Highlanders move away from their homes?
    a. The bagpipes were too loud.
    b. The crofts were converted to castles.
    c. The land was converted from crop farming to sheep farming.
    d. None of the above

3. What is tartan?
    a. Plaid fabric
    b. A fur pocket
    c. Highland music
    d. A bagpipe

4. What is peat?
    a. A dark brown soil-like material found in blogs, mires, mores, and peatlands
    b. A material that can be cut like bricks and dried for use as fuel
    c. A Scottish form of the name "Peter"
    d. Both a and b

Sheep grazing, Elgol, Scotland

Loch Ness Monster Mystery

Answer the following questions.

1. What did you learn about the Loch Ness Monster, or "Nessie," legend?

_____

_____

_____

_____

The Loch Ness Monster is of interest to cryptozoologists, who study and search for legendary animals. There are many mysteries surrounding stories of these cryptids, or creatures whose existence has not been verified, making the field of cryptozoology a pseudoscience.

Perhaps the Loch Ness Monster is a mythical creature that people have imagined seeing or created tales about. Or maybe it has been confused with another animal like a seal or oversized eel. Or possibly the creature is a plesiosaur that is not extinct from Day 6 of creation 6,000 years ago.

2. What do you think about the Loch Ness Monster legend?

_____

_____

_____

_____

Optional: Teacher's Discretion   ☐ No   ☐ Yes Due Date: _____

To learn more about the legend of the Loch Ness Monster, explore the Answers in Genesis website.

Melodies of Scotland

Optional: Teacher's Discretion   ☐ No   ☐ Yes Due Date: _____

Locate online or in other sources the following music and listen.

1. Scottish bagpipes
2. *Hebrides Overture* by Felix Mendelssohn (inspired by visiting Fingal's Cave, "the melodious cave")

Describe your reactions to and reflections on the music.

_____

_____

_____

Mapping It Out!

Complete the map of the country of Scotland in the box below. Refer to the map on page 383.

Label the following places on your map. You can use colored pencils to shade areas of land or water, draw rivers and mountains, etc.

☐ Scotland

☐ Inner Hebrides

☐ Outer Hebrides

☐ Orkney Islands

☐ Shetland Islands

☐ Glasgow

☐ Add a star ★ for the capital city of Edinburgh.

Scottish terrier

Flashcards

Make flashcards of the bolded glossary words from this lesson. Then, either add drawings of the terms or act them out in charades. Be creative!

Learn Geography Terms

Page 342 is a reference page for understanding the terms geographers use to describe landforms.

We are thankful for the people and landscapes of Scotland, from the inviting views of the Scottish Highlands to the archipelagos. The land is majestic, dotted by islands, flatlands, and mountains. The magnificence of Your creation, Lord, is remarkable. Your Word tells us in Psalm 90:2, "Before the mountains were born Or You gave birth to the earth and the world, Even from everlasting to everlasting, You are God." As the earth changed as a result of the dramatic impact of the Flood, Your handiwork continues to be evidenced.

Edinburgh's annual New Year's fireworks display is a sight to see! But that's not all you can see or do during Scotland's world-famous New Year's celebration, known as Hogmanay, a word referring to the last day of the "old year," or New Year's Eve. Scots celebrate the New Year for a whole four days, with traditions such as visiting family and friends to give them gifts (or lumps of coal), street processions, concerts, food and attractions, traditional Scottish dancing, and the Loony Dook. What is the Loony Dook, you ask? It's an event in which many people dive into the frigid waters of the estuary of several Scottish rivers, often while wearing fancy clothes. I don't think I would want to participate, but it might be fun to watch!

If you're willing to stay up late, we can see the amazing fireworks show, which starts at midnight after the cannon fires at Edinburgh Castle. What say you — do you think you can stay awake?

250 Lesson 12. Day 116

A Child's Geography. Vol. 5: Explore Viking Realms

Talk About It

The oldest crown jewels of Great Britain rest in Edinburgh Castle along with the sceptre and sword of state. The Scotts refer to them as the "Honours of Scotland." Immense care is used to protect and care for these prized items and other displays in the exhibition. Other than for ceremonial events like a coronation, these special royal items, known as regalia, are otherwise secured and preserved.

Scotland Crown Jewels - silver and gold headdress adorned with Scottish pearls. garnets. and amethysts

Sceptre (scepter) - silver hexagonal rod with a polished crystal globe and a gold orb that is topped with a pearl

Sword of State - blade embellished with engravings of acorns and oak leaves to symbolize the risen Christ

In addition to the description of their great worth in terms of money, heritage, and historic value, the precious objects hold greater symbols. A crown represents power or dignity, a scepter is a sign of supreme authority, and a sword symbolizes protection.

In 1507, King James IV of Scotland receives the new Sword of State in the Holyrood Abbey. Alexander Stewart, Archbishop of Saint Andrews, holds the scepter. The Honors, the Scottish Crown Jewels, Edinburgh Castle, Scotland.

These items of outstanding value are a small comparison to the immeasurable worth of Christ the King. Items and symbols of royalty are described in various Bible passages in reference to Christ, the Holy Spirit, and God. Search the Bible for some verses that reference royalty or symbols of royalty.

Talk with your family or a friend about symbols of royalty in the Bible.

Conversation starter ideas:

🌍 What gemstones are in Revelation?

🌍 Where in the Bible is the Lord compared to a scepter, and what does that mean?

🌍 What are key ideas and words related to a sword in the Bible?

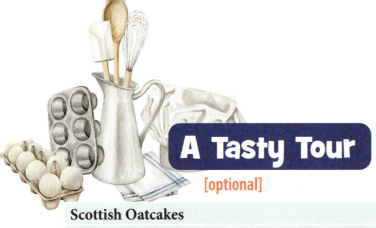

A Tasty Tour

[optional]

Scottish Oatcakes

Ingredients:

1½ cup Scottish oats

¼ teaspoon baking powder

½ cup all-purpose flour

¼ cup melted butter (½ stick)

¼ teaspoon sugar

⅓ cup hot water

¼ teaspoon salt

NOTE: Requires adult supervision and participation.

Optional: Teacher's Discretion

☐ No   ☐ Yes

Due Date: _____

Directions:

1. Preheat oven to 325°. Grease a baking sheet.

2. Combine flour, sugar, salt, baking powder, and oats. Stir until combined. Add butter until evenly incorporated. With a fork, mix in hot water until evenly moistened.

3. Roll dough out ½ inch thick. Cut with round cookie or scone cutter, approximately 2½ to 3 inches in diameter. Bake for 25 minutes until golden. Cool on rack.

4. Store oatcakes at room temperature in airtight container for two days.

13

Wales: The Hammer and the Dragon

South Stack Lighthouse, Holyhead

Our last stop on the isle of Great Britain is Wales, but this is not the final country we'll visit in the United Kingdom. There is one more, but it is not located on this large island. While we could drive back down through Scotland and England to reach Wales, it would be much more interesting to take a ship, don't you think?

We'll take the local Caledonia MacBrayne ferry down to the seaport town of Cairnryan on the southwest coast of Scotland, just north of the English border, then we'll board the great Stena Line ferry, the largest ferry in Europe, serving Scotland, England, Wales, Ireland, and France. Our destination is Holyhead, Wales.

As we glide through the Irish Sea, we can faintly see the coast of Northern Ireland off in the distance to our right and the Isle of Man more clearly to the left before we arrive in northern Wales. Wales has been politically connected to England since the 16th century, but she has a distinct cultural identity all her own.

Geographically speaking, Wales is stunning. From the craggy cliffs above the shoreline to the verdant green hills further afield, Wales is like a surreal photograph come to life. Culturally speaking, Wales is charming. Formidable castles spike the coastline. Fleecy sheep speckle the countryside, and children laugh and play on every corner.

Snowdonia National Park

The Welsh are more expressive and perhaps more exuberant than their English cousins. They are warm and winsome. The majority of people living in Wales speak English, but many speak Welsh at home and with their fellow countrymen. Officially, Wales is a bilingual nation. Welsh is an old Celtic language closely related to Cornish, which is spoken farther south on the English coast, and to Breton, spoken even farther south across the English Channel on the northern coast of France. It is one of Europe's oldest living languages, spoken since the 6th century.

In Welsh, the name of this country is Cymru (pronounced *Camry*). Their language is called Cymraeg. This melodic language is poetic and descriptive, considered to be one of the great treasures of Wales. It defines the nation and its people. It's what makes Wales, Wales.

Wales is littered with impressive castles. Let's visit one nearby at Caernarfon, which is the current seat of English government in North Wales. Caernarfon Castle is also the site where Prince Charles, son of Queen Elizabeth II, was crowned Prince of Wales in 1969. Just like his father's title — the Duke of Edinburgh — the Prince of Wales is a title of honor only. When Prince Charles ascended to the throne, his son William became the next Prince of Wales.

Caernarfon Castle was built by Edward I after his invasion of North Wales in 1282. After defeating the local Welsh princes, he began a concentrated crusade to colonize the entire region. He built fortified towns in the shadows of the mighty fortresses he constructed — towns where English citizens could settle safely in the newly conquered territory. Edward's massive building project was extremely expensive and nearly bankrupted the English Crown.

The fact that the coastline of Wales is dotted with English strongholds proves that the feisty Welsh were not easily subdued by their neighbor to the east. King Edward I, the fiery monarch of England

during the late 13th century, was determined to claim the entire island for England. He was known as the Hammer because of his brutish treatment toward both the Welsh and the Scots.

Llywelyn ap Gruffudd, the ruler of Gwynedd in Wales at that time, refused to pay homage to the great and terrible Edward I, prompting the English invasion of Gwynedd and the surrounding region. King Edward desperately wanted to control this region, so he built mighty castles throughout Wales to both flaunt the power of England and squelch any possible future uprisings.

Caernarfon Castle, along with several others located in the nearby towns of Conwy, Beaumaris, and Harlech, are among the finest examples of medieval military architecture in all of Europe. The last time this castle was stormed was in 1415, when the Welsh, led by Owain Glyndwr, revolted against English rule in the Last War of Independence. Roughly a hundred years later, Wales was officially incorporated into England by the Laws in Wales Acts of 1535 and 1542.

Just a short ways inland is Snowdonia, the first and largest national park in Wales, which is named after Snowdon, its highest peak at 3,560 feet. "Snowdon" in Welsh does not translate to mean snow. It means "the land of eagles" because eagles prefer to live at higher elevations, and they love living here.

Caernarfon Castle

Betws-y-Coed

Most visitors to the park either hike to the summit of the mountain or ride the train to the top to enjoy the spectacular view. From there, you can see Crib Goch, with its distinctive knife-edge crest. Curiously, Crib Goch means "the red ridge" in Welsh. This rugged ridge sits under a nearly permanent rain cloud. It is the wettest spot in the entire United Kingdom, receiving nearly 180 inches of rain each year.

While others are going up Snowdonia, we are going down — down into the slate mining caves to have an even more extraordinary adventure. Outside the small town of Betws-y-Coed is an old slate mine that has been turned into a thrilling adventure challenge. We descend to the deepest point in the United Kingdom to test our skills and our nerve. After we **rappel** to the center of the mountain, we spend the afternoon ziplining through hollow caverns, boating across an underground lake, scaling up vertical shafts, traversing the abyss, scrambling up a hidden waterfall, and then doing it all over again. Isn't this a great adventure?

After that cave adventure, we are downright exhausted! Let's grab a quick dinner of Welsh **rarebit** and **cawl** and then settle into a countryside bed and breakfast for the night. The word rarebit is a corrupted form of "rabbit," but there is no rabbit in rarebit. Welsh rarebit is essentially melted cheese on toast, and cawl is a broth-based soup with vegetables and bacon. Doesn't that sound like a good way to finish off this great day? I think so, too.

rappel: descend a rock face or other near-vertical surface by using a doubled rope coiled around the body and fixed at a higher point

rarebit: dish of melted and seasoned cheese on toast, sometimes with other ingredients

cawl: in the Welsh language, the word is used to refer to any broth-based soup

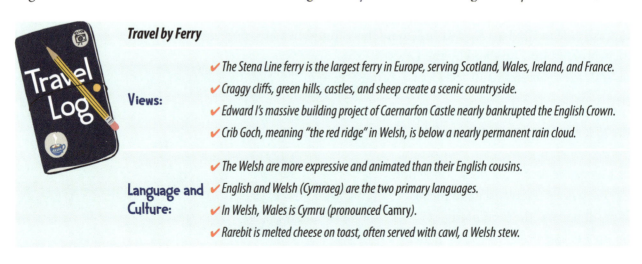

Travel Log

Travel by Ferry

Views:
✔ The Stena Line ferry is the largest ferry in Europe, serving Scotland, Wales, Ireland, and France.
✔ Craggy cliffs, green hills, castles, and sheep create a scenic countryside.
✔ Edward I's massive building project of Caernarfon Castle nearly bankrupted the English Crown.
✔ Crib Goch, meaning "the red ridge" in Welsh, is below a nearly permanent rain cloud.

Language and Culture:
✔ The Welsh are more expressive and animated than their English cousins.
✔ English and Welsh (Cymraeg) are the two primary languages.
✔ In Welsh, Wales is Cymru (pronounced Camry).
✔ Rarebit is melted cheese on toast, often served with cawl, a Welsh stew.

Medieval Military Architecture

Answer the following questions and follow the instructions

1. What are two things you learned about Caernarfon Castle?

    a. _____

       _____

       _____

    b. _____

       _____

       _____

2. Based on the descriptions of the terms, check the boxes that are part of Caernarfon Castle's structure.

☐ Crenellation - top row of stones on a wall or tower with alternating raised sections and lower sections to offer spaces for protection and line of fire

☐ Merlon - raised section of a crenellation   ☐ Crenet - lower section of a crenellation

☐ Curtain wall - the outer wall of a castle   ☐ Moat - ditch that is dry or with water around all or part of a castle

☐ Slit - opening in wall for firing arrows   ☐ Bailey - courtyard of level ground with enclosed spaces called wards

☐ Tower - tall. narrow structure that stands by itself or connected to another structure

3. What observations can you make about how the castle was designed for military purposes?

_____

_____

4. Why is the coast of Wales dotted by massive English castles?

_____

_____

Stena Line Ferry

Ports are the landing place for ships where cargo and people are loaded and unloaded. They are a vital part of maritime infrastructure. Cargo or products need to move for commerce. People and vehicles on ferries depend on an organized system for travel.

Materials needed:
- ☐ Various-sized small game pieces, small toy cars, or both
- ☐ Paper or cardboard
- ☐ Scissors
- ☐ Ruler

With the Stena Line ferry being the largest ferry in Europe, a systematic process is needed for loading and unloading vehicles along with people. Algorithms — instructions to solve a problem — can be used. Mathematical formulas help create a systematic process to maximize the use of space and provide order while also setting safety parameters.

At the port, there is a terminal where vehicles are assigned how to enter the ferry via a ramp. Lanes are used to help create order, and the size of vehicles must be considered. Vehicles must be closely arranged yet not too snug that doors cannot be opened.

With scissors, cut out paper or cardboard to represent a ferry and ramp. Draw lanes. Create a plan for loading and unloading that takes into account the different sizes of vehicles, the need for a system with some efficiency, and the possibility of some vehicles arriving close to departure time. Arrange and move various-sized small game pieces, small toy cars, or both to represent loading and unloading the ferry.

How do you create order in your own life? While there are things that happen that are unexpected, having some order can help as we navigate challenging situations.

Optional: Teacher's Discretion   ☐ No   ☐ Yes

Due Date: _____

With parent permission or guidance, explore books or online sources about the loading and unloading process for different ferries.

Cardiff Castle

→ It's a new day! And today, we are driving to south Wales. Two-thirds of the population of Wales lives in or around Cardiff, the capital city, located on the southern coast of Wales. While most visitors to Wales spend some time in the capital, our destination is just east of Cardiff. We are on our way to Caerleon, an old Roman villa and the supposed location of King Arthur's Camelot.

Are you familiar with the tales of King Arthur? Arthur was a legendary warrior king who led Britain to defeat the Saxon invaders at the close of the 5th century. Whether King Arthur was fact or fiction has long been debated by historians. Arthur's name occurs in Old English poetry and in such texts as Geoffrey of Monmouth's 12th-century *Historia Regum Brittanniae (A History of the Kings of Britain)*. But are any of them true?

Many tales have been handed down through the tradition of oral storytelling in the regions of southern Wales and Brittany in northern France. Celtic folklore depicts King Arthur as a mighty and moral hero of the realm, surrounded by trusted friends and mortal enemies. He was the Red Dragon of Wales. His family's royal crest is proudly represented on the Welsh flag even to this day. Stories of King Arthur, his wife Guinevere, and his most trusted knight Lancelot have been told and retold for over a thousand years. Arthurian literature thrived during the Middle Ages and then died away in the centuries that followed. However, there was a major

A view of Camelot Castle Hotel on the coast of Cornwall

resurgence in fascination with this British king and his company of extraordinary companions during the 19th century. Even today, in the 21st century, the legend lives on not only in literature but also in film, theater, and other media.

Key figures in the Arthurian tales are the gallant Knights of the Round Table. The famous circular table was supposedly constructed especially for this imposing group of men to signify that all were of equal rank in Arthur's kingdom. It was located in Camelot, King Arthur's primary fortress and the place he held court. Most scholars place the location of Camelot here in Caerleon, and local businesses are proud to promote this myth by selling an assortment of King Arthur souvenirs. While no ruins have been found of Arthur's castle, other fascinating ruins certainly do exist here.

In Caerleon, we find the remains of Isca Augusta, a Roman legionary fortress dating back to A.D. 43, and an even older hilltop fortification dating back to around the Iron Age, likely built more than 3,000 years ago. Camelot or no Camelot, this place gives us a glimpse into some very ancient history.

Driving back north, we have one more place to visit in Wales before we leave the island of Great Britain. The town names here seem awfully difficult to pronounce, don't they? On the highway, we see signs for Llanvihangel Crucorney, Cwmystwyth, Llanrhaeadr-ym-Mochnant, and Llanarmon Dyffryn Ceiriog. Can you pronounce any of these words? Here's a little bit of help. The "w" is actually a long vowel, which sounds like an English double-o as in "pool," but the double-l is unlike any sound we use in the English language. In the field of **linguistics** — the study of language — this is called a *voiceless alveolar lateral fricative*, and it is pronounced like a silent L or a forward S. Now that you have had one short language lesson in Welsh, you may feel more prepared to pronounce one of the longest town names in the entire world. The town is in north Wales. Its name is Llanfairpwllgwyngyllgogerychwyrndrobwllllantysiliogogogoch.

linguistics: scientific study of language or speech

Wow, what a name! It means, "Saint Mary's church in the hollow of the white hazel near to the fierce whirlpool of Saint Tysilio of the red cave."

While the name of this town is intriguing, this is not our final stop in Wales. But don't worry! We are almost there! However, as we drive through the Welsh countryside, reading the various signs in both languages, we are suddenly struck by the view. It is almost like we stepped into an animated story, as the scenery is so picture perfect. The curving hillsides slope gently down to meet each other in a lush green valley, meticulously manicured and divided into lots by low stone walls enclosing fluffy white Welsh mountain sheep and curly-haired Welsh black cattle. This postcard-perfect scene is too good to miss. Let's stop to take some photos.

Look there! On the ground moving along at quite a rapid pace is a rainbow leaf beetle, *Chrysolina cerealis*, unique to the Welsh habitat; it is considered endangered in the United Kingdom. Snap a photo of that beautiful bug to show your friends at home. With some stunning photos captured, let's pile back into the car and finish our journey.

We are now pulling into the quaint Welsh town of Ruthin. This much simpler name comes from the Welsh words *rhudd*, which means "red," and *din*, which means "fort." "Red fort" refers to the color of the red sandstone used to build the castle here in 1277. The original name for the castle was Castell Coch yng Ngwern-fôr, meaning "Red Castle in the Sea Swamps." Ruthin has had its fair share of flooding over the years, as it is situated in a low valley where the water flows during heavy rains. Castell Coch, which was originally the residence of Edward I's brother, was the first castle to be stormed by Owain Glyndwr during the Last War of Independence. Now the castle is a hotel. This is where we'll spend our final night in Great Britain!

Before we turn in for the night, let's stroll around the charming town center. After the Last War, Ruthin was rebuilt into a fine medieval marketplace town. There is a lovely old church here that is still used as a church today, but the old courthouse building with its original gibbet (gallows) still visible just below the eaves has been converted into a bank.

Bara brith

The last time the gibbet was used was in the year 1679. Father Charles Mahoney, an Irish Franciscan monk, was shipwrecked off the coast near Pembrokeshire in south Wales yet somehow managed to survive and swim ashore. He traveled north in hopes of completing his homeward journey to Ireland but was arrested because he was wearing a **habit**, the traditional garb of monks. He was tried and convicted of the crime of being a Catholic priest in an era when Catholicism was against the law in Britain. He was sentenced to death here at the old courthouse.

That is some tragic history for you, and you can learn quite a lot more about past criminals (or supposed criminals) and their punishments down at the Ruthin Gaol, which is the Old English spelling of "jail." Or, if you would rather, we can pop into the corner bakery instead and enjoy some Welsh baked goods, such as Welsh cakes or bara brith, which means "speckled bread." Welsh cakes are a bit like biscuits with a sprinkling of sugar over the top, and bara brith is a fruit loaf made with chopped dried fruit bits and sweet spices, similar to a Christmas fruitcake. Usually, bara brith is served sliced with butter alongside a cup of hot tea in the afternoon. It sounds like that will hit the spot.

With full stomachs and the anticipation of staying overnight in an 800-year-old castle, we practically skip up the hill to reach our hotel. What a beautiful country Wales is! And such a fascinating if complicated history it shares with her neighbor, England. It has been such a delight to roam around this huge island nation exploring all Great Britain has to offer. Where will we go next?

habit: long, loose garment worn by a member of a religious order

Say "oo" for "w" while in Wales!

Myth or Legend:
✔ The supposed location of King Arthur's Camelot is the old Roman villa of Caerleon.
✔ King Arthur's royal crest from his family is represented on the Welsh flag.
✔ Lancelot and the Knights of the Round Table met in Camelot.

Locations:
✔ Two-thirds of Wales' population live in the capital city of Cardiff.
✔ Town names include Llanvihangel, Cwmystwyth, and Llanarmon Dyffryn Ceirog.
✔ The "w" in Welsh is pronounced like the English double-o as in "pool."
✔ Llanfairpwllgwyngyllgogerychwyrndrobwllllantysiliogogogoch is a town with one of the longest names in the world.
✔ Ruthin was named "Red fort" after the red sandstone used to build Castell Coch.

TIMELINE

1282 ▶ Edward I invades Wales and builds Caernarfon Castle.

1535 ▶ Wales is officially incorporated into England by the Laws in Wales Acts.

Short Answer

Write a short answer to the questions.

1.   Two-thirds of the population of Wales live in what city? _____

2.   What is mined for in Wales? _____

3.   What are some of the animals that live in Wales? _____

4.   What does Red Castle or Castell Coch yng Ngwern-fôr mean?_____

_____

5.   What is the name of Welsh cakes? _____

Rename Your Town or City

Llanfairpwllgwyngyllgogerychwyrndrobwllllantysiliogogogoch has claimed the title of one of the longest town names in the world.

The original name for Llanfairpwllgwyngyllgogerychwyrndrobwllllantysiliogogogoch in Wales was originally shorter until it reached this length. Without a doubt, the meaning of the long name gives details on its location. Landmarks, church buildings, and landscape shape its meaning.

What does it mean in Welsh? "Saint Mary's Church in the hollow of the white hazel near the rapid whirlpool and the Church of Saint Tysilio of the red cave."

Bring your creativity and knowledge of where you live to create a new long name for your town or city. What are landmarks, buildings or other structures of significance to your faith, and descriptions of landscape? Try combining all your words together without spaces to form a creative new name for your town or city.

_____

_____

Search for Insects

Chrysolina cerealis is classified as the rainbow beetle's species in the animal kingdom. The rainbow beetle is found in Wales and in a few other locations in Europe. When we learn in Genesis of every "kind" being created, we are learning about the family or order. This is the classification system: kingdom, phylum, class, order, family, genus, species. The "kind" in Genesis comes from the word *baramin* that may be associated with order or family. So, there are variations in an order or family to create uniquely designed beetles that adapt to their habitat and showcase originality within God's ordered creation. The multicolored iridescent shell of the rainbow leaf beetle glimmers in the sunlight.

Materials needed:
- ☐ Magnifying glass
- ☐ Drawing paper and drawing supplies

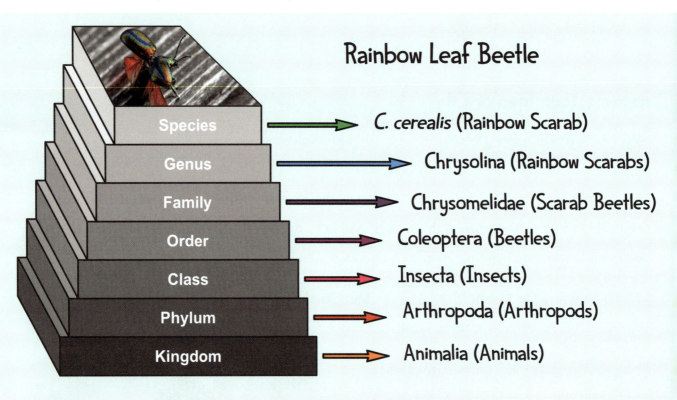

Rainbow Leaf Beetle

- Species → *C. cerealis* (Rainbow Scarab)
- Genus → Chrysolina (Rainbow Scarabs)
- Family → Chrysomelidae (Scarab Beetles)
- Order → Coleoptera (Beetles)
- Class → Insecta (Insects)
- Phylum → Arthropoda (Arthropods)
- Kingdom → Animalia (Animals)

Optional: Teacher's Discretion   ☐ No   ☐ Yes   Due Date: _____

With your parent's permission or guidance, explore outside or even go for a hike or walk to discover insects where you live. Use a magnifying glass to examine the unique characteristics of the insects you locate. Draw one or more insects you locate. To learn more about the Rainbow Beetle, explore the Answers in Genesis website.

Then God said, "Let the earth bring forth living creatures after their kind:
cattle and creeping things and beasts of the earth after their kind": and it was so.

—Genesis 1:24

Mapping It Out!

Complete the map of the country of Wales in the box below. Refer to the map on page 383.

Label the following places on your map. You can use colored pencils to shade areas of land or water, draw rivers and mountains, etc.

☐ Wales

☐ Irish Sea

☐ Holyhead

☐ Caernarfon

☐ Add a star ★ for the capital city of Cardiff.

Flashcards

Make flashcards of the bolded glossary words from this lesson. Then, either add drawings of the terms or act them out in charades. Be creative!

Welsh corgi

A Tasty Tour

[optional]

Rarebit

Ingredients:

4 slices thick bread

2 egg yolks

2 tablespoons sour cream

¾ teaspoon Worcestershire sauce

1 teaspoon mustard (Dijon for spicy)

2 cups cheddar cheese, grated

NOTE: Requires adult supervision and participation.

Optional: Teacher's Discretion

☐ No   ☐ Yes   Due Date: _____

Directions:

1. Toast the bread on both sides.

2. In a bowl, whisk together the egg yolks, sour cream, mustard, and Worcestershire sauce.

3. Stir in the grated cheese and any other ingredients you want to add.

4. Spread the egg and cheese sauce mixture right up to the edges of the toast and grill for 2–3 minutes until golden brown.

Learn Geography Terms

Page 342 is a reference page for understanding the terms geographers use to describe landforms.

Love your neighbor

Christianity is the religion of more than 40% of Wales, and a slightly larger percentage are non-religious. Just like other parts of the world, there are people God created who do not recognize Him. We humbly ask you, Lord, for wisdom and boldness. James 1:5 tells us, "But if any of you lacks wisdom, let him ask of God, who gives to all generously and without reproach, and it will be given to him."

Crossword Puzzle

Complete the crossword puzzle using the hints below.

ACROSS

3. Rhudd in Welsh means _____

5. Largest park in Wales

6. Nickname for King Edward the First

7. Broth soups are known as

9. Old English spelling of "jail"

10. Welsh for "the red ridge"

12. Welsh language is called _____

DOWN

1. Roman legionary fortress

2. A knight of the Round Table of Camelot

4. Majority of people in Wales speak this language

8. Melted cheese on toast is called _____

11. Welsh name for Wales

Make a Topographical Map: Part 1

Let's create a topographical map.

1. Choose between creating a map of Wales or of Wales and England.

2. Cut cardboard to desired size.

3. With a pencil and yardstick or ruler, draw and label the lines of latitude and longitude on your cardboard.

4. Using the latitude and longitude lines as a guide, draw the outline of Wales or Wales and England.

5. In a mixing bowl, stir together 4 cups flour and 2 cups salt. Gradually add 2 cups of water. Knead salt dough until smooth.

6. Arrange the salt dough on your map space and form higher elevations according to the topographical map information.

7. Allow map to dry for 1 to 2 days.

Materials needed:
☐ Cardboard
☐ Scissors
☐ Yardstick or ruler
☐ 4 cups flour
☐ 2 cups salt
☐ 2 cups water
☐ Mixing bowl

You will be painting and labeling your topographical map on Day 130 of the course as Part 2 of this activity.

Welsh Lovespoons

The Welsh have a special tradition centered around a spoon. Wooden lovespoons would be carefully-crafted by a young man, who would then give the spoon to the girl he loves. It was a way to show how much he loved her and that he was skilled and could make money for his future wife and family.

Let's get creative – using markers, colored pencils, or crayons, use the three spoons to tell a story through your designs.

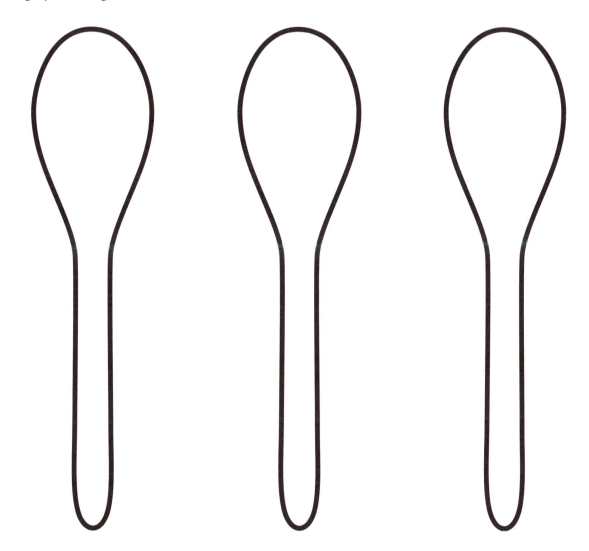

When you have finished, write the short story your design reveals on the lines below.

_____

_____

_____

_____

Make a Topographical Map: Part 2

Refer back to this topographical map and key for Wales as a guide. Paint your plaster topographical map. Then redraw and label the lines of latitude and longitude. Label key sites of water and the capital city.

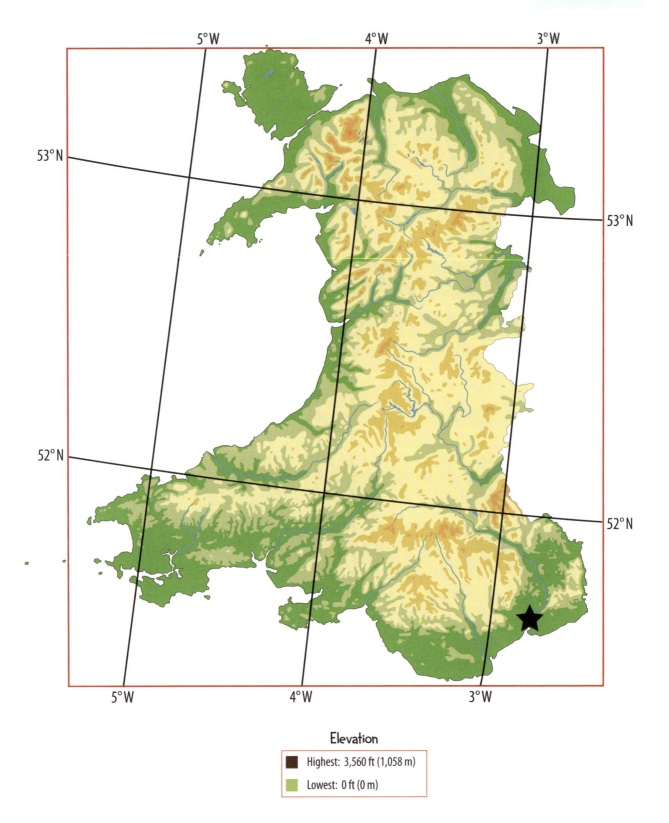

Elevation

■ Highest: 3,560 ft (1,058 m)

■ Lowest: 0 ft (0 m)

14

Northern Ireland: The Giant's Narrow Escape

Belfast Castle

When is a country not really a country? When is a people not sure where they belong? After a short drive up to Liverpool in England, we'll hop on the ferry and cross the Irish Sea to visit our next country. Only this country isn't considered a country in its own right by some people. This "country" is in many ways more like a province — a province of the United Kingdom. Yes, we are on our way west to Northern Ireland!

The history, culture, and political landscape of Ireland are complicated. Let's learn a bit of Irish history so that it all makes sense.

England began ruling over the island of Ireland way back in the 12th century. For almost 900 years, England has controlled all or part of Ireland. Before this time, the island was occupied by multiple Celtic tribes, each ruled by its own chieftain, who submitted to one central High King. Then when revolutions began cropping up

Ardara

in various parts of the world, such as the United States and France, toward the end of the 18th century, Ireland wanted to join the movement for independence and fight for her own freedom. England worked furiously to stamp out the uprisings that were springing up all over the island.

In an effort to put a final stop to the rebellion and to claim Ireland officially as its own, England reorganized the nation to include itself and Ireland in the name. Great Britain would now be called the United Kingdom of Great Britain and Ireland. Ireland wasn't happy with this new, yet more official, arrangement. Nothing had actually changed but the name. Ireland didn't feel like equal partners with Great Britain, so for the next 120 years, Ireland revolted. To make the island feel more British, England encouraged her citizens to **emigrate** from England to Northern Ireland, to a region known as Ulster. Over time, the British outnumbered the Irish in the northern part of the island. Life in Ireland was getting more complex and divided.

Robinson and Cleaver Department Store in Belfast for the State Opening of the first Northern Ireland parliament, 1921

The native Irish in the south wanted a free Ireland, free from British rule. The British in the north wanted to remain part of Great Britain. Then, in 1921, Ireland declared its independence from Britain to become the Irish Free State. The next day, Northern Ireland seceded from the Irish Free State and requested to remain a province of Great Britain. England agreed and changed her name once again. Now she would be known as the United Kingdom of Great Britain and Northern Ireland.

emigrate: leave one's own country in order to settle permanently in another

The countries that are included in the United Kingdom are England, Wales, Scotland, and Northern Ireland. Besides Northern Ireland, the other three countries govern themselves with British oversight. Northern Ireland has never governed itself and does not to this day. That is why people argue whether Northern Ireland is a country at all. It acts more like a province of Great Britain.

Sadly, peace did not settle over the land after the 1922 agreement. Next came **The Troubles**, a time in Irish history when the people of Northern Ireland fought against each other. The native Irish, who were also primarily Catholic and members of the Nationalist political party, fought for a united Ireland, a free Ireland where England had no business, authority, or control. But the British citizens, who were mostly Protestant and members of the Unionist political party, fought to remain under British rule, preserving their more English way of life.

The Troubles continued for more than 75 years. Finally, in 1998, the two halves of Ireland resolved to make peace and let bygones be bygones. That doesn't mean that everyone in Ireland today is happy with the arrangement, but they have chosen to live with it and live with one another in peace and harmony. It is now safe to walk the streets of Northern Ireland without fear of violence. However, local businesses and individual homes and neighborhoods continue to identify themselves by which side of the issue they land on by waving British or Irish flags outside their doors and displaying them inside their buildings. In this way, everyone knows what topics to avoid in order to keep the peace.

The flag of Northern Ireland

The Troubles: violence between the groups of British-supporting unionists and Irish nationalists

Here is how it can still be complicated today: When you meet people from Northern Ireland, they may identify themselves as Irish or British, but never both. When it comes to sports, the island of Ireland may form a single team, or athletes from Northern Ireland may compete for Great Britain. At the Olympic games, you will see both scenarios take place. Cultural links in Northern Ireland are shared with both the Republic of Ireland to the south and Great Britain to the east to form one big, complicated community.

The ferry pulls into Belfast, the capital city of Northern Ireland, and cars emerge from below deck in single file. We are eager to explore this Irish city even if it is a bit brisk outside. Today is a day for hats and scarves, but leave your umbrella in your backpack. It would turn inside out for sure in this windy weather.

Now that you grasp a little about the thorny history of Ireland, and Northern Ireland in particular, you can understand why you see either Irish (orange, white, and green) or Union Jack (red, white, and blue) flags displayed on every corner and stretched as banners across every street. You will also be able to comprehend why large concrete walls were once built to separate neighborhoods and why partisan parades, both scheduled and spontaneous, are frequent even today, especially here in Belfast. You can probably also understand some of the emotion behind the graffiti painted on once bare concrete walls, the signer indicating on which side of the issue he stands.

Finally, you know why there are so many British government buildings here and fine examples of Victorian and Georgian architecture, including Queen's University, named for Queen Victoria of England. Northern Ireland is both strongly British and fiercely Irish. This combination doesn't always mix well, like oil and water.

Belfast is both the capital city and the largest city in Northern Ireland. By the early 1800s, Belfast was a major shipping port and played a key role in the Industrial Revolution. Flax grows incredibly well in the north of Ireland, and it is from this tiny humble plant that fine linen is spun. Belfast quickly became the leading linen producer in the world, earning the nickname "Linenopolis."

Other industries thrived here as well, such as tobacco processing, rope making, and shipbuilding. In fact, the RMS *Titanic* was built right here at the Harland and Wolff shipyard, the biggest shipyard in the world. You can still see the **berth** where she was built and launched before the "unsinkable" ship sank to the bottom of the Atlantic Ocean during her maiden voyage to New York in 1912.

berth: area for ships at a port or harbor

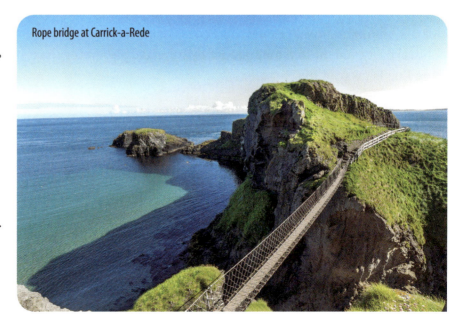
Rope bridge at Carrick-a-Rede

274 Lesson 14. Day 131

A Child's Geography. Vol. 5: Explore Viking Realms

Queen's University

Belfast suffered greatly during the time known as The Troubles. During the 1970s and 1980s, Belfast was considered one of the most dangerous cities in the world because of all the fighting. However, the city then became one of the safest cities, if not the safest city, in the United Kingdom. Belfast has come a long way, and its citizens are a happy, welcoming community who love to host visitors and neighbors alike.

If you look up, you can see that the city is flanked on the north and west by a series of rocky cliffs. These crags are believed to be the inspiration for an imaginative author, Jonathan Swift. When Swift was living at Lilliput Cottage near the bottom of Belfast's Limestone Road, he imagined that the shape of the rocky hillside resembled the profile of a sleeping giant safeguarding the city. The pointy bluff, in particular, he thought looked like a giant nose. This point is known locally as Napoleon's Nose, as it does resemble the shape of the French emperor's well-defined snout.

The Great Hunger: It is believed that the potato was introduced as a crop in Ireland in the 1500s, though how it got there is a story with many versions. However it got there, it proved to be easily grown and soon became the staple food for the poor among the Irish people. Then in 1845, tragedy struck.

The potato crops were ravaged by a fungus that destroyed much of the crops. As it spread, there was little else for the Irish to eat, as much of the other crops were exported to Great Britain, which also was in control of Ireland at the time and offered little help. And the price of what was available for other crops was beyond what they could pay.

By the time the crisis ended in 1852, an estimated one million people had died of starvation, and a million or so left the country for places like the United States. Those who remained never forgot the tragedy and the British lack of response to it, and sought even more to throw off British control of Ireland.

It would take decades to determine the cause of the blight, which was a fungus that would be named *Phytophthora infestans*.

Napoleon's Nose

And speaking of snouts, I smell something zesty and comforting all at the same time. The smells are wafting from the restaurant on the corner — Spuds. Let's check it out.

Ireland is famous for its potatoes. Potatoes have both blessed and cursed the people who live here on this island, so it seems only fitting that we stop in for lunch at Spuds and enjoy some Irish-grown potatoes. Spuds' specialty is baked potatoes, and they serve them with every topping you could ever imagine and then some. I think I'll order the Buffalo Spud that's loaded with chicken, Buffalo sauce, Gorgonzola cheese, sour cream, and chives. What will you have? Perhaps the Mac & Cheese Spud, the Bacon 'n Eggs Spud, or maybe you'd like to go all out with the Kitchen Sink Spud?

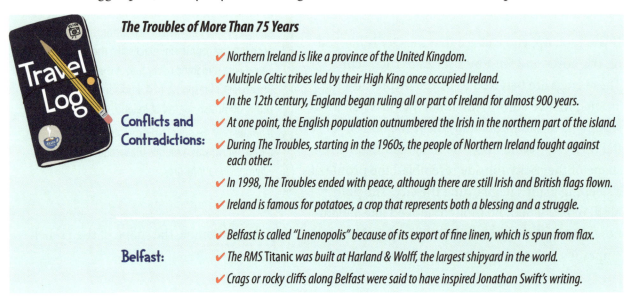

The Troubles of More Than 75 Years

Conflicts and Contradictions:

✔ Northern Ireland is like a province of the United Kingdom.

✔ Multiple Celtic tribes led by their High King once occupied Ireland.

✔ In the 12th century, England began ruling all or part of Ireland for almost 900 years.

✔ At one point, the English population outnumbered the Irish in the northern part of the island.

✔ During The Troubles, starting in the 1960s, the people of Northern Ireland fought against each other.

✔ In 1998, The Troubles ended with peace, although there are still Irish and British flags flown.

✔ Ireland is famous for potatoes, a crop that represents both a blessing and a struggle.

Belfast:

✔ Belfast is called "Linenopolis" because of its export of fine linen, which is spun from flax.

✔ The RMS Titanic was built at Harland & Wolff, the largest shipyard in the world.

✔ Crags or rocky cliffs along Belfast were said to have inspired Jonathan Swift's writing.

276 Lesson 14. Day 131

A Child's Geography. Vol. 5: Explore Viking Realms

Short Answer

Answer the following questions.

1. What led up to The Troubles?

_____

_____

_____

_____

_____

_____

2. What took place that started The Troubles and lasted 75 years?

_____

_____

_____

_____

3. What took place in 1998 that ended The Troubles?

_____

_____

_____

_____

4. Even after The Troubles, what symbols are displayed to represent different positions?

_____

_____

_____

_____

Scottish Gaelic vs. Irish Gaelic

When visiting Scotland, we learned about Scottish Gaelic. Now as we learn about Northern Ireland, let's examine the similarities and differences in both. The Lord's Prayer is commonly recited from Jesus' words in Matthew 6:9b–13. Try reading a few lines in Scottish Gaelic or Irish Gaelic.

Scottish Gaelic	English (KJV)	Irish Gaelic
Ar n-Athair a tha air nèamh,	Our Father which art in heaven,	Ár nAthair atá ar neamh,
Gu naomhaichear d'ainm.	Hallowed be thy name.	Naofa d'ainm.
Thigeadh do rìoghachd	Thy kingdom come,	Go dtiocfaidh do ríocht
Dèanar do thoil air an talamh,	Thy will be done on earth, .	Go ndéanfar do thoil ar domhan,
mar a nithear air nèamh.	As it is in heaven.	Mar atá ar neamh.
Tabhair dhuinn an-diugh ar n-aran làitheil.	Give us this day our daily bread	Tabhair dúinn inniu ár n-arán laethúil
Agus maith dhuinn ar fiachan,	And forgive us our debts,	Agus maith dúinn ár bhfiacha,
amhail a mhaitheas sinne dar luchd-fiach.	As we forgive our debtors.	Mar a mhaithimid dár bhféichiúnaithe.
Agus na leig ann am buaireadh sinn;	And lead us not into temptation,	Agus ná lig dúinn a bheith cathaithe,
ach saor sinn o olc:	But deliver us from evil:	Ach saor sinn ón olc.
oir is leatsa an rìoghachd,	for thine is the kingdom,	Óir is leatsa an Ríocht
agus an cumhachd,	and the power,	agus an Chumhacht
agus a' ghlòir,	and the glory,	agus an Ghlóir,
gu sìorraidh. Amen.	for ever. Amen	trí shaol na saol. Áiméan.

Answer the following questions.

1. What are some similarities between Scottish Gaelic and Irish Gaelic?

_____

_____

_____

_____

2. What are some differences between Scottish Gaelic and Irish Gaelic?

_____

_____

_____

_____

Can you recite the Lord's Prayer? If not, practice reciting it for someone else. If you can already recite the Lord's Prayer, then try teaching someone else.

Lough Neagh

➜ An hour later after being full of potato goodness, we're back on the road. Our next stop is Derry, also known as Londonderry. I'll explain why it has two names in a minute. But first, we are passing the massive **Lough** Neagh on our left. It almost looks like another ocean, but it is in fact a freshwater lake. It is the largest freshwater lake in the British Isles. The shore is home to a variety of flora and fauna, but the lake itself is known for its prized Lough Neagh eel. Fishermen cannot catch enough to keep up with the demand from high-end chefs who serve them on their menu.

There are a handful of ancient Irish folktales that try to explain how the lake came to be here. One is that the legendary giant Fionn mac Cumhaill scooped up a chunk of earth and tossed it at the giant Benandonner, his archrival in Scotland. The chunk of land fell into the Irish Sea and formed the Isle of Man, and the crater left behind filled with water to form Lough Neagh. While these stories are fanciful, we know that the lake was formed by our strong and creative God, who shaped the earth at creation. In recent times, the lake has been under the Earl of Shaftesbury's ownership, all the way from East Dorset, England. Imagine owning the biggest lake in the British Isles!

Onward to Londonderry! Or Derry! Or whatever you want to call the quaint medieval city on the River Foyle.

lough: a lake

People do not call Londonderry Derry because it is shorter or easier to say. No, this city has two names because Irish Catholic Nationalists will not associate their town with London, England. The original name of the Irish settlement here was Derry, dating back to the 6th century. On the other hand, British Protestant Unionists are proud to refer to their medieval walled town as Londonderry, the name given

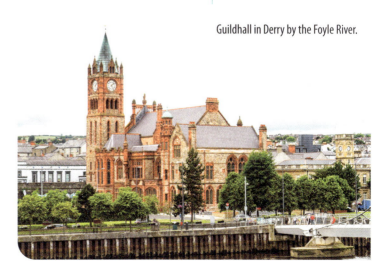

Guildhall in Derry by the Foyle River.

by the British who renamed it in 1613 when it was properly built up by the London **Guilds** and surrounded by a fine city wall.

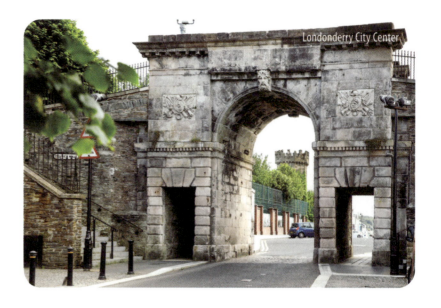
Londonderry City Center

Derry is the only remaining walled city in Ireland. Not only is its wall completely intact, but it is one of the most spectacular examples of a walled city in all of Europe. The walls were built in 1613 as a defense for the early British settlers from England and Scotland. The walls are approximately a mile in circumference and form a walkway around the inner city. This wide **earthen** and stone promenade provides a unique view of the original layout of the town and its preserved Renaissance-style street plan. There are seven gates that lead into the old city, and many historic buildings are preserved within, including the old Gothic Cathedral of St. Columba. The monastery next to the cathedral was founded here by Columba, the famous Irish missionary who later set out to convert the people of Scotland across the sea.

If we set off north from Derry, we'll find ourselves driving along the Antrim Coast, one of the most beautiful areas in all of Ireland and unsurprisingly designated as an Area of Outstanding Natural Beauty (AONB). This is a photographer's paradise. Get your cameras ready because we are about to see some spectacular scenery, and you might just take a stunning photograph.

Along the Antrim Coast is another natural phenomenon that you have to see to believe. Known as the Giant's Causeway, it is an expanse of approximately 40,000 interlocking basalt columns lining the coast and plunging into the swirling ocean tide. The tops of the columns form natural stepping stones that lead from the tops of the cliffs to the depths of the sea. An ancient volcanic eruption caused the hexagonal basalt patterns to form what residents and visitors alike consider the fourth-greatest natural wonder in the United Kingdom.

guilds: organizations of people in the same occupation

earthen: made of baked clay

Derry

280 Lesson 14. Day 135

A Child's Geography. Vol. 5: Explore Viking Realms

A couple of grade-school boys are hopping joyfully from column to column. Their mother, who is standing quite close to us, begins to wave and shout to get their attention. Her calls and gestures cannot compete with the roar of the ocean, so she puts two fingers in her mouth and pierces the air with a loud, shrill whistle. The boys immediately look up and run toward her.

Giant's Causeway

"Boys, do not stray so far from me," she scolds. "You never know when a large wave might rise up and sweep you out to sea."

She turns to us and smiles. "Hello, there. I heard you talking just now, and you don't sound like you are from around these parts. My name is Bronagh. I was just about to tell my wee lads here a story. This is Emmet and Fergus, my six-year-old twins. I wonder if you would like to hear it as well. It is a mythical tale about how this incredible landscape came into being."

"We'd love to hear the story," we nod.

"Well then . . . while we know scientifically that it was volcanic activity that formed these amazing interlocking columns, the Irish still love to tell an old, old tale that claims to explain its unusual existence," Bronagh begins.

"In the legendary tale, the columns are the remains of a great causeway built by a so-called Irish giant."

"Is this the same giant that scooped out the earth to form the Isle of Man out at sea, leaving behind a big hole that is now the great lake, Lough Neagh?" we ask.

"Indeed it is, my young friends!" Bronagh exclaims, impressed. "Most visitors to Northern Ireland are not as well versed in our folklore as you are. The myth goes like this," she continues. "The Irish

giant was challenged to a fight by his great nemesis, the Scottish giant, and he accepted. So that the two giants could meet halfway between their countries, the Irish giant built an expansive causeway across the channel with his own two hands. Supposedly, when he had finished, he looked up and caught a glimpse of the Scottish giant off in the distance, who seemed to be bigger than he was. Afraid, he looked for a place to hide. Unsure what to do, according to the story, he asked his wife for help.

She disguised him as a baby in a cradle. When the Scottish giant saw the "baby", it is told that he thought the Irish giant must be a giant among giants. He fled back to Scotland in fright, frantically destroying the causeway behind him so the Irish giant could not follow. And that is the fictional story of why the columns seem to fall away into the ocean. The site is actually an amazing wonder of the natural processes that God created."

Her young sons, realizing the story is over, stand and begin to run in circles around the group of us marveling at the size and symmetry of this geological phenomenon.

Bronagh goes on to explain that almost identical basalt columns, all part of the same ancient lava flow, can be found on the Scottish side of the sea at Fingal's Cave on the Isle of Staffa. Now we have seen both sides of the incredible Giant's Causeway!

And on that great note, it is time to leave Northern Ireland and indeed the entire realm of the United Kingdom of Great Britain and Northern Ireland. What a beautiful and hospitable kingdom it is! We have loved the landscape, architecture, pathways, and people. We will never be the same now that we have spent time exploring the shores, learning about the legends, enjoying the food, and getting to know the people. Cheerio! Perhaps we'll come back soon!

Photography Paradise in Northern Ireland

Londonderry or Derry:
- ✔ Londonderry, or Derry, the last walled city in Ireland, sits on the River Foyle.
- ✔ The name Derry dates back to the Irish settlement in the 6th century.
- ✔ The British renamed it Londonderry in 1613 when the London Guilds built it up.
- ✔ Seven gates are in the approximate one-mile circumference walled-in city.
- ✔ A Renaissance-style street plan leads to the Cathedral of St. Columbia.

Formations:
- ✔ Lough Neagh is the largest freshwater lake in the British Isles.
- ✔ The Antrim Coast provides spectacular scenery for photographers.
- ✔ An ancient volcanic eruption led to the 40,000 basalt columns called the Giant's Causeway.
- ✔ Folklore are fictional stories, like how Lough Neagh was formed by a giant scooping a big hole.

TIMELINE

1613	▶	Derry is renamed Londonderry by the British who kept a strong presence there.
1921	▶	Northern Ireland secedes from the Irish Free State one day after it is formed.
1998	▶	The Troubles end in Northern Ireland.

Industries of Belfast

In a cartoon or caricature style, draw images of Belfast. With creative handwriting, write keywords, including Belfast's nickname, to represent Belfast and the industries that shaped it. Use colored pencils to color and outline with a fine-tip black marker.

Materials needed:
- ☐ Colored pencils
- ☐ Fine-tip black marker

Antrim Coast Photography

The Antrim Coast offers photographers brilliant greens and blues of waters, basalt columns, and rocky cliffs. Based on one of the photographs, write a descriptive paragraph that uses vivid details. (Your paragraph should include a topic sentence, three or more detail sentences, and a concluding sentence.)

_____

_____

_____

_____

_____

_____

_____

_____

_____

_____

_____

_____

_____

_____

_____

Mapping It Out!

Complete the map of the country of Northern Ireland in the box below. Refer to the map on page 383.

Label the following places on your map. You can use colored pencils to shade areas of land or water, draw rivers and mountains, etc.

- ☐ Northern Ireland
- ☐ Londonderry/Derry
- ☐ Lough Neagh Lake
- ☐ Antrim
- ☐ Add a star ★ for the capital city of Belfast.

Flashcards

Make flashcards of the bolded glossary words from this lesson. Then, either add drawings of the terms or act them out in charades. Be creative!

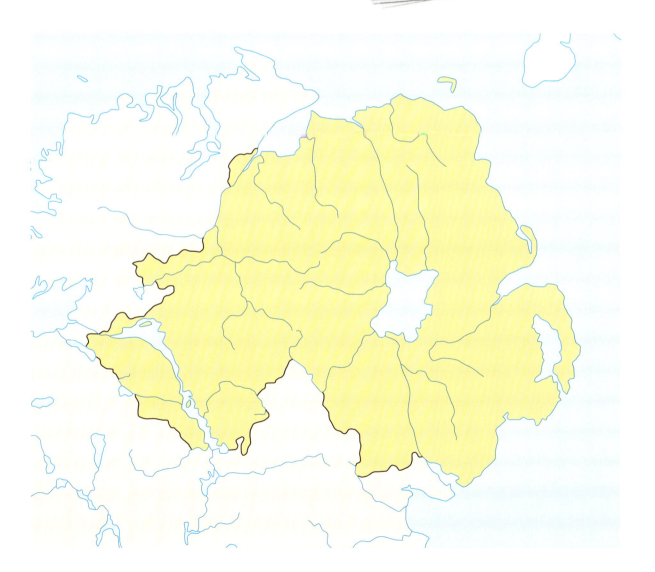

Renaissance-Style Street Plan

Londonderry has a Renaissance-style street plan that leads to the Cathedral of St. Columbia. Observe the map to note how symmetry is used to create a design for the streets.

Design a Renaissance-style street plan of your own.

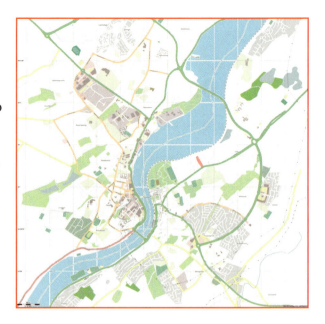

Love your neighbor

The crags along the rocky cliffs of Northern Ireland represent the rugged countryside and the resilience of people surrounded by windy seas. As recorded in Matthew 7:24, Jesus says, "Therefore, everyone who hears these words of Mine, and acts on them, will be like a wise man who built his house on the rock." May we seek to build our lives on the solid foundation of Jesus.

Ireland: The Garden Island

15

Doonagore Castle

Chugging along south just a wee bit past the city of Londonderry, we cross the swift River Foyle and find ourselves in a new country, one that is not part of the United Kingdom but still located in the British Isles. We are now in Ireland — the Republic of Ireland to be exact.

The southern portion of the island of Ireland, which makes up about five-sixths of the island, broke away from the United Kingdom in 1922 to become an independent country. This is why the official name of the UK is now the United Kingdom of Great Britain and Northern Ireland, instead of the United Kingdom of Great Britain and Ireland, as it once was before 1922. Let's start at the beginning.

Flag of Ireland

Ireland is known as the "garden island" because of its breathtaking scenery and lovely landscapes. But Ireland is not all rainbows and roses. It has a deep and complicated past, which is part of what makes it so beautiful today. The Irish are fiercely independent, resilient, passionate, and sentimental. The people of Ireland have carved out their island way of life through hard work and hard-fought determination. We'll learn all about it as we travel around this stunningly gorgeous isle of green.

Who lived here before the British arrived on the island, or before the Vikings, or even before the Celts, or the missionaries from abroad? Who was here first? The people who settled here after the Flood were descendants of Japheth through Gomer and Magog, as well as perhaps other descendants.

We'll find out more at Brú na Bóinne, an early megalithic site that was constructed before the pyramids were built in Egypt, located just outside the town of Drogheda on the eastern coast of Ireland. There are over a thousand such megaliths strewn about Ireland, but we'll visit the biggest and best preserved one of all.

Along the River Boyne, where it begins to bend and form an **oxbow**, a series of earth mounds were raised around 4,200 years ago, creating one of the most significant landscapes in the world. These mounds are mostly tombs, many of them **passage tombs**, while others are believed to be gathering places for ceremonies and even pagan rituals for some people who did not believe in the One true God. A combination of resources, including cut stone, timber, mud, and grass, were used to create these staggeringly massive mounds that have hardly changed over thousands of years.

The three largest mounds were structured to align with the skies in order to keep track of days and times. At Newgrange — the largest megalith covering over an acre of earth — the sun only shines down the narrow

oxbow: section of a river that forms a "U" shape

passage tombs: graves consisting of a narrow passage made of large stones and one or multiple burial chambers covered in earth or stone

Oxbow in the River Boyne

passageway on the winter **solstice** one day a year, setting aglow the interior with golden light for 17 full minutes on the darkest day of all.

Brú na Bóinne means "Mansion of the Boyne," possibly because there are hundreds of little satellite mounds encircling the larger ones, creating a massive network of underground rooms.

While we do not know a great deal about the people who built these impressive earth mounds, we do know some things. Keeping a calendar was important to them, and they measured days and time by the movement of the earth, moon, sun, and stars. They had a good understanding of astronomy and mathematics, especially geometry, and they were artistic. Many beautiful carved stones have been left behind, which influenced the artistic pursuits of the Celtic tribes who would arrive centuries later. They made useful tools and built sound structures that have stood strong for thousands of years. God created people to be intelligent from the beginning. Even when people do not give credit to the One true God, it is He who created them.

> **solstice:** either of the two times in the year, the summer solstice or the winter solstice, when the sun reaches its highest or lowest point in the sky at noon, marked by the longest and shortest days.

This is just about all we know of that time, yet even this information is significant because it indicates that an intelligent society dwelt on this island at some point before other people groups arrived to alter and influence the Irish culture. It helps us to understand what makes Ireland so unique. Resilience, strength, and determination have been woven into the very fabric of the people on the island.

While Ireland boasts some amazing manmade monuments that have stood the test of time, it also possesses more than its fair share of incredible landscape features as formed during the Flood of Genesis. It's amazing to see the unique beauty and wonder of places like this one that came from the cataclysmic event. We'll crisscross the island to reach the Cliffs of Moher before nightfall so we can watch the sun set over the Atlantic Ocean. That's right! It only takes about three hours to cross all of Ireland from east to west!

The twisty country road we take passes green pastures, quaint villages, and desolate ruins scattered about the countryside. Over time, the native ancient Irish were joined by waves of Celtic tribes who sailed across the seas and heaved their boats up on Ireland's shores.

The Celts brought folklore, poetry, artwork, more efficient farming methods, and advanced weapons and warfare strategies. They didn't overrun the people who lived here before them but rather peacefully fused their different ways of life into one.

While the Celts were fearsome warriors, it would be many years before another group would storm Ireland's coast to put their mettle to the test, especially since the Romans never made it this far north or west. In fact, the next newcomers would be messengers of peace, not war.

After the Celts came the missionaries, the first and most famous being St. Patrick. Patrick was born in the northern part of Britain around the end of the 4th century. When he was 16 years old, Patrick was kidnapped by pirates and taken to Ireland as a slave. For six long years, Patrick toiled as a shepherd in Northern Ireland. He slept in the cold and went days without food.

In his agony, he called out to God and asked to be saved from his plight. Previously an unreligious man, Patrick turned to prayer for relief and continued to ask for an end to his tragedy. One night, he dreamed that a ship was waiting to take him home to England. Patrick escaped from his master and traveled 200 miles to reach the ship.

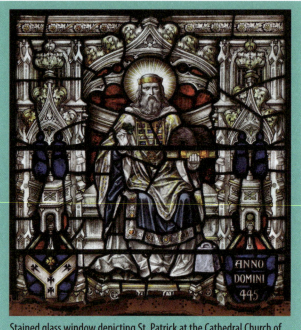

Stained glass window depicting St. Patrick at the Cathedral Church of St. Patrick, Armagh

After his escape, Patrick journeyed to Gaul (now modern-day France) to study in a monastery. While there, he had another dream, telling Patrick to return to Ireland to spread the good news of the gospel. After the dream, he did the unthinkable and returned to the land where he had been enslaved. He traveled all around Ireland, preaching the Word of God and converting peasants and kings alike to Christianity.

He set up his own monastery for teaching missionaries and began the important Irish monastic tradition of studiously learning the word of God and applying its principles to one's personal life. At a time when most of Europe was plunging into chaos and ignorance, Ireland was exploding with profound thought and higher education.

Today, St. Patrick is celebrated every year on March 17th for bringing the light of the gospel to Ireland. Traditional Irish music keeps the beat for festive parades and dancing that may continue for several days. The Irish love to celebrate their heritage. If only we could be here on St. Patrick's Day to celebrate with them!

Back to St. Patrick and his missionary training school: St. Patrick started the tradition of building monasteries in Ireland for Christians who wanted to share the gospel like he did. This is why we see so many monastic ruins strewn about the Irish countryside. The monasteries of Ireland became a epicenter for monks and missionaries to study and learn their faith before taking it further afield to the wide world beyond. Columba, the first missionary to Scotland, hailed from Ireland. And the *Book of Kells*, the most famous and possibly the most beautiful illuminated medieval book, which contains the four Gospels of the New Testament, was carefully hand-copied and illustrated by

290 Lesson 15. Day 140

A Child's Geography. Vol. 5: Explore Viking Realms

monks at the Abbey of Kells, which we are passing on our right. The *Book of Kells* is now on display at Trinity College in Dublin — perhaps we'll be able to see it during our Ireland adventure!

Our short road trip across the country is almost complete! The rather small city of Galway is the largest on the western side of the island with just 80,000 people who call it home. Galway is known as one of the most quintessentially "Irish" places in Ireland. In other words, you get a good dose of "Irishness" when you spend time in Galway.

One of the reasons for this is that most of the people that live on the west coast speak Irish as either their first or second language. Irish is an old Celtic language that has been spoken for thousands of years, but less than 20% of the people of Ireland speak it fluently today. Everyone in Ireland speaks English, but Galway is a truly bilingual city.

Every other door in Galway seems to lead to an establishment overflowing with smiling people and joyous music. Traditional Irish dance and music, known as trad, is kept alive in Galway and other parts of Ireland, enjoying a resurgence among the young and old alike. You can't help but smile when you hear the unmistakably Irish melodies floating through the air.

Just south of Galway are the magnificent Cliffs of Moher. Over a million people travel from all over the world to foolishly belly crawl to the edge and hang their heads over these grand cliffs to boast that they have been past the edge of the world — or at least past the western edge of Europe. Combine wind gusts with visitors taking risky photos, and an average of nine people die from the edges of the cliffs each year in addition to accidents that people survive.

Don't forget your raincoat! The mist and rain which frequents this area can quickly soak unprepared travelers. Kara and Nate, American travelers who host a travel show, have invited us along to hike the Cliffs of Moher with them and their drone. The scenery is spectacular, and their cheerful company is delightful.

Cliffs of Moher

King John's Castle

Because of the enormous scale, the sheer rock faces on these cliffs, and being well known in popular culture, the Cliffs of Moher have been given the nickname of "the Cliffs of Insanity." Now that it is dark, it's time to drive to our charming bed and breakfast in nearby Limerick, located directly across the bridge from King John's Castle. After a good night's sleep, we'll drive a short ways to Ireland's southern shore and explore the famous Ring of Kerry!

———◆———

The early morning sunshine spills across the towers and turrets of King John's Castle, washing the medieval citadel in a splash of golden light. The massive stone fortress was built on the orders of King John of England in the year 1200 on an island in the middle of the River Shannon to protect the town of Limerick as well as the entire island of Ireland from invaders from the sea.

Centuries before the castle existed, a Viking stronghold was founded on this same piece of ground. In the year 812, a fleet of Danish Vikings sailed up the river, burned the peaceful monastery that flourished here, and established a bustling trading center in its stead. The Vikings had begun their descent upon Ireland in earnest a few years prior in the year A.D. 795, changing the Irish landscape and ushering in a new era for the island country.

Crossing the seas in their dragon-headed longships, the Scandinavian pirates attacked monasteries and isolated villages, burning, looting, and pillaging in search of gold and treasure. For nearly 35 years, they launched amphibious assaults all around the coast of Ireland, but the worst was yet to come. During the 9th century, small Viking raids were replaced by complete onslaughts. Fleets of 50 ships or more appeared at the mouths of Ireland's great rivers. The shallow hulls of their ships allowed the Vikings to row into the interior of Ireland, sacking quiet monastic communities and establishing permanent bases for themselves.

These fortified harbors became known as **longphorts**, which the Vikings used to overwinter their ships when dangerous weather made sailing perilous. Over time, the longphorts became the first true towns

longphorts: ship harbors or Viking base camps in Ireland

in Ireland. While the monasteries had created a culture of higher learning and beautiful art, the Vikings added a new element by establishing towns and important centers of trade. The Vikings were master sailors and traders, and it wasn't long until goods from all over Europe made their way into the Viking towns of Limerick, Cork, and Dublin.

The Vikings retained their power and control over Ireland for about 300 years until the era of the Vikings came to a close all over Europe. At this time in Ireland, local Irish chieftains began to rise to power and take back control of their regional areas. One powerful lord — his name was Brian Boru — used his influence and strength to unite Ireland for the first and last time. He became the great High King of Ireland for the better part of his lifetime. After his death, however, regional chieftains began fighting for control, and the political unity of Ireland crumbled.

Into this power struggle came Diarmait Mac Murchada. It was the middle of the 12th century when Diarmait became the king of Leinster, a large kingdom in the middle-eastern part of the country. He had a falling out with a neighboring warlord and requested aid from King Henry II of England. Henry, consumed by his own conflict with France, recruited some Norman allies led by Richard Fitzgerald de Clare (nicknamed Richard Strongbow) to help this Irish king in return for his loyalty to the English crown.

This alliance marked the beginning of England's involvement in Ireland. Dairmait and Richard conquered Ireland in small waves. Diarmait had set his sights on becoming the next High King of Ireland. To secure his alliance with England, he gave his daughter in marriage to his Norman ally, Richard Strongbow. When Diarmait died, it was unlawful for his title and lands to pass through his daughter's **line**, but Strongbow overcame opposition and took control of the kingdom of Ireland anyway.

line: descendants

Henry II approved of Richard Strongbow's success but wanted Ireland for himself. He granted the lordship of all of Ireland to his son, Prince John. When John's brother, King Richard the Lionhearted, died in 1199, John became the king of England and the lord of Ireland — the first to bear this title. Ireland had officially become lost to the Irish. King John built this great castle at the mouth of the River Shannon to symbolize his victory and to stamp out any threats to his lordship from both within Ireland and without.

Here we are! It's time to explore the Ring of Kerry, the most visited region of Ireland outside of the capital city of Dublin. The Ring of Kerry is not a destination but a journey, an opportunity to inhale the beauty of Ireland not as one single snapshot, but as a photo album of lavish green and

Ring of Kerry

wildly remote grandeur. The Ring of Kerry consists of a circular driving route, during which we'll pass through quaint seaside villages, explore Viking ruins, and marvel at stunning views of the Atlantic Ocean.

Because so many locals and visitors to Ireland enjoy this drive around the southern horn of Ireland so much, the traffic congestion on the road can become unbearable. In addition, the road in places is so narrow and the drop-off to the sea so steep that drivers and passengers alike can feel claustrophobic and even frightened. Giant coaches transport tourists along this route, but they all drive one single direction to aid in traffic flow — counter-clockwise. For this reason, most cars drive in the opposite direction because who wants to get stuck behind a long line of tour buses? Not us, thank you very much. Let's be off!

Land of Resilient People

Travel Log

Views:

✔ "Mansion of the Boyne" is the meaning of Brú na Bóinne with small mounds around large mounds and underground rooms.

✔ The Book of Kells, the ornately illustrated copy of the Gospels, is on display at Trinity College in Dublin.

✔ The city of Galway is the most "Irish" city in Ireland.

✔ The Cliffs of Moher feature sharp drop-offs, magnificent views, and misty rains.

✔ Visitors take in the scenic circular driving route of the Ring of Kerry.

Resilience:

✔ The southern portion of Ireland broke free from the United Kingdom in 1922 to become the Republic of Ireland.

✔ The Irish were joined by Celts, who were warriors, followed by missionaries.

✔ Following kidnapping and slavery by pirates, Patrick escaped to study in a monastery in France.

✔ King John's Castle was built to protect Limerick and all of Ireland from invaders.

Label Viking Artifacts

Fill in the blanks to label each artifact according to type. Some words may be used more than once.

Silver   Ironworking   Raw amber   Stone

Bronze   Wood   Antler. whalebone. horn. or walrus ivory

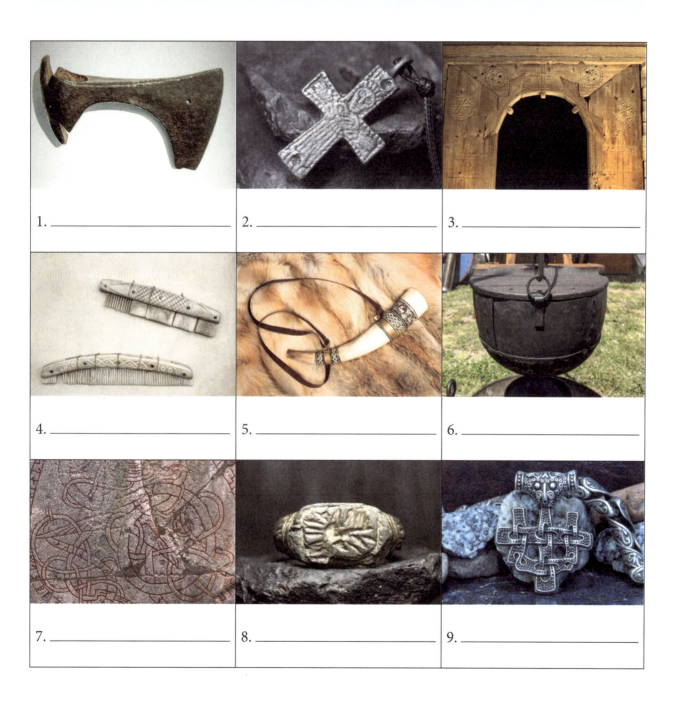

1. _____   2. _____   3. _____

4. _____   5. _____   6. _____

7. _____   8. _____   9. _____

Irish Melodies

Ireland's landscape and the resilience of the people have helped create lively music and poetry. From the traditional Irish dance music known as trad, to Celtic hymns, to more modern expressive music. One can't help but smile when you hear the unmistakably Irish melodies floating through the air.

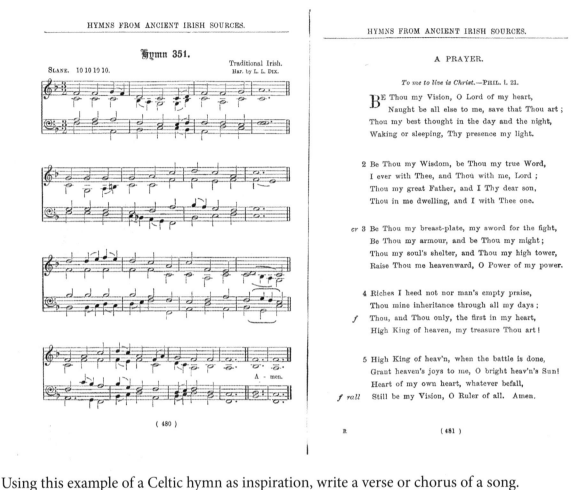

Using this example of a Celtic hymn as inspiration, write a verse or chorus of a song.

_____

_____

_____

_____

_____

_____

_____

Sing to the LORD. all the earth: Proclaim good news of His salvation from day to day.

–1 Chronicles 16:23

Cathedral and colored houses, Cork

→ The gorgeous Ring of Kerry behind us, we are on our way to Cork. Cork is the third-largest city on the island, after Dublin and Belfast. This thousand-year-old city is a lively place where nearly all its residents believe in the same central idea — one which they have held onto tightly for hundreds of years: Ireland should be one country, not two. Politically speaking, this is the "nationalist" viewpoint: Ireland deserves to be united under self-rule (or Home Rule, as it is called here).

As you remember, Ireland was "given" to Prince John by his father, Henry II, the King of England in 1185. When John became king after the death of his brother, Richard the Lionhearted, he was the first British ruler to claim the entire island of Ireland for his own. Since that time, Ireland has been either fully or partially ruled by England, a situation the majority of Irish people have despised ever since.

While Corkians, and the Irish people in general, are content to live peacefully in a divided Ireland at this time in history, they still dream of a united Ireland in the future where the government of the United Kingdom has no part. A mindset of peace despite the division has been carefully nurtured and has slowly grown over the past two decades, so this serenity is a relatively new phenomenon in Ireland.

Since the beginning of English involvement in Irish affairs more than 800 years ago, the Irish have struggled and fought for their independence. Countless wars, uprisings, riots, and causes have raged through Ireland to gain that independence, and for three-quarters of the country, those efforts have paid off.

Ireland: The Garden Island

The Republic of Ireland broke away from the United Kingdom in 1922, and the Irish finally achieved their hard-won independence. But for many Irish, five-sixths of the island is not enough. They want it all to fall under Irish rule. However, with the majority of the residents in Northern Ireland of British or Scottish descent, it's not that simple. Most citizens of Northern Ireland prefer to identify themselves as British, not Irish. So, it's complicated.

But not here in Cork! In Cork, the belief of the people is simple; one day, Ireland will be united — and for the first time in centuries, they are willing to wait patiently for that day.

Just outside Cork is the most famous and most visited of all Irish castles. Blarney Castle is the medieval fortress that houses the Blarney Stone, a limestone block enclosing one of the **machicolations** of the castle. A machicolation is an opening in the floor between the **corbels** of the **battlement**, through which stones or other material, such as boiling hot water or cooking oil, could be dropped on attackers at the base of a defensive wall.

Scripture says, "Have nothing to do with godless myths and old wives' tales; rather, train yourself to be godly" (I Timothy 4:7; NIV). However, people around the world often do just that! According to a false legend, kissing the stone at Blarney Castle bestows the kisser with the gift of eloquence of speech to flatter and please the listener. The builder of the castle, Cormac MacCarthy, decided to incorporate this stone into the structure of the castle. Since the 15th century, millions of people have kissed the stone. In the past, in order to touch one's lips to the stone, the aspiring kisser must climb the castle's tower then foolishly lean backward over the edge of the parapet, dangling by the ankles a dangerous distance above the ground below. Today, participants receive the help of an assistant, wrought iron handrails, and protective crossbars to prevent a deadly fall. The Bible tells us that God will give us the wisdom we need just by asking Him for it and believing He will give it to us. There is no need to risk your life for the gift of gab!

machicolations: openings between the supporting corbels of a projecting parapet or the vault of a gate, through which stones or burning objects could be dropped on attackers

corbels: projections jutting out from a wall to support a structure above it

battlement: parapet at the top of a wall, usually of a fort or castle, that has regularly spaced, squared openings for shooting through

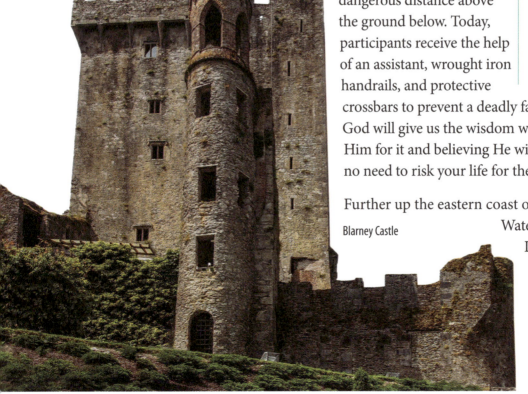
Blarney Castle

Further up the eastern coast of Ireland is the town of Waterford. Like Cork and Limerick, Waterford was a humble monastic settlement until the Vikings came along and greatly expanded the community, turning it into a bustling town in the 9th century. Here too, as in the other towns, Vikings established their longphort trading center at the mouth of the river.

Reginald's Tower still stands as a proud reminder of that once powerful society, the only landmark in Ireland to retain its Viking name. Over the years, it has been used as a mint, a prison, and a military storehouse. It is also famous for being the location of the wedding between Richard de Clare (Richard Strongbow) and Aoife (pronounced *Eefa*), the daughter of the King of Leinster, the one who gave his daughter in marriage to strengthen his alliance between Ireland and England.

Today, Waterford is best known for Waterford Crystal, which has been manufactured in the city since 1783. The crystal company has employed thousands of Waterford residents who have taken great pride in their work and the products they produced. For centuries, young couples all over the world have bought Waterford Crystal to grace their dining tables in their new homes after they were married. The name "Waterford" is equated with the highest quality crystal in the world.

It's about a two-hour drive from Waterford to Dublin, the capital city of the Republic of Ireland and our last stop on our exploration around the island of Ireland. Along the way, we can enjoy the beautiful green rolling countryside that is abloom with flowers, fruit trees, and rows of healthy-looking crops. Some of these fields are growing potatoes, but you may be surprised to discover that most of the fields do not.

The single greatest tragedy in modern Irish history was the potato famine that struck during the 1840s. The British government conducted a study in 1843 to investigate the effect of the ballooning Irish population on Irish land and its farming operations. The commission wrote up its findings in a report, noting that as many as three million Irish residents (over one-third of the population) were wholly dependent on the potato crop for food.

A couple years later, in 1846, the unthinkable happened. A potato blight struck Ireland, and most of the potato crop failed before harvest. The Prime Minister of Great Britain, Robert Peel, responded quickly to the crisis. He spent one million pounds (a pound is a type of British currency) on American corn and had it shipped and distributed to the hungry in Ireland. Later that year,

a political party who opposed his actions removed Peel from power. Sadly, the potato blight returned with a fury the following year. This time, all the potato crops across the island were destroyed.

When the second blight struck the island, the British didn't step in to help, and the Irish people

River Liffey in Dublin

felt abandoned to their disaster. Hunger and sickness killed poor Irish families by the thousands. Yet all the while, the grain crops harvested that year in Ireland were still exported to Britain. The government refused to stop the exports and use this alternate food source to feed the hungry in Ireland.

Where the British government failed to avert the crises, others stepped in to help. The Quakers set up food kitchens, and many compassionate people from America and other parts of the world sent food and money to Ireland. But these efforts weren't enough to avert disaster. The number of fatalities continued to climb, and the Irish became desperate for an escape from the deadly island, beginning a mass emigration from Ireland to other countries.

The poor and hungry people of Ireland crowded onto any ship that would take them away from the island in search of a better life. Corrupt sea captains took advantage of their desperate plight, cramming more people than was healthy into the tiny holds of their ships. Thousands died during the trans-Atlantic voyages to the United States in what became known as "coffin ships."

By the year 1850, a quarter of the population had been wiped from the face of Ireland as the population dropped from 8 million to 6 million; one million were dead and a million more fled.

With the blight finally gone, the Irish who remained behind began to rebuild their island way of life, but many did so with an even greater hatred for the British who ruled them.

The Irish continued to protest, boycott, and strike against the British government throughout the second half of the 19th century, but it wasn't until World War I when the people of Ireland began to gain some serious ground for their cause. While the British were preoccupied fighting alongside their allies against the Central Powers in Europe, the Irish began to fight against the powers-that-be within their own country. Uprising after uprising, the Irish began to frighten and weaken the British government on their own soil, little by little.

The British government retaliated, and after many bloody and unscrupulous battles, both sides were weary from the fight. King George V made a bold and brave move when he decided to travel to Belfast to talk with the people of Ireland. He said, "I appeal to all Irishmen to pause and join in the making for a land which they love a new era of peace, contentment, and good will." The king's speech was echoed across the land and printed in newspapers from coast to coast.

Record Tower and Chapel Royal in Dublin Castle

A few weeks later, a truce was called, and a delegation from Ireland went to London to work out the details for lasting peace. By 1922, the United Kingdom of Great Britain and Ireland was no more. The new Irish Free State had been born.

However, as you know from our visit to Northern Ireland, that corner of the country decided to remain loyal to Great Britain and not join the Irish Free State in 1922. The Troubles soon followed, but now, since 1998, a true and lasting peace has settled over the land. Ireland, once a troubled country filled with violence and hatred, then became one of the safest and most hospitable places in the world.

Entrance door to Dublin Castle

We have arrived in Dublin, the capital and largest city in Ireland. It is 60 degrees outside with clear blue skies overhead. This is a beautiful day to stroll through downtown and inhale all this city has to offer. Plus, today we get to meet up with an American friend who is visiting family here in Dublin. April agreed to meet us at Dublin Castle and accompany us on a little sightseeing tour around the city.

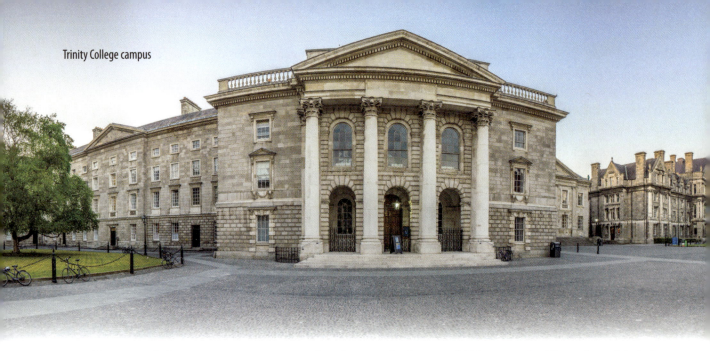

Trinity College campus

April has traveled to every continent on the planet, which was a lifelong goal of hers, but this is her first visit to Ireland.

"April!" I shout as I spot her at the entrance to the enormous Norman fortress.

"My favorite people!" she replies and laughs her unmistakable laugh, hugging each one of us. "Have you seen this castle yet? It's humongous. I guess it was built here shortly after the Norman invasion on the orders of King John of England. Yes, I'm talking about the same evil Prince John from the Robin Hood stories. He was actually a real villain in history who treated the Irish miserably."

"Well, he definitely wanted to make his presence known here in Ireland," I reply. "This isn't the first castle we have come across that he had built here."

"Apparently, this is the oldest structure standing in Dublin. It was built in 1204. There was a town here before the castle existed that was established by the Celts in the 7th century. Then there was a monastic settlement, then a Viking trading port, and then this Norman stronghold. See, I have my Dublin history down." April trills out her musical laugh. "Better take notes for that book you're writing," she says with a wink.

It seems that most of the cities we have visited in Ireland share a similar story — native Irish were here first, then Celts, then monks, then Vikings, then Normans. As least we are getting the Irish timeline cemented into our brains.

April continues, "I think the most impressive part of this castle is the gardens. There is a lake in the rear garden, which is actually a tidal pool that refills when the ocean tide pours in. In fact, my friends who live here told me that the name Dublin means 'the black pool,' referring to this very tidal pool behind Dublin Castle that once defended the mouth of the River Liffey. Pretty fascinating, don't you think?"

"Yes, it certainly is," we respond. "You know, something we really want to see while we are here in Dublin is the *Book of Kells*, located inside the library at Trinity College. I noticed on my map that it is just over Ha'penny Bridge, that iron footbridge there that crosses the River Liffey."

Let's take a selfie on the bridge, because it is one of Dublin's most iconic landmarks and is supposedly the most photographed sight in the city. A photo with all of us together will help us remember the amazing day we spent with our friend in this historic city.

The *Book of Kells* does not disappoint. It is the most spectacular book we have ever seen. Its glimmering illuminated pages lined with Celtic embellishments and extraordinary illustrations give us an idea of just how much work the monks put into the creation of this masterpiece.

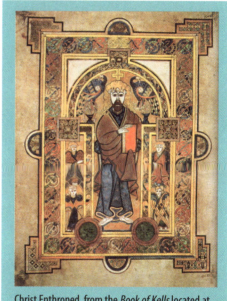

Christ Enthroned, from the *Book of Kells* located at Trinity College, Dublin

"I'm starting to get hungry! What about you? There's a food court outside the museum. Let's grab a bite to eat at Leo Burdock Fish and Chips. They say many famous people have eaten here and signed their names on the walls of the popular eatery. We can top it off with a sweet treat from the Lemon Crepe Company down the way. How does that sound?"

April looks at her watch and her eyes grow big. "Oh my! I don't have time! I have tickets to a concert tonight. Gotta run!"

Before April scurries off down the street, she pauses just long enough to say, "I'm so glad you spent the day with me today. It was so good to spend time with friends from home. See you later!"

Books in the Long Room Library, Trinity College

Fireworks over Ha'penny Bridge

We say goodbye to dear, exuberant April. We must also say goodbye to the dear, passionate people of Ireland. What an amazing visit we have had here in the Republic of Ireland these last few days. We learned some complicated history, explored some beautiful cities, traipsed through some old dusty castles, and enjoyed some delicious food and drink. See you later, Ireland! I hope we'll be back one day.

TIMELINE

795	▶	The Vikings invade Ireland.
1185	▶	Ireland is "given" to Prince John from his father, Henry II.
1200	▶	King John's Castle is built at the mouth of the River Shannon in Limerick, Ireland.
1921	▶	Ireland becomes the Irish Free State.

304 🌐 Lesson 15. Day 143

A Child's Geography. Vol. 5: Explore Viking Realms

Unscramble the Words

Unscramble the words to complete the sentences.

Most of the cities we have visited in Ireland share a similar story:

1. Native _____ were here first,

    hIrsi
    _____

2. _____ were next.

    eslCt
    _____

3. Followed by _____ , who studied.

    nkoms
    _____

4. Then the _____ arrived.

    kingsVi
    _____

5. They were followed by the _____, who invaded and settled.

    romaNns
    _____

Complete the Travel Log

Using previous travel logs as examples, create a travel log for Ireland.

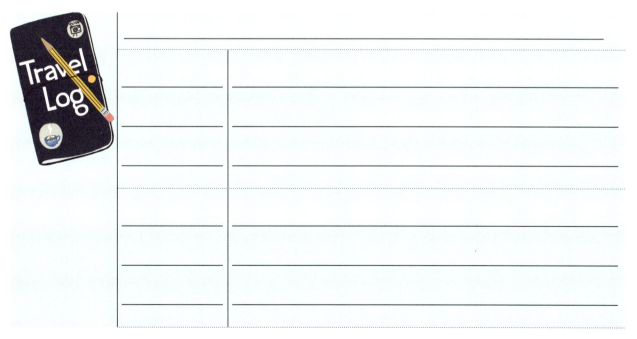

Illuminated Manuscript

The *Book of Kells* containing the four Gospels of the New Testament is a stunning example of an illuminated medieval book. The pigments for the vibrant colors were from animals, plants, and minerals. They were then illuminated with gold. The process of adding the gold accents is referred to as gilding — the process of applying gold leaf or gold paint.

To make your own illuminated manuscript, follow the steps.

1. Begin by lightly brushing a sheet of smooth cardstock or watercolor paper with tea. This will give the appearance of a medieval design on parchment paper.

2. While your paper dries, choose a selection from Matthew, Mark, Luke, or John to copy. One idea is the Lord's Prayer in Matthew 6:9–13.

3. With a ruler and pencil, draw a one-inch border around the edge of your paper.

4. Either use your ruler to draw lines inside the border or place dots where you will write each line.

5. Make the first letter of your text an oversized letter.

6. Carefully carve the quill of the feather and dip in black paint or use a calligraphy pen to write your manuscript.

7. With a pencil, draw embellishments and designs around the first letter and around the border.

8. Using the gold marker along with markers and paints, finish your design.

Materials needed:
- ☐ Smooth cardstock or watercolor paper
- ☐ Small glass of tea
- ☐ Paintbrush
- ☐ Ruler
- ☐ Feather, scissors, and black paint or calligraphy pen
- ☐ Gold marker or gold paint
- ☐ Markers or paint

The symbols of the Four Evangelists (clockwise from top left): an angel (Matthew), a lion (Mark), an eagle (John), and an ox (Luke) from the *Book of Kells.*

Optional: Teacher's Discretion ☐ No ☐ Yes Due Date: _____

*To carve the quill of a feather, seek parent permission and guidance to select a large feather. With a pair of scissors, cut the end of the feather. Cut an angle at the end of the feather.

Mapping It Out!

Complete the map of the Republic of Ireland in the box below. Refer to the map on page 383.

Label the following places on your map. You can use colored pencils to shade areas of land or water, draw rivers and mountains, etc.

☐   Ireland

☐   Cork

☐   Waterford

☐   Limerick

☐   Add a star ★ for the capital city of Dublin.

Irish setter

Flashcards

Make flashcards of the bolded glossary words from this lesson. Then, either add drawings of the terms or act them out in charades. Be creative!

Learn Geography Terms

Page 342 is a reference page for understanding the terms geographers use to describe landforms.

Love your neighbor

Some of the expressive music of Ireland tells about the political struggles of Ireland over the centuries mixed with the personal struggles of the human heart seeking to connect with God during the highs and lows of a person's life on earth. Psalm 63:7 proclaims, "For You have been my help, And in the shadow of Your wings I sing for joy."

Wood-sorrel (oxalis acetosella),
flowering plants native to Ireland

Create a Castle

Throughout your readings of Ireland and other countries, you've learned about various styles and designs of castles, including Dublin Castle. Now you will create your own 3D castle using cylindrical objects that you may find in your recycle bin.

Materials needed:

☐ Cylindrical objects (paper towel rolls, wrapping paper rolls, nut or potato chip container)

☐ Hot glue gun (with parental supervision)

☐ Brown paper, brown sacks, or cardboard

☐ Black marker

☐ Scissors

☐ Paintbrush

☐ Black and white paint

☐ Cornmeal

1. You are the designer! Imagine how large or small you want your castle to be. You may choose to design and complete part of a castle or an entire castle. Decide what castle principles and features to include. You may even choose to sketch your ideas first. Review Adventure Challenge 25 about castle design for ideas along with other images from your readings as inspiration.

2. Using scissors and a hot glue gun, carefully, construct your castle with cylindrical objects and brown paper, brown sacks, or cardboard to fit the architectural style you have selected. Be careful with the glue gun or you can get burned.

3. Mix white and black paint to create a gray-scaled color. For a stone-like texture, mix your paint with cornmeal.

4. After the paint has dried, use a black marker to accent features.

5. With a parent's permission, use other objects available to finish your design.

Malahide Castle near Dublin

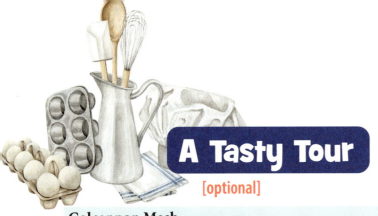

A Tasty Tour

[optional]

Colcannon Mash

Ingredients:

5 large potatoes

4 cloves of garlic

7 ounces of butter

Whole cabbage (thinly sliced)

3 ounces of spring onions

½ cup single cream

½ ounce fresh chives (chopped finely)

Salt and ground black pepper to taste

NOTE: *Requires adult supervision and participation.*

Optional: Teacher's Discretion

☐ No   ☐ Yes

Due Date: _____

Directions:

1. Boil the potatoes with the garlic for 15-20 minutes until cooked through.

2. While the potatoes are cooking, melt 7 ounces of the butter in a small frying pan and saute the cabbage and spring onions for 3-4 minutes until softened.

3. Drain the potatoes and mash (leave the garlic in).

4. Add the cabbage and spring onions (including the butter they were cooked in) to the potatoes.

5. Meanwhile warm the remaining butter and cream until the butter is melted. Add to the potato and cabbage mixture.

6. Add the chives and plenty of salt and pepper and stir until thoroughly combined. Serve with extra butter and chives to garnish.

Iceland: Fire and Ice

16

Iceland puffin

The pain and fatigue were beginning to feel like lightning bolts shooting down his thighs as he crawled up the steep incline, hoping it would be the last one. The grueling discomfort in his muscles kept his mind on conquering the great mountain, pushing aside his grief for a brief moment. A few more agonizing steps and Flóki, gasping for oxygen, pulled himself over a rocky ledge to find himself at the summit. Exhausted, he sat down to catch his breath.

Once his breath was coming in even drafts, he surveyed his surroundings. In wonder, he stood again and gazed out toward the sea. The sea … the monster that took his little girl from him. *The sea is nothing more than a watery grave*, he thought to himself, as he wiped an escaped tear away from his face.

Images pounded through his brain as Flóki recalled the day his family decided to make the dangerous voyage. The four of them sat down together over a meal of steamed fish and vegetables in the longhouse, and Flóki announced, "I think we should join the next expedition to Snæland. They say the fishing there is just as good as it is here in Norway and that the farming opportunities are even better because there is more land to go around. But the voyage will be long and possibly treacherous. I want this to be a family decision, not just mine."

The beautiful faces of his wife and two teenage daughters smiled back at him with confident reassurance. Those faces. He promised not to forget a single line or detail of them. Instead of four family members pulling up on the shore of their new country, there were only two — he and his wife, Skara. Their eldest daughter stayed behind in the Shetland Islands to marry a fine man with a large farm. And his baby… oh, his baby! The sea snatched her away from him when the tempests rose. She was tossed by a great wave from the ship and drowned within sight of the Faroe Islands.

His hot tears came in earnest now. He and Skara would be starting over. Their livestock died shortly after making landfall on Snæland. They had nothing but a few seeds and a wild hope that their efforts would succeed.

After wiping the salty tears from his face and blinking to clear the blurriness from his eyes, Flóki scanned his surroundings once more. To his right, he could see steam rising from a nearby mountain peak and black lava fields spreading out below. Fire. To his left, he saw steep fjords, such a dear reminder of home. But these fjords were packed with giant glistening icebergs. Ice.

House with green roof in Saksun, Faroe Islands

312 Lesson 16. Day 155

A Child's Geography. Vol. 5: Explore Viking Realms

Fire and ice. He thought to himself, *This country should not be named 'snow land,' for it is so much more than that. This country is Iceland. May the coming spring melt both the ice in the fjords and the ice in my heart.*

When the first Norwegian Viking reached this remote island in the North Atlantic Ocean, it was snowing. He named it Snæland, or "snow land." Shortly thereafter, this Viking arrived, the one who had lost his daughter at sea. He renamed the island Iceland, and the name stuck.

Iceland is considered a European country even though it is located closer to North America than Europe. The island sits atop the Mid-Atlantic Ridge, a ridge that runs along the bottom of the ocean floor. The Mid-Atlantic Ridge is the longest mountain range in the world, as well as a divergent tectonic plate, which means these huge continental plates in the earth's crust are moving apart and creating rifts along the mountain tops way down in the deep blue sea.

All this tectonic activity in the ocean below turns Iceland into a geological hot bed of activity with many burbling volcanoes, gushing geysers, and thermal hot springs. Geysers, which are springs of water pushed turbulently into the air at regular intervals, are a rare phenomenon that occur only in a few places on earth and generally near active volcanic sites. Iceland has many geysers, one named Geysir, from which our English word is derived. Iceland's most

Whale-watching boat in the fjords of Husavik, Iceland

famous geyser is Strokkur, which erupts like clockwork every 8–10 minutes and has been doing so for thousands of years.

Iceland experienced another eruption with great impact but this time of a volcanic nature. Grimsvötn volcano, located under the thick ice of Europe's largest glacier, is Iceland's most active volcano. It erupted in May of 2011 and hurled lava and ash 12 miles into the atmosphere, creating a huge mushroom cloud of volcanic ash and causing a major disruption to air travel across Europe and the Atlantic Ocean.

The Nordic nation of Iceland is the world's 18th-largest island at 40,000 square miles and Europe's second largest after Great Britain. Thirty smaller surrounding islands belong to Iceland. Still, it is the most sparsely populated country in Europe. Two-thirds of the population live in the capital city of Reykjavik on the southwest coast. While the main island is located completely below the Arctic Circle, its most northern island of Grimsey with a population of 87 straddles the Arctic line of latitude.

Iceland is known for its dramatic landscape. Jagged mountain ridges, gushing waterfalls, and chiseled fjords lend a majestic air to the topography. Lava fields and glaciers flow in patchwork across the flatter ground. Iceland is very literally made from fire and ice.

It's pretty much always chilly in Iceland, even with the aid of the warm North Atlantic Current (NAC) that passes right by its southern shore — the NAC is an offshoot of the Gulf Stream that we learned about when we were visiting England in Lesson 9. However, it would be colder still if the NAC didn't flow by the island.

Still, the cold is not unbearable. In fact, it is not nearly as cold as Greenland, which is located less than 200 miles west and is almost completely covered by an ice sheet. Average temperatures in the capital city of Reykjavik during the winter are in the 20s and reach up into the 60s during the summer. But extremes are possible here. The coldest temperature recorded on the island was -36 degrees Fahrenheit in January of 1918, and the highest temperature was 87 degrees Fahrenheit in June of 1939.

There are several distinctive animals who live in Iceland. If we're patient and attentive, we may see some, so let's keep our eyes peeled! Of the unique animals that make Iceland home, the only native land animal is the Arctic fox. The rest have either been intentionally brought here by humans or arrived accidentally by iceberg. Polar bears are known to "visit" Iceland, but they do not generally stay. They come to Iceland by traveling on icebergs from neighboring but distant Greenland.

Other wild mammals you may spot are the majestic reindeer, silky mink, and Arctic hare. Domesticated animals include Icelandic sheep, the Icelandic sheepdog to herd those Icelandic sheep, and the sturdy Icelandic horse. Birds — mostly seabirds — are abundant in Iceland, particularly puffins, skuas, and kittiwakes that nest along the sea cliff walls.

Out at sea, there lives an abundance of sea creatures, such as seals, whales, and countless varieties of fish. The fishing industry is a major contributor to Iceland's economy, accounting for roughly half of

Icelandic sheep

the country's total exports to other countries. Commercial whaling declined through the years.

The reason why Icelanders whale less is because that industry is in conflict with the other huge moneymaker for the island — tourism. Iceland receives three times as many tourists to the country as residents who live here. The tourists come to see the incredible scenery, climb icebergs, fly by helicopter over active volcanoes, and whale watch. For this reason, some Icelanders are inclined to leave as many whales as possible in the sea for visitors to enjoy.

Formerly Snowland

Awe-Inspiring Beauty:

- ✔ The Mid-Atlantic Ridge is the longest mountain range in the world.
- ✔ Geysers, volcanoes, and hot springs result from the divergent tectonic plate.
- ✔ Strokkur is Iceland's most famous geyser.
- ✔ Iceland's most active volcano is Grimsvötn.
- ✔ The most sparsely populated country in Europe, Iceland has the capital city of Reykjavík.
- ✔ Waterfall, fjords, and mountain ridges make for an amazing landscape.

By Water, Land, and Iceberg:

- ✔ The warm North Atlantic Current (NAC) is an offshoot of the Trans-Atlantic Gulfstream.
- ✔ The Arctic fox is the only native land animal of Iceland.
- ✔ Polar bears travel by iceberg from Greenland.

Short Answer

Answer the following questions.

1. How did Iceland get its name?

_____

_____

_____

_____

_____

_____

2. Iceland is located on what mountain range?

_____

_____

3. How do polar bears "visit" Iceland?

_____

_____

4. What other animals live in Iceland?

_____

_____

_____

_____

_____

_____

Animals of Iceland

Optional: Teacher's Discretion   ☐ No   ☐ Yes   Due Date: _____

We have learned about various animals of Iceland. God has uniquely created the animal kinds with the potential and ability to adapt to different environments. For example, as the bear began to make its habitat in various areas after the Flood, variations and the ability to adapt took place. That is why a polar bear in Iceland is different from a grizzly bear in another region.

Choose one of the animals from the lesson to learn more about. With your parent's permission or guidance, learn more about the animal from the Answers in Genesis website and other online sources and books. Discover God's unique design for the animal, unique features, and habitat.

Create an outline of what you learned. Main points have Roman numerals, followed by points that are capitalized letters, and then supporting details are numbered.

> **Animals of Iceland**
>
> I. Main Point 1
>
>   A. Secondary Point
>
>   1. Supporting Detail

Make a Geyser

Optional: Teacher's Discretion   ☐ No   ☐ Yes   Due Date: _____

1. With your parent's permission or guidance, locate an open outdoor space for your geyser.

2. Make a tube from the piece of paper, taping it so it doesn't unroll.

3. Place a toothpick horizontally through the tube about an inch from the bottom.

4. Drop the Mentos® into the tube of paper, letting the toothpick stop them from sliding through.

5. Remove the cap from the 2-liter soda bottle and place the bottle on a flat surface outside.

6. Carefully lower the tube inside the opening of the bottle up to the toothpick.

7. Gently grasp the tube with one hand and the toothpick with the other.

8. Quickly pull the toothpick out of the paper tube, dropping the Mentos® into the bottle, and jumping out of the way with the tube before the soda geyser begins.

9. Enjoy watching the geyser you created!

Materials needed:
- ☐ Mentos®
- ☐ toothpick
- ☐ tape
- ☐ 2-liter soda
- ☐ Piece of paper (rolled up to make a tube)

According to ancient Icelandic literature, the permanent settlement of Iceland began in A.D. 874 when the Norwegian Viking chieftain Ingólfr Arnarson built his homestead on the island at the site of modern-day Reykjavík. Multitudes of Viking families looking for suitable farmland soon followed. But this same saga, as well as others, mention an earlier people who came to inhabit the land but didn't stay. These were Papar monks who traveled from distant Ireland and Scotland only to find the island utterly desolate and uninhabited. Archaeologists have discovered the ruins of a cabin in Hafnir that was abandoned approximately one hundred years before the Vikings appeared.

Around that same time, however, Swedish Viking explorer Garöar Svavarsson circumnavigated Iceland to establish that it was indeed an island. He built a longhouse and overwintered in Húsavik then departed the following summer, leaving a few of his men behind.

Over the course of the next few centuries, more Norwegians and some Danes followed, bringing with them their **thralls** from the British Isles. They also brought their form of government with them, known as the **Althing**, a ruling assembly body that is still in place today, making it the oldest parliament in the world. Within fifty years of the first Viking landing, most of the arable land on the island had been claimed. By 986, Viking families were sailing farther west to Greenland in hopes of finding suitable living conditions.

thralls: slaves

Althing: legislative assembly of Iceland

There once was a Viking named Erik. His father, Thorvald, killed a man in Norway, and so he was banished from the land. Thorvald and his

Reykjavík

10-year-old son, Erik, left for Iceland and found a new life there. Erik grew up, married, and began a family of his own.

One day, a conflict resulted in a neighbor killing one of Erik's slaves. Erik took revenge, leading to another death. Now Erik, like his father before him, was banished from his homeland. But Erik's banishment from Iceland was only for a duration of three years. With his 10-year-old son, Leif, Erik the Red, nicknamed for his fiery hot temper as well as his fiery red hair, sailed west with his family to a land he would name Greenland. Like father, like son, repeat.

Leif Erikson statue

According to the saga of Erik the Red, he spent his three years of exile exploring this new land. When Erik returned to Iceland, he told everyone tall tales about "Greenland," hoping to lure more settlers to the desolate island. Less than a year later, Erik returned to Greenland with his family and a large number of colonists.

Erik's son Leif grew up in the harsh conditions of Greenland, but when he came of age, he sailed back to Norway to work as a companion to Olaf, the king of Norway. There, he became a Christian and felt led to return to Greenland to share the good news of the gospel with his kinsfolk.

On his return voyage, he was blown off course and arrived at a land where wheat and grapevines grew wild. Leif Erikson had landed on the North American continent in the region of Newfoundland, Canada. He named the place Vinland because of the wild vines and then, as his father before him, returned to Greenland with a cargo of grapes and timber to lure more settlers to this bountiful land.

In the end, Vinland was never permanently colonized by Vikings, but a Norse settlement was uncovered by archaeologists in the 1960s, confirming that Vikings did indeed discover North America 500 years before Christopher Columbus sailed the oceans blue in 1492.

———✦———

Reykjavík is a city built for strolling, so let's get walking! The streets are wide and flat, named after fabled warriors and false Viking gods, and the buildings are colorful and inviting, giving it a bright Nordic atmosphere. Here the air is cool and fresh even though Reykjavík translates to mean "smoky bay." Icelanders, like the Finnish, love a warm swimming pool, but Iceland pools are typically located outside and heated by geysers and thermal hot springs. Sounds like fun, doesn't it?

I suggest we take a soak in the pool then grab a bite to eat at one of Iceland's world-famous restaurants. We are nearing the end of our tour of northern Europe, so I think we can splurge a little before we travel back home. Reykjavík boasts some truly outstanding local and international cuisine. Local cuisine focuses on seafood and lamb, and you can never go wrong by ordering the fish of the day in one of Reykjavík's restaurants.

Golden Circle Road

Icelandic chefs like to surprise you when your food is brought to the table. If you order cod, you may get the whole cod's head. Other unusual dishes you might want to try are boiled sheep's head or fermented shark. If these Icelandic classics sound a little too daring for you, you can always order an Icelandic hot dog. Apparently, they serve up some of the best in the world.

Let's order, and then I'll finish telling you about the history of Iceland.

After a few hundred years, the original Iceland Commonwealth was crumbling as powerful Icelandic chieftains fought with each other, creating a civil war on their island home. With the disintegration of their native leadership, the Norwegian crown stepped in to help and formed a union between Iceland and Norway in 1262 when they signed the Old Covenant, making Iceland a Norwegian dependency.

During the centuries that followed, Iceland became one of the poorest countries in Europe. With its harsh weather, volcanic eruptions, and infertile soil, Icelandic society barely subsisted on their own agricultural crops. Then, the **Black Death** swept through — not once, but twice — leaving the island devastated with two-thirds of the population wiped out.

By the 16th century, at the height of the Protestant Reformation, Denmark ruled Norway, which meant they ruled Iceland too. Denmark's king, Christian III, imposed Lutheranism on all his subjects, including those in faraway Iceland. The country officially became Lutheran, and Lutheranism has been the dominant Christian denomination here ever since. God gives us free will, and salvation is not truly authentic unless you recognize your need for a Savior rather than following the command of an earthly king.

Hardships continued for the poor island nation. Within a hundred years of occupation, Denmark began imposing harsh trade restrictions on Iceland. Along with these harsh new laws, Iceland was suffering through multiple natural disasters, including volcanic eruptions and disease. They were also the target of pirates from several countries, who began raiding the coastal cities and abducting people into slavery. The final straw fell with the Laki volcanic eruption of 1783, which caused devastating effects across the country. Over half of all the livestock in Iceland died from the ash fallout, causing a famine from which a quarter of the population died.

Black Death: also known as the Bubonic Plague, the Black Death was an epidemic spread by rats. This disease killed about one-third of the European population between A.D. 1348 and 1352.

Amazing landscape at Diamond Beach, Iceland

With the climate becoming increasingly cold, less food available to eat, pirates raiding the coast, and volcanoes erupting in the interior, Icelanders began to flee. A mass immigration to the New World ensued, particularly to the region of Gimli, Manitoba, in Canada, which is sometimes referred to as "New Iceland."

Then, finally, something good happened.

Active volcano at Mount Fagradalsfjall, Iceland

Denmark-Norway split into two separate kingdoms following the Napoleonic Wars in 1814. Iceland remained a Danish dependency at this time, but something was brewing. National loyalty was resurfacing after the dust settled from the clash of the two Scandinavian superpowers. By 1874, Denmark agreed to allow Iceland the opportunity of limited home rule. Then, in 1918, Denmark signed an agreement that recognized Iceland as a fully sovereign and independent state, although still united with Denmark as her overseer, or decision-maker, and protector for the next 25 years.

When Denmark was invaded by Germany during World War II, Iceland declared itself independent, claiming she would take care of her own affairs. Within a month, British armed forces invaded Iceland against her wishes to keep the Germans out.

Two years later, the 25-year provision set by Denmark expired, and Icelanders voted on whether to remain in a personal union with Denmark or absolve it. The vote was 97% in favor of abolishing the union and setting up a new constitution. On the 17th of June in the year 1944, Iceland officially became a free country and appointed its first president.

Today, Iceland is a free and prosperous nation. It is an oasis of light and warmth in the midst of the cold Atlantic separating the Old World from the New World. Its long history gives perspective, and its newfound freedom gives exuberance. Hurrah for Iceland, the crown jewel of the North Atlantic Sea!

Our tour of the Viking realms of Northern Europe has come to an end, and it is time to travel home. Are you ready? I hope you have enjoyed our adventure together. I loved having you along!

Keep asking questions, recording notes, and taking photographs, storing all these wonderful memories in your heart and mind. Having the heart of a geographer means having a heart for the world.

Come! Let's go into all the world together, learn from one another, appreciate the cultures of the people groups, and help the lost find truth through spreading the gospel.

The Viking Influence in Iceland

Vikings:
- ✔ Numerous Vikings explored Iceland in search of farmland but few stayed.
- ✔ After banishment from Norway, Thorvald the Viking landed in Iceland.
- ✔ Erik the Red, son of Thorvald, was banished from Iceland and traveled to Greenland.
- ✔ Leif Erikson, who was the son of Erik, became a Christian and spread the gospel.

Struggles:
- ✔ After much hardship in the late 1700s, mass emigration from Iceland began, particularly to Manitoba in Canada.
- ✔ Iceland became fully sovereign and independent from Denmark in 1918 but with a 25-year oversight.
- ✔ In 1944, Iceland officially became a free country with its first president.

TIMELINE

874 ▶	Norwegian Viking chieftain Ingólfr Arnarson builds his homestead on the island at the site of modern-day Reykjavík.
986 ▶	Vikings begin leaving Iceland in hopes of finding more farmable land in Greenland.
1262 ▶	Iceland and Norway are united under the Old Covenant.
1814 ▶	Iceland becomes a Danish dependency.
1874 ▶	Denmark agrees to allow Iceland the opportunity of limited home rule.
1918 ▶	Denmark signs an agreement that recognizes Iceland as a fully sovereign and independent state.
1944 ▶	Iceland officially becomes a free country and appoints its first president.
2011 ▶	Grimsvötn volcano erupts and hurls ash 12 miles into the atmosphere.

324 Lesson 16. Day 158

A Child's Geography. Vol. 5: Explore Viking Realms

The Erikson Family

Write answers to the following prompts.

1. Review the highlights (or lowlights) of the three Eriksons described in the text. Write a brief summary of each.

_____

_____

_____

_____

_____

_____

2. What is a biblical example of someone who chooses a different way than the troubled generation before? You may brainstorm with your family for ideas.

_____

_____

_____

_____

_____

_____

3. Write a summary of what happened in the biblical example you found.

_____

_____

_____

_____

_____

_____

4. Copy a portion of the Scripture from the events you summarized in question 3.

_____
_____
_____
_____
_____
_____

5. What is a present-day example of someone who chooses a different way than the troubled generation before? You may brainstorm with your family for ideas.

_____
_____
_____
_____
_____
_____

6. What is your reaction to this present-day example and what have you learned from it?

_____
_____
_____
_____
_____
_____

Mapping It Out!

Complete the map of Iceland in the box below. Refer to the map on page 384.

Label the following places on your map. You can use colored pencils to shade areas of land or water, draw rivers and mountains, etc.

☐ Iceland   ☐ Atlantic Ocean

☐ Add a star ★ for the capital city of Reykjavík.

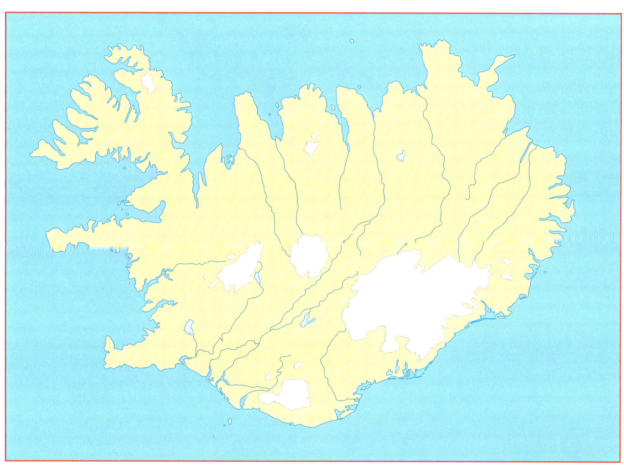

Icelandic sheepdog

Flashcards

Make flashcards of the bolded glossary words from this lesson. Then, either add drawings of the terms or act them out in charades. Be creative!

Geospatial Data on a Map

Geography and spatial information combine to create geospatial data on a map. The information presented can help reveal more about objects, people, and the environment. Vector geospatial data uses lines or dates. Raster data can include photographs and satellite imagery.

Observe information about the map of Iceland with geospatial data. It is one example of the many types of maps with geospatial data.

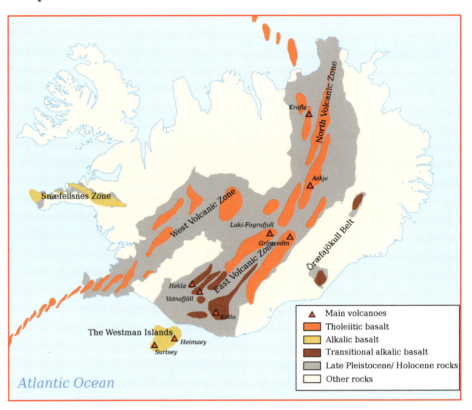

What are three observations you can make based on the map?

1. _____

2. _____

3. _____

As we have visited our last country on our tour, it's your turn to write and say a prayer for Iceland and her people.

_____

_____

_____

_____

Travel Itinerary

The travel itineraries are included in the daily schedule.

Travel Itinerary 1: The Baltic States

We have now toured the Baltic States: Lithuania, Latvia, and Estonia. Write your own travel itinerary (plan) of top explorations if you were planning a travel adventure.

	Lithuania	Latvia	Estonia
Must-See Place to Visit and Description			
Geographic Feature to Explore and Description			
Food to Try and Description			

Travel Itinerary 2: Scandinavia

We have now toured Scandinavia: Finland, Sweden, Norway, and Denmark. Write your own travel itinerary (plan) of top explorations if you were planning a travel adventure.

	Finland	Sweden	Norway	Denmark
Must-See Place to Visit and Description				
Geographic Feature to Explore and Description				
Food to Try and Description				

Page intentionally left blank.

Travel Itinerary 3: The British Isles

We have now toured The British Isles: the City of London (in England), England, Scotland, Wales, Northern Ireland, and Ireland. Write your own travel itinerary (plan) of top explorations if you were planning a travel adventure.

	City of London	Southern England	Central England	Northern England
Must-See Place to Visit and Description				
Geographic Feature to Explore and Description				
Food to Try and Description				

Exercise continued on the next page.

Travel Itinerary 3: The British Isles (continued)

We have now toured The British Isles: the City of London (in England), England, Scotland, Wales, Northern Ireland, and Ireland. Write your own travel itinerary (plan) of top explorations if you were planning a travel adventure.

	Scotland	Wales	Northern Ireland	Ireland
Must-See Place to Visit and Description				
Geographic Feature to Explore and Description				
Food to Try and Description				

Travel Itinerary 4: North Atlantic

We have now toured the North Atlantic: Iceland. Write your own travel itinerary (plan) of top explorations if you were planning a travel adventure.

Iceland

Must-See Place to Visit and Description	_____ _____ _____ _____ _____
Geographic Feature to Explore and Description	_____ _____ _____ _____ _____
Food to Try and Description	_____ _____ _____ _____ _____

Good Job!

BALTIC STATES TIMELINE

1800 B.C.	▶ Maarahvas build fort settlements.
1500 B.C.	▶ Five meteorites crash into the island of Saaremaa in Estonia.
A.D. 1000	▶ A Viking named Gunnar Hámundarson of Iceland raids the island of Saaremaa in Estonia.
1061	▶ Estonians prevails against barbarian invaders from Russia.
1199	▶ Pope Innocent III orders a crusade to Estonia to establish Christian church in the north.
1201	▶ Bishop Albert claimed Riga, Latvia as the new capital for the Christian church.
1208	▶ A crusade is dispatched to subdue the Vikings in Estonia.
1227	▶ Crusaders defeated the Estonian Vikings.
1248	▶ The capital city of Estonia, Tallinn, is established by the Danes.
1253	▶ King Mindaugus of Lithuania crowned.
1291	▶ Lithuanian Crusade begins.
1385	▶ Jogaila crowned King of Poland and Grand Duke of Lithuania.
1390	▶ Welsh raiders storm Vilnius Castle (AKA Crooked Castle).
1410	▶ Battle of Grunwald takes place in Lithuania.
1625	▶ St. Olaf's Church in Tallinn is the tallest building in the world.
1655	▶ Sweden attacks Poland and Lithuania.
1710	▶ Russian occupation of Latvia.
1917	▶ The end of Russian occupation of Latvia.
1918	▶ Latvia declares her independence from Russia.
1918	▶ Estonia declares her independence from Russia.
1941	▶ Germany conquers Latvia.
1990	▶ Lithuania declares her independence.
1991	▶ Latvia regains her independence.
2014	▶ Riga recognized as a European Capital of Culture.

283 ▶	Lucia, Sweden's patron saint, is born into wealthy Italian family.
820 ▶	The Oseberg Ship built by the Vikings.
980 ▶	Erik the Red discovers Greenland.
988 ▶	The city of Odense in Denmark is founded.
1000 ▶	Leif Erikson discovers Newfoundland in North America.
1049 ▶	The city of Oslo, Norway is established.
1070 ▶	Bergen, Norway is established by King Olav Kyrre, son of Harald Hardrada.
1150 ▶	Hopperstad Stave Church built along the Sognefjord in Norway.
1219 ▶	The oldest flag in the world - Denmark's - is designed.
1252 ▶	Birger Jarl founded Stockholm, Sweden.
1349 ▶	The Black Death arrives in Norway.
1429 ▶	Pirates, the Victual Brothers, burns down much of Bergen, Norway.
1500 ▶	Denmark rules all of Norway and much of Sweden.
1523 ▶	Stockholm liberated from the Danes.
1621 ▶	Galileo Galilei witnesses and names the aurora borealis.
1665 ▶	The Battle of Vågen waged between the Dutch and English in Bergen Harbor, Norway.
1714 ▶	Greater Wrath battle between Russia and Sweden.
1742 ▶	Lesser Wrath battle between Russian and Sweden.
1805 ▶	Hans Christian Anderson is born in Odense, Denmark.
1888 ▶	Alfred Nobel reads his obituary in the newspaper.
1901 ▶	The first Nobel Peace Prize is awarded to Jean Henri Dunant for his role in founding the International Red Cross.
1903 ▶	The Oseberg Ship uncovered in Norway.
1932 ▶	LEGO® company is founded in Denmark.
1947 ▶	The Kon-Tiki raft built to prove the Polynesian Islands may have been settled by peoples from South America.
1953 ▶	Midsommar became an official national holiday.
1971 ▶	A large group of homeless people storms a military base, taking possession of it for their new home, now called Christiania.
1972 ▶	Margrethe II, Queen of Denmark, begins her reign.
2018 ▶	A 66-foot Viking longship is discovered in southern Norway.

BRITISH ISLES TIMELINE

3200 B.C.	▶ The stone circle of Castlerigg is erected.
3000 B.C.	▶ Stonehenge is built in England.
3000 B.C.	▶ Brú na Bóinne passage tombs are constructed in Ireland.
1450 B.C.	▶ Cleopatra's Needle is erected in Egypt by Thutmose III.
43	▶ Roman Empire invades Britain.
60	▶ The Romans build a bath house in Bath.
71	▶ The wall around York is built by the Romans.
122	▶ Hadrian's Wall is built by the Romans.
460	▶ St. Patrick returns to Ireland as a missionary.
563	▶ Columba establishes an abbey on the island of Iona in Scotland.
627	▶ The first version of York Minster is built; the final version is completed 850 years later.
793	▶ Viking attack on Lindisfarne in northern England.
795	▶ The Vikings invade Ireland.
1066	▶ William the Conqueror builds Dover Castle.
1068	▶ William the Conqueror orders the construction of Nottingham Castle.
1078	▶ William the Conqueror begins the construction of the Tower of London.
1096	▶ Oxford University is established.
1170	▶ Thomas Becket is murdered in Canterbury Cathedral.
1185	▶ Ireland is "given" to Prince John from his father, Henry II.
1194	▶ Battle between King Richard and Prince John occurs at Nottingham Castle.
1200	▶ King John's Castle is built at the mouth of the River Shannon in Limerick, Ireland.
1209	▶ Cambridge University is established.
1244	▶ King Henry III orders the construction of Clifford's Tower for his daughter's wedding.
1282	▶ Edward I invades Wales and builds Caernarfon Castle.
1295	▶ The Tower of London is completed under the rule of Edward I.
1387	▶ The Canterbury Tales was written by Geoffrey Chaucer.
1450	▶ First recipe for black pudding is published.
1535	▶ Wales is officially incorporated into England by the Laws in Wales Acts.
1613	▶ Derry is renamed Londonderry by the British who kept a strong presence there.
1666	▶ The Great Fire of London devastates the City of London.
1707	▶ The Treaty of Union - England and Scotland are united.
1725	▶ The Highland Clearance begin in Scotland.
1730	▶ Dr. Richard Russell prescribes seawater as a cure for a variety of illnesses.
1745	▶ Prince Charlie incites a rebellion among the highlanders to reclaim the Scottish throne.

1759	►	The Guinness Brewery is founded in Dublin.
1783	►	The Waterford Crystal company is established.
1819	►	Cleopatra's Needle is given as a gift from the King of Egypt.
1831	►	Like the song, London Bridge is falling down; so it is replaced by a stone bridge.
1837	►	Buckingham Palace becomes the official residence of the British monarchy.
1846	►	The great potato famine in Ireland begins.
1880	►	The largest recorded earthquake along the Great Glen Fault in Scotland.
1901	►	Beatrix Potter self-publishes *The Tale of Peter Rabbit*.
1921	►	Ireland declares her independence from Britain to become the Irish Free State.
1921	►	Northern Ireland secedes from the Irish Free State one day after it is formed.
1922	►	The Troubles begin in Northern Ireland.
1925	►	London is the largest city in the world.
1936	►	George VI becomes King of England after his brother, Edward, abdicates the throne.
1952	►	Elizabeth II is crowned Queen of England.
1967	►	The second London Bridge is sinking, so it too is replaced.
1981	►	Charles, Prince of Wales, and Lady Diana Spencer are married.
2011	►	Prince William and Catherine Middleton are married at Westminster Abbey.

340 🌐 Timeline

A Child's Geography. Vol. 5: Explore Viking Realms

ICELAND & NORTH ATLANTIC TIMELINE

874 ▶	Norwegian Viking chieftain Ingólfr Arnarson built his homestead on the island at the site of modern-day Reykjavík.
986 ▶	Vikings begin leaving Iceland in hopes of finding more farmable land in Greenland.
1000 ▶	Leif Erikson discovers Newfoundland in North America.
1262 ▶	Iceland and Norway are united under the Old Covenant.
1814 ▶	Iceland becomes a Danish dependency.
1874 ▶	Denmark agrees to allow Iceland the opportunity of limited home rule.
1918 ▶	Denmark signs an agreement that recognizes Iceland as a fully sovereign and independent state.
1944 ▶	Iceland officially becomes a free country and appoints its first president.
2011 ▶	Grimsvötn volcano erupts and hurls ash 12 miles into the atmosphere.

Blank timeline books to record your entries can be found at the Master Books website.

GEOGRAPHY TERMS

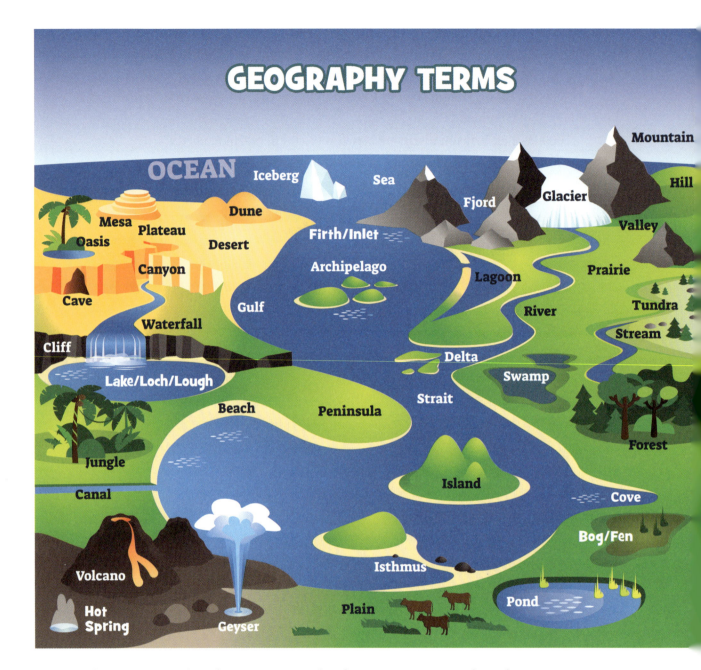

NOTE: These are examples of various geographic features you can use for reference.

342 Geography Terms

A Child's Geography. Vol. 5: Explore Viking Realms

Glossary

Abdication — To renounce or give up the right to the throne.

Althing — The legislative assembly of Iceland.

Amber — Hard translucent fossilized resin produced by coniferous trees, typically yellowish in color. Amber has been used in jewelry since antiquity. It is found chiefly along the southern shores of the Baltic Sea; pieces often contain the bodies of trapped insects. When rubbed, amber becomes charged with static electricity: the word electric is derived from the Greek word for amber.

Archipelagos — A group of islands.

Arctic Circle — The parallel of latitude 66° 33° north of the equator. It marks the northernmost point at which the sun is visible on the northern winter solstice and the southernmost point at which the midnight sun can be seen on the northern summer solstice.

Artifact — A man-made object, especially one of cultural or archaeological significance.

Assassinate — To murder an important person in a surprise attack for political or religious reasons.

Atgeir — A type of polearm, or spear-like weapon, used during the Viking Age in Scandinavia and Norse colonies in the British Isles and Iceland.

Aurora borealis — A natural electrical phenomenon characterized by the appearance of streamers of reddish or greenish light in the sky seen near the north pole. The effect is caused by the collision of charged particles from the sun with atoms in the ionosphere, the upper atmosphere.

Autonomy — To self-govern; freedom from external control or influence; independence.

Barbarian — Person lacking social skills and manners; rough or violent

Basalt — A dark, fine-grained volcanic rock that sometimes displays a columnar structure.

Battlement — A parapet at the top of a wall, usually of a fort or castle, that has regularly spaced, squared openings for shooting through.

Bishopric — District led by bishop; diocese.

Black Death — Also known as the Bubonic Plague, the Black Death was an epidemic spread by rats. This disease killed about one third of the European population between A.D. 1348 and 1352.

Bog — Wet muddy ground too soft to support a heavy object or body. It is a wetland that accumulates peat, a deposit of dead plant material. Other names for bogs include mire, quagmire, muskeg, and fen.

Bog-shoeing — To wear special footwear so as to walk along the top of the bog without sinking into it.

Cathedral — A large church that is run by a bishop.

Catholic — Relating to the Roman Catholic Church.

Cawl — In the Welsh language, the word is used to refer to any broth-based soup.

Chips — French fries.

Chuffed — Very pleased.

Circumnavigate — To go all the way around something.

Communism — A state in which all property is publicly owned and shared equally.

Concentration camps — A type of prison where many people are held, often under terrible conditions.

Corbel — A projection jutting out from a wall to support a structure above it.

Coronation — A ceremony for crowning a new king or queen.

Croft — A small, rented farm, especially one in Scotland, comprising a plot of arable land attached to a house and with a right of pasturage held in common with other such farms.

Crusaders — Fighters for political, social, or religious causes during medieval times.

Dala horses — A traditional carved, painted wooden statue of a horse originating in the Swedish province of Dalarna.

Divergent tectonic plate — A linear geographical feature that exists between two tectonic plates causing them to move away from each other.

Emigrate — To leave one's own country in order to settle permanently in another.

Enclave — A country, or portion of a country, that is entirely surrounded by another country.

Exmoor ponies — A horse breed that has roamed the bleak, open moors of southwestern England, known as Exmoor, for centuries.

Fen — A low and marshy or frequently flooded area of land.

Firth — A narrow inlet of the sea; an estuary.

Fjord — A narrow channel of the sea between high cliffs or hills.

Garrison — The troops stationed in a fortress to defend it. The term also refers to the building occupied by the troops stationed in a town to defend it.

Geyser — A hot spring in which water intermittently boils, sending a tall column of water and steam into the air.

Gibbet — A gallows or an upright post with an arm on which to hang criminals.

Glaciers — A large body of continuously accumulating ice and compacted snow, formed in mountain valleys or at the poles, that deforms under its own weight and slowly moves.

Guild — An organization of people in the same occupation.

Habit — A long, loose garment worn by a member of a religious order.

Haggis — A Scottish dish consisting of a sheep's or calf's offal mixed with suet, oatmeal, and seasoning, then boiled in a bag, traditionally one made from the animal's stomach.

Hanseatic — A medieval association of northern German cities, formed in 1241 and surviving until the 19th century. In the later Middle Ages, it included over 100 towns and functioned as an independent political power.

Hanseatic League — Group formed to protect and control trade.

Hardtack — A hard dry bread or biscuit, especially used as rations for sailors.

Heir apparent — An heir whose claim cannot be set aside by the birth of another heir; a person likely to succeed to the throne.

Helipad — A landing and takeoff area for helicopters.

Hot springs — A place where hot water comes up out of the ground.

Home Rule — The government of a colony, country, or region by its own citizens.

Immigration — The action of coming to live permanently in a foreign country.

Inclusions — A body or particle recognizably distinct from the substance in which it is embedded.

Inlet — A narrow bay off of a lake or the sea.

Jarl — A Norse or Danish chief.

Kaffee-klatsch — An informal social gathering at which coffee is served.

Kissing gate — A small gate hung in a U- or V-shaped enclosure, letting one person through at a time.

Kybyns — A Lithuanian pastry, often stuffed with chopped mutton or beef. However, this versatile pastry can also be filled with mushrooms, vegetables, curd, nuts, or even chocolate.

Lagoon — A pool of water that is separated from the main body of water by a reef, sandbar, or other barrier.

Loch — Scottish word for lake.

Longphorts — A ship harbor or Viking base camp in Ireland.

Lough — Irish word for lake.

Machicolations — An opening between the supporting corbels of a projecting parapet or the vault of a gate, through which stones or burning objects could be dropped on attackers.

Magnum Opus — A large and important work of art, music, or literature, especially one regarded as the most important work of an artist or writer.

Marzipan — A sweet, yellowish paste of ground almonds, sugar, and egg whites, often colored and used to make small cakes or confections.

Megalith — A large, rough-hewn rock used as a monument or as part of a building.

Menagerie — Unique collection of animals, often exotic

Midsommer — The middle part of summer; a Scandinavian holiday.

Milecastle — A small fort or rectangular fortification built during the period of the Roman Empire placed at intervals of approximately one Roman mile along several major frontiers, such as Hadrian's Wall.

Monarchy — A country ruled by a king or queen.

Monolith — A large single upright block of stone serving as a pillar or monument.

Nave — The long central part of a church.

Northmen — Barbaric pirates who were Vikings from Scandinavia

Oxbow — A section of a river that forms a "U" shape.

Pagan — A person holding religious beliefs other than those of the main world religions.

Passage tombs — A grave consisting of a narrow passage made of large stones and one or multiple burial chambers covered in earth or stone.

Peninsula — A piece of land that is bordered by water on three sides but connected to mainland.

Peppercorn rent — A very small payment or a nominal rent used to satisfy the requirements for the creation of a legal contract.

Pilgrimage — A journey taken for religious purposes.

Plague — A contagious disease that spreads rapidly and kills many people.

Prime Meridian — The earth's zero of longitude, which by convention passes through Greenwich, England.

Protestant — A member of any Christian church that is not part of the Roman Catholic Church.

Quarry — A place from which rock and stone is extracted.

Ramparts — Tall, thick walls built for protection.

Rappel — Descend a rock face or other near-vertical surface by using a doubled rope coiled around the body and fixed at a higher point.

Rarebit — A dish of melted and seasoned cheese on toast, sometimes with other ingredients.

Refuge — A condition of being safe or sheltered from pursuit, danger, or trouble.

Resin — A sticky flammable organic substance, insoluble in water, exuded by some trees and other plants.

Rune stones — Large stone carved with symbols or letters by ancient Scandinavians or Anglo-Saxons.

Saint — A person who is holy and set apart for God's work.

Sea level — The average height of the sea's surface. Often used as the baseline for measuring elevation.

Smorgasbord — A buffet offering a variety of hot and cold meats, salads, hors d'oeuvres, etc.

Snickelways — A collection of small streets and footpaths in the city of York, England.

Solstice — Either of the two times in the year, the summer solstice or the winter solstice, when the sun reaches its highest or lowest point in the sky at noon, marked by the longest and shortest days.

Sovietization — Under the control and influence of the Soviet Union.

Spit — A narrow point of land projecting into the sea.

Summer solstice — Also known as midsummer, the summer solstice occurs when one of Earth's poles has its maximum tilt toward the sun.

Sycophant — A person who acts obedient or loyal toward someone important in order to gain advantage.

Taiga — The sometimes-swampy coniferous forest of high northern latitudes.

Thrall — The state of being in someone's power or having great power over someone; a slave.

Thynghowe — An important Viking Era open-air assembly place or thing, located at Sherwood Forest, in Nottinghamshire, England.

Trans-Atlantic Gulf Stream — A warm and swift Atlantic ocean current that originates in the Gulf of Mexico and stretches to the tip of Florida, and follows the eastern coastlines of the United States and Newfoundland before crossing the Atlantic Ocean.

Tuff — A light, porous rock formed by consolidation of volcanic ash.

Tunics — Ancient Greek and Roman-style clothing that was sleeveless and reached the knees.

UNESCO World Heritage Site — A place designated by the United Nations Educational, Scientific and Cultural Organization as a place of historical or cultural significance.

Vellum — A smooth material made from animal skin used for making books.

Welsh Cat — Similar to a battering ram, only a Welsh cat clawed away at a defensive wall rather than ramming it.

Winter solstice — Also known as midwinter, the winter solstice occurs when one of Earth's poles has its maximum tilt away from the sun.

348 Glossary

A Child's Geography. Vol. 5: Explore Viking Realms

Before the Quiz

To review for each quiz, review for that section:

🌍 Notecards of glossary words

🌍 Adventure Challenges

🌍 Mapping It Out!

To review for the Final Exam, review the four quizzes.

A Child's Geography. Vol. 5   Quiz 1   Day   Total Score   Name:

The Baltic States   Lessons 1-3   33   _____ of 100

Matching

Match each word or phrase to the correct description.

1. _____ Person lacking social skills and manners; rough or violent

2. _____ Fighters for political, social, or religious causes during medieval times

3. _____ A condition of being safe or sheltered from pursuit, danger, or trouble

4. _____ A person holding religious beliefs other than those of the main world religions

5. _____ A state in which all property is owned and shared equally

a. Barbarian

b. Pagan

c. Refuge

d. Crusaders

e. Communism

Fill in the Blank

Complete the correct answer in the blanks provided.

1. Riga is the capital city of Latvia and was once a _____ fishing village.

2. The white wagtail is the national bird of _____.

3. The _____ _____ refers to the materials created of various objects, such as tools and jewelry, from stone and bronze.

4. _____ won the Battle of Grunwald.

5. The Curonian Spit is a UNESCO World _____ Site.

Multiple Choice

Circle the letter of the correct answer.

1. In 1390, Welsh raiders stormed the Crooked Castle in Lithuania using a weapon called the
   _____.

   a. Welsh raider

   b. Welsh dog

   c. Fierce dog

   d. Welsh cat

2. A translucent honey-colored substance, amber is from fossilized tree _____.

   a. Storks

   b. Resin

   c. Bark

   d. Crosses

3. In Estonia, you may try _____ through wet, spongy ground.

   a. Playing basketball

   b. Sandboarding

   c. Taking a ferry

   d. Bog-shoeing

4. The Curonian Spit is located in

   a. Lithuania

   b. Latvia

   c. Estonia

   d. Finland

5. A sweet confection made from sugar or honey and almond meal is _____ that is used to
   craft cakes, confections, and even large creations.

   a. Saint

   b. Rye bread

   c. Marzipan

   d. Biezpiena Sierins

Finish the Map

Label the following locations on the map:

1. Baltic Sea   2. Lithuania   3. Latvia   4. Estonia   5. Tallinn

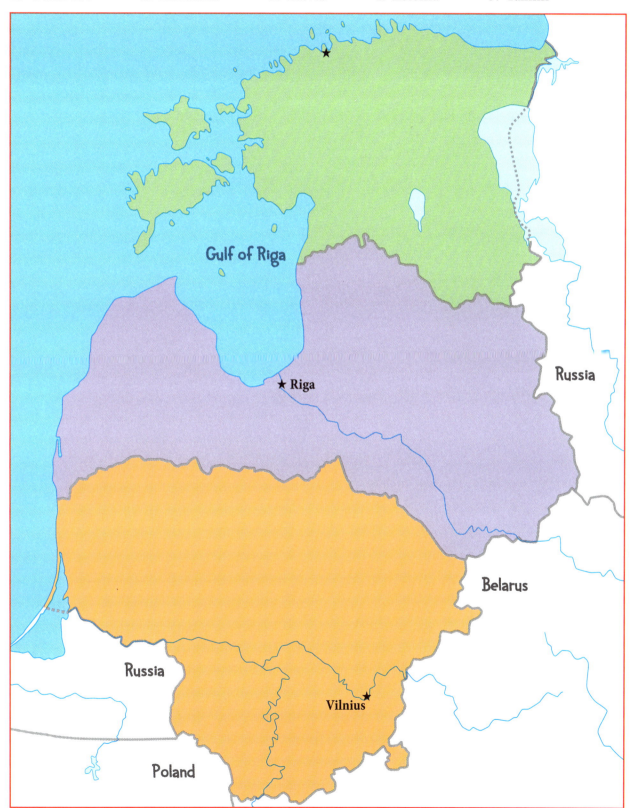

The Baltic States

Page intentionally left blank.

Multiple Choice

Circle the letter of the correct answer.

1. _____ witnessed and named the aurora borealis in 1621.

   a. Birger Jarl

   b. Galileo Galilei

   c. Lucia

   d. Christopher Columbus

2. The _____ carries warm water up from the equator, which cools in the northern hemisphere and then returns to the southern hemisphere.

   a. Saaremaa Island

   b. Crusader

   c. Maarahvas

   d. Trans-Atlantic Gulf Stream

3. The famous Icehotel is located in _____.

   a. Stockholm

   b. Jukkasjärvi

   c. Finland

   d. Norway

4. Vikings got their name from _____, meaning fjord or inlet.

   a. Vik

   b. Minke

   c. Stave

   d. Ship

5. The Oseburg Viking Ship is made of _____, a strong wood.

   a. Birch

   b. Pine

   c. Acacia

   d. Oak

Matching

Match each word or phrase to the correct description.

1. _____ An informal social gathering at which coffee is served

2. _____ A buffet with a variety of food

3. _____ A group of islands

4. _____ Part of a broken-off glacier

5. _____ Roskilde is the site of this Danish museum

6. _____ This famous house found in Billund.

a. Archipelago

b. LEGO House

c. Iceberg

d. Kaffee-klatsch

e. Smorgasbord

Fill in the Blank.

Write a similarity and a difference for each term. (Wording may vary for answers.)

Taiga vs. fen

1. Similarity: _____

2. Difference: _____

Trade surplus vs. trade deficit

3. Similarity: _____

4. Difference: _____

Finish the Map

Label the following locations on the map:

1. Gulf of Bothnia   2. Oslo   3. Stockholm   4. Sweden   5. Helsinki

Scandinavia

Page intentionally left blank.

A Child's Geography. Vol. 5   Quiz 3   Day   Total Score   Name:

The British Isles   Lessons 8–15   153   _____ of 100

Multiple Choice

Circle the letter of the correct answer.

1. A small rented farm, especially one in Scotland, comprising a plot of arable land attached to a house and with a right of pasturage held in common with other such farms.

    a. Basalt

    b. Croft

    c. Loft

    d. Basalt column

2. _____ is a layer of rock between the crust of the earth and the outer core.

    a. Mantle

    b. Legend

    c. Minster

    d. Knackered

3. The White Cliffs of _____ can be seen across the English Channel in the country of France on a clear day.

    a. Clover

    b. Rover

    c. Stover

    d. Dover

4. "Right of access" gates and paths are _____.

    a. Private

    b. Public

    c. Toll booths

    d. Only for Cotswold sheep

5. Cambridge was a farm, then a trading center for _____, and then a location for the University of Cambridge.

    a. Kings

    b. Sheep

    c. Charlotte Mason

    d. Vikings

Fill in the Blank

Complete the correct answer in the blanks provided.

1. Longphorts are where the Vikings used to overwinter their _____.

2. In 1831, London Bridge was _____ _____ (like the song). It was replaced by a stone bridge.

3. In 1837, _____ Palace became the official residence of the British monarchy.

4. Mini-_____ or milecastles spaced approximately a mile apart were designed to protect against Viking raids along Hadrian's Wall and other locations.

5. To descend a rock face or near-vertical surface by using a doubled rope coiled around the body and fixed at a higher point is to _____.

Short Answer

Write a short paragraph about this topic. (Wording will vary for responses.)

Caernarfon Castle in Wales represents medieval military architecture through what types of features?

_____

_____

_____

_____

_____

_____

_____

_____

_____

_____

Finish the Map

Label the following locations on the map:

1. London   2. England   3. Scotland   4. Wales   5. Northern Ireland

Page intentionally left blank.

Matching

Match each word or phrase to the correct description.

1. _____ Also known as the Bubonic Plague, an epidemic spread by rats

2. _____ A linear geographical feature that exists causing part movement of the earth's crust

3. _____ The legislative assembly of Iceland

4. _____ Mountain range on which Iceland is located

5. _____ Can be depicted with Mentos® and soda

a. Divergent tectonic plate

b. Black Death

c. Althing

d. Geyser

e. Mid-Atlantic

List the Animals

List five animals that live in Iceland.

1. _____

2. _____

3. _____

4. _____

5. _____

Fill in the Blanks

1. A _____ is a spring of water pushed turbulently into the air at regular intervals.

2. Iceland has _____ smaller islands that surround it.

3. The _____ _____ is the only native animal in Iceland.

4. _____ is the huge moneymaker.

5. This disease, the _____ _____, swept through Iceland _____, killing two-thirds of the population.

Bonus Activity (optional)

Draw your image based on the description in the five points below. Ensure your illustration includes all five details and identifies the type of animal described.

1. Type of animal
2. Travels by iceberg
3. Arrives in Iceland
4. Comes from Greenland
5. Does not usually stay

Finish the Map

Label the following locations on the map:

1. Iceland   2. Reykjavík   3. Atlantic Ocean

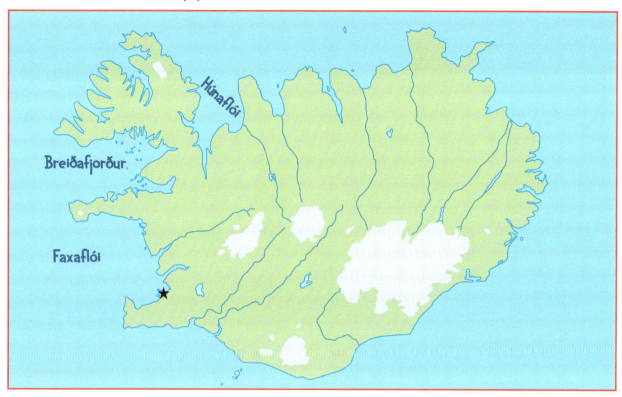

Unscramble the Answer

Use the hints to unscramble the words of the locations.

1. The first name given to Iceland:

       eandlSna   _____

2. This nation of Iceland is the world's 18th largest island:

       Noicrd   _____

3. Iceland's main island is below this:

       ctAric eclric   _____

4. This current passes by Iceland's southern shore:

       thorN tAlatic rrtneCu   _____

5. A major contributor to Iceland's economy:

       finshgi   _____

Page intentionally left blank.

Name _____

Multiple Choice

Circle the letter of the correct answer.

1. A translucent honey-colored substance, amber is from fossilized tree _____.

    a. Storks

    b. Resin

    c. Bark

    d. Crosses

2. The White Cliffs of _____ can be seen across the English Channel in the country of France on a clear day.

    a. Clover

    b. Rover

    c. Stover

    d. Dover

3. The _____ carries warm water up from the equator, which cools in the northern hemisphere and then returns to the southern hemisphere.

    a. Saaremaa Island

    b. Crusader

    c. Maarahvas

    d. Trans-Atlantic Gulf Stream

4. In Estonia, you may try _____ through wet, spongy ground.

    a. Playing basketball

    b. Sandboarding

    c. Taking a ferry

    d. Bog-shoeing

Fill in the Blank

1. Cambridge was a farm, then a trading center for _____, then a location for the University of Cambridge.

2. Riga is the capital city of Latvia and was once a _____ fishing village.

3. The _____ _____ refers to the materials created of various objects, such as tools and jewelry, from stone and bronze.

4. An archipelago is a group of _____.

5. The polar bear travels by _____, arrives in Iceland, comes from Greenland, and does not usually stay.

Finish the Map

Label the following locations on the map:

1. The Baltic Sea
2. Sweden
3. London
4. England
5. Scotland
6. Wales
7. Northern Ireland
8. North Sea
9. Lithuania
10. Latvia
11. Iceland
12. Reykjavík
13. Atlantic Ocean
14. Stockholm
15. Oslo
16. Estonia

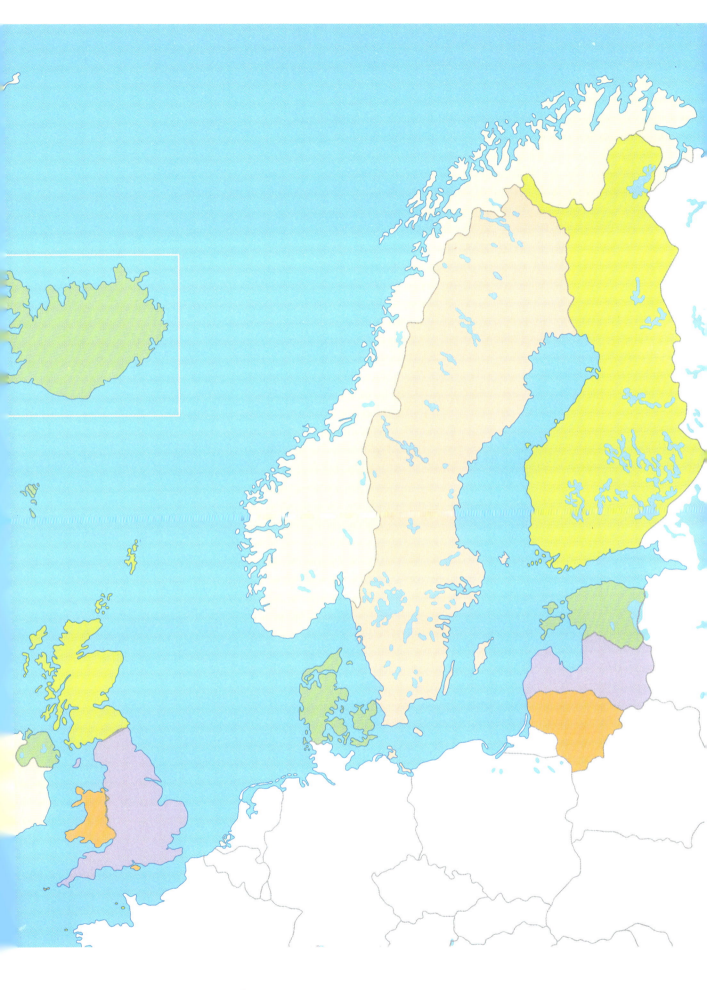

A Child's Geography. Vol. 5: Explore Viking Realms

Final Exam. Day 180 369

Page intentionally left blank.

Answer Keys

While students may not always give the exact answer found in the answer key, they should express the basic ideas given.

Lesson 1

Adventure Challenge 1, Day 5, pages 25-26

Share What You Remember About Lithuania

1. They wanted to convert Lithuanians to Christianity. If they could not, they would destroy.
2. Yes, they were victorious.
3. Lithuania won the Battle of Grunwald.
4. The Curonian Spit is a remarkable geographic feature of Lithuania.
5. People in Lithuania enjoy sandboarding.

Adventure Challenge 2, Day 8, pages 33-34

Fill in the Blank

1. Poland
2. Germany
3. independence
4. Mindaugus
5. 1291
6. Welsh cat
7. Christian
8. Grunwald
9. Questions and answers will vary.

Share What You Remember About Lithuania

1. It is white throughout it.
2. Lithuania is famous for basketball.

Lesson 2

Adventure Challenge 3, Day 13, pages 41-42

The Amazing Outdoors in Latvia

1. g
2. k
3. o
4. m
5. d
6. n
7. j
8. b
9. f
10. c
11. e
12. l
13. h
14. i
15. a

Fill in the Blank

1. amber, resin
2. bronze
3. wolf, lynx
4. birds
5. Russia

Adventure Challenge 4, Day 16, pages 47-49

Fill in the Blank

1. Sovietization
2. 1991
3. Daugava

Lesson 3

Adventure Challenge 5, Day 23, pages 63-64

Short Answer

1. Maarahvas means "country people" or "people of the land."
2. Saaremaa means "Island land" or "the land on the island."
3. Meteorites crashed to the ground approximately 3,500 years ago in Saaremaa.

Adventure Challenge 6, Day 26, pages 69-70

Short Answer

1. St. Olaf's Church was once the tallest building in the world.
2. A bog is a stretch of wet, spongy ground with soil that is composed mainly of decayed vegetable matter.
3. Bog shoes can be worn to walk through a bog

Matching

1. b
2. a
3. d
4. c

Lesson 4

Adventure Challenge 7, Day 36, pages 77-78

Exports and the Economy

1. 60.96
2. deficit
3. surplus

Fill in the Blank

1. lakes
2. equator

Adventure Challenge 8, Day 40, pages 83-84

Fill in the Blank

1. Russia, Sweden
2. coffee

3. health, pool

4. Questions and answers will vary.

Lesson 5

Adventure Challenge 10, Day 50, pages 101-102

Find the Dates in the Royal Palace

1. 1953
2. 1252
3. 1500
4. 1523
5. 1621

Unscramble the Locations

1. Lake Vänern
2. Lake Vättern
3. Lake Mälaren
4. Finland
5. Denmark
6. Stockholm

Lesson 6

Adventure Challenge 11, Day 55, pages 119-120

Match the Norwegian Foods

1. c
2. d
3. b
4. a
5. h
6. e
7. f
8. g

Adventure Challenge 12, Day 58, pages 125-126

Fill in the Blank

1. fjord
2. riches
3. Viking Ship
4. better
5. Minke

Lesson 7

Adventure Challenge 13, Day 63, pages 133-134

Find the Viking Artifacts

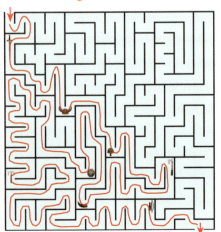

Playwright and Poet from Denmark

1. Answers will vary but should show a connection to the phrase and concept emotionally of being "brokenhearted" or deeply sad.

2. Answers will vary - students should note while the author used his writing abilities to create happy endings, people today have many ways to not only experience heartbreak, but also find find happiness.

3. Answers will vary, but essentially that God cares for us and wants to help us with our heartbreaks.

4. Answers will vary. Students should give a clear definition of what the word means, and also why and how it is experienced. Even examples can demonstrate the understanding of the concept.

Adventure Challenge 14, Day 66, pages 141-142

LEGO® House vs. Danish Viking Ship Museum

1. Answers will vary per student, but they should be able to clearly note a couple of details of what they found interesting.

2. Answers can vary but they need to note a specific feature of the ship museum.

3. Answer will vary. Student will choose one of the two options and then should give two or more reasons for their choice.

Norway vs. Denmark

1. Answers will vary, though they should have picked a color on the map to answer what shows the highest points of the country.

2. two

3. He, You (3 times), Your (2 times)

4. Answers could include: established, totter, covered, standing, fled, hurried, rose, sank down, established, set, pass, return, cover.

5. not appears 3 times in the verses

Lesson 8

Adventure Challenge 15, Day 78, pages 157-158

Word Search

```
S           R
T           O
P   P I C C A D I L L Y   C I R C U S
A                 L
B U C K I N G H A M P A L A C E
L                 O
S           W E S T M I N S T E R A B B E Y
C                 E
A   T R A F A L G A R S Q U A R E
T                 V
H                 A
E                 T
D       T O W E R O F L O N D O N
R                 R
A L   L O N D O N E Y E
L
```

Adventure Challenge 16, Day 81, pages 165-166

Rank the Choices

1. Student should put the sites in order of their preference and give a reason why it is placed as it is in the order. Example: 1. Big Ben; because its a unique clock that is famous and has a nickname.

2. Answers will vary.

3. Answers will vary.

Design a Palace

1. 52 royal and guest bedrooms

2. 188 staff bedrooms

3. 78 bathrooms

Lesson 9

Adventure Challenge 17, Day 86, pages 177-178

Fill in the Blank

1. France

2. William the Conqueror, tunnels

3. Plymouth

Adventure Challenge 18, Day 90, pages 187-188

Fill in the Blank

1. a. Cornwall, b. Brittany, c. Ireland, d. the Isle of Man, e. Scotland, and f. Wales

2. ophiolite, green

3. Bath

4. crust

5. Answer will vary, however, student must write their own fill in the blank question and give a complete answer to it.

Archaeoastronomy

1. 4,000, 10,000

2. 50,000

3. Answers vary and may point toward use of an animal or a group of people, and the method to move, push, or pull.

4. Architecture in ancient times related to astronomy

5. Answers vary and point to intelligence. Answers may also focus on cooperative efforts of a group or community or how the site must have been important for some reason to put in such precision or effort.

Lesson 10

Adventure Challenge 19, Day 95, pages 199-200

Crossword Puzzle

Across	Down
1. peppercorn	2. private
3. Inklings	5. Oxford
4. Cotswold	7. *Mea*
6. Cambridge	
8. Ancient	

Activity 13, Day 100, page 211

Draw the Triangle

1a. Scotland   1b. Wales

Lesson 11

Adventure Challenge 21, Day 103, pages 219-220

Fill in the Blank

1. (Wording may vary.) Since Roman times, the primary industry was sheep.

2. (Wording may vary.) Many ancient axes have been found along the fellsides. The Lake District ("stone axes factory) was a major source of stone axes.

3. (Wording may vary.) During medieval times, mining was a major source of income. Mining for copper, silver, and lead has mostly stopped. Some graphite and slate is still mined. The mining of graphite led to the pencil industry.

4. (Wording may vary.) Bobbins are the little metal thread holders inserted into sewing machines. More than half of the world's bobbin supply came from the Lake District in the 19th century. Tourism has now replaced the bobbin industry.

5. Instead of sheep (wool) and bobbins, tourism brings in money.

Adventure Challenge 22, Day 106, pages 227-228

Short Answer

1. Answers may vary, but should give specific examples, at least two to three; this could be specific sites, towns, cultural traditions, food, tourist attractions or other information.

2. Answers may vary. May reference that they are both stone circles.

3. Answers may vary. May observe that it is smaller than Stonehenge.

4. Answers may vary. May mention intimidating barbarians or showing power or a suitable other answer.

5. Wording may vary. Hardtack (dry bread), hard cheeses, and beef jerky.

Lesson 12

Adventure Challenge 23, Day 111, pages 237-238

Archipelagos

1. approximately 56 miles

2. approximately 4 miles

3. approximately 19 miles

Short Answer

1. Loch Ness Lake

2. Inner Hebrides, Outer Hebrides, Orkney, and Shetland

Faults Exploration

1. 306 inches (25.5 feet)

2. Fault lines will vary, but should mention at least two historical fault lines, as well as location, and at least one earthquake which occurred there historically.

Adventure Challenge 24, Day 115, pages 247-248

Multiple Choice

1. c. Building made of stone on agricultural land

2. c. The land was converted from crop farming to sheep farming.

3. a. Plaid fabric

4. d. Both "a" and "b"

Loch Ness Monster Mystery

1. Answers will vary, but should give a couple of examples of what they learned about Nessie.

2. Answers will vary. There could be a range of responses to this question - it could be they find it interesting and intriguing or the student may go into why he thinks there may or may not be a Nessie; or the student could try to explain how and why it became a legend.

Lesson 13

Adventure Challenge 25, Day 121, pages 257-258

Medieval Military Architecture

1. a. Answers vary, but for full credit, should note two distinct things. Ex. The last time this castle was stormed was in 1415.

   b. Answers vary. Owain Glyndwr, revolted against English rule in the Last War of Independence.

2. It contains all of the mentioned. All boxes should be checked.

3. Answers will vary. For the crenellations, the merlons provided protection, and the crenets allowed for fire of arrows, the curtain wall was a protective stronghold, the moat helped prevent an attack, slits allowed for firing arrows, and the tower allowed a visual overlook of the fortress

4. Answers to this will vary. Ex.: The Welsh were not easily subdued by their neighbor England to the east.

Adventure Challenge 26, Day 125, pages 263-264

Short Answer

1. Cardiff

2. Slate

3. Welsh mountain sheep, Welsh black cattle

4. Red Castle in the Sea Swamps

5. Bara brith

Activity 18, Day 128, pages 267-268

Crossword Puzzle

Across	Down
3. Red	1. Isca Augusta
5. Snowdonia	2. Lancelot
6. Hammer	4. English
7. Cawl	8. Rarebit
9. Ruthin Gaol	11. Cymru
10. Crib Goch	
12. Cymraeg	

374 Answer Keys

A Child's Geography. Vol. 5: Explore Viking Realms

Lesson 14

Adventure Challenge 27, Day 133, pages 277-288

Short Answer (Wording of answers may vary.)

1. Ireland declared its independence from Britain. Northern Ireland requested to remain a province of Great Britain.

2. Nationalist party wanted freedom and Unionists wanted British rule

3. The two parts of Ireland decided to make peace.

4. Irish and British flags

Scottish Gaelic vs. Irish Gaelic

1. Similarities will vary. For example, some words are spelled the same or almost the same.

2. Differences will vary. For example: Some words are spelled differently and accent marks are different as well.

Lesson 15

Adventure Challenge 29, Day 141, pages 295-296

Label Viking Artifacts

1. Ironworking   6. Ironworking
2. Silver   7. Stone
3. Wood   8. Bronze
4. Whalebone   9. Silver
5. Horn

Adventure Challenge 30, Day 145, pages 305–306

Unscramble the Words

1. Irish   4. Vikings
2. Celts   5. Normans
3. monks

Lesson 16

Adventure Challenge 31, Day 156, pages 317-318

Short Answer

1. A Norwegian Viking named it Snæland or "snow land." It was later renamed Iceland by another Viking.

2. Mid-Atlantic Range

3. On icebergs from Greenland

4. Arctic fox, reindeer, mink, Arctic hare, Icelandic sheep, Icelandic sheepdog, puffins, skuas, kittiwakes, seals, whales, and fish

Adventure Challenge 32, Day 160, pages 325-326

The Erikson Family

1. After banishment from Norway, Thorvald the Viking landed in Iceland.

2. Answer will vary but should focus on someone in the Bible who did something better or different than their parents or grandparents or previous generation. Ex. Moses or Abel or other biblical figure.

3. The summary written should be connected with the biblical figure decided upon in the second question above and show the difference in their actions vs the previous generation.

4. Scripture will vary.

5. Answer will vary but should name a specific person.

6. Reactions will vary in wording and focus, but see if the student connects to the positive actions of that person or expresses their opinion of the person chosen or what that person did differently.

Activity 23, Day 161, pages 328

Geospatial Data on a Map

Answers 1-3 will vary. Should include points such as volcanoes and their locations, volcanic zones where volcanic activity could occur, where various types of basalt are found as a resource that could be used, and other rock layers.

Page intentionally left blank.

Quizzes

While students may not always give the exact answer found in the answer key, they should express the basic ideas given.

Quiz One (Lessons 1–3)

Matching

1. a
2. d
3. c
4. b
5. e

Fill in the Blank

1. Viking
2. Latvia
3. Bronze Age
4. Lithuania
5. Heritage

Multiple Choice

1. d
2. b
3. d
4. a
5. c

Finish the Map

The Baltic States Map

Note: If you have concerns about placement of sites on the map, there are reference maps in the resource section of this book.

Student should have identified the following sites on the map of the Baltic States, Baltic Sea, Lithuania, Latvia, Estonia, and Tallinn. Reference map on page 20.

Quiz Two (Lessons 4–8)

Multiple Choice

1. b
2. d
3. b
4. a
5. d

Matching

1. e
2. f
3. a
4. c
5. d
6. b

Similarities and Differences

Fill in the Blank

1. Both are swampy or marshy.

2. Taiga is a forest of high northern latitudes; a fen is a low and frequently flooded area.

3. Both are measured by the value of exports and imports.

4. Trade surplus is when the value of a country's exports is greater than the imports. Trade deficit is when the value of a country's imports is greater than its exports.

Finish the Map

The Nordic States Map

Note: If you have concerns about placement of sites on the map, there are reference maps in the resource section of this book.

Student should have identified the following sites on the map of the Nordic States: Gulf of Bothnia, Oslo, Stockholm, Sweden, and Helsinki. Reference map on page 20.

Quiz Three (Lessons 9–15)

Multiple Choice

1. b
2. a
3. d
4. a
5. d

Fill in the Blank

1. ships
2. falling down
3. Buckingham
4. forts
5. rappel

Short Answer

If writing about Caernarfon Castle in Wales, features that describe medieval military architecture include crenellations, merlon, slits, and tower. Different features may be described.

Finish the Map

The British Isles Map

Note: If you have concerns about placement of sites on the map, there are reference maps in the resource section of this book.

Student should have identified the following sites on the map of the British Isles: London, England, Scotland, Wales, and Northern Ireland. Reference map on page 20.

Quiz Four (Lesson 16)

Matching

1. b
2. a
3. c
4. e
5. d

List the Animals

Five of the animals from Iceland should be listed: Arctic fox, reindeer, mink, Arctic hare, Icelandic sheep, Icelandic sheepdog, puffins, skuas, kittiwakes, seals, whales, and fish.

Fill in the Blank

1. geyser
2. 30
3. Arctic fox
4. Tourism
5. Black Death (or Bubonic Plague), twice

Draw the Answer

Drawing should depict a polar bear on an iceberg from Greenland to Iceland but not staying.

Finish the Map

North Atlantic Map

Note: If you have concerns about placement of sites on the map, there are reference maps in the resource section of this book.

Student should have identified the following sites on the map of North Atlantic: Iceland, Reykjavik, and Atlantic Ocean.

Unscramble the Answer

1. Snaeland
2. Nordic
3. Arctic Circle
4. North Atlantic Current
5. fishing

Final Exam

Multiple Choice

1. b
2. d
3. d
4. d

Fill in the Blank

1. Vikings
2. Viking
3. Bronze Age
4. islands
5. iceberg

Finish the Map

Northern Europe map

Note: If you have concerns about placement of sites on the map, there are reference maps in the resource section of this book. Reference map on page 20.

Grading

It is always the prerogative of an educator to assess student grades however he or she might deem best. The following is only a suggested guideline based on the material presented through this course. To calculate the percentage of the worksheets and tests, the educator may use the following guide. Divide total number of questions correct (example: 43) by the total number of questions possible (example: 46) to calculate the percentage out of 100 possible. 43/46 = 93 percent correct.

The suggested grade values are noted as follows:

90 to 100 percent = A

80 to 89 percent = B

70 to 79 percent = C

60 to 69 percent = D

0 to 59 percent = F

Note: The answer key starting on page 369 provides answers for the numbered question in this course.

Maps

Recommended Resource: Map Trek is a wonderful resource for maps for any course. It includes maps and outlined maps that can be filled in and used as worksheets.

Northern European Map

NORTHERN EUROPE MAP

North Cape

Jan Mayen
(Norway)

Norwegian Sea

Iceland

★
Reykjavik

North Atlantic Ocean

Faroe Islands
(Denmark)

Finland

Gulf
of
Bothnia

Shetland Islands
(UK)

Norway

Sweden

Helsinki
★

Gulf of Finland
★ Tallinn

Estonia

Scotland

Oslo ★

Stockholm
★

Latvia

Riga
★

Northern
Ireland

Edinburgh

North Sea

Slagerrak

Baltic Sea

Lithuania

Belfast
Dublin

Denmark

Copenhagen
★

Vilnius
★ Belar

Ireland

★

England

Germany

Poland

Wales
Cardiff ★

★ London

Netherlands

Celtic Sea

Belgium

English Channel

France

380 Northern Europe Map

A Child's Geography. Vol. 5: Explore Viking Realms

THE BALTIC STATES MAP

Finland

Gulf of Finland

★ Tallinn
Paldiski
Rakvere
Tapa
Kohtla-Lärve
Narva

Hiiumaa

Haapsalu

Estonia

Lake Peipus

Saaremaa

Pärnu
Viljandi
Tartu

Lake Pskov

Kuressaare

Baltic Sea

Gulf of Riga

Kolka

Valga

Voro

Ventspils
Mersrags

Valmiera
Cesis

Aluksne

Gulbene

Stende
Tukums

★ Riga

Latvia

Russia

Jurmala
Ogre

Saldus
Jelgava

Liepaja

Rezekne

Jekabpils

Daugava

Mazeiliai

Daugavpils

Kretinga
Klaipeda
Rietavas

Siauliai

Panevezys

Belarus

uronian Spit

Lithuania

Silute

Ukmerge
Svencioneliai

Taurage

Kedainiai

Nemen

Nemunas
Jonava

Neris

Russia

Kaunas

Lake Galve
★ Vilnius

Alytus

Poland

Druskininkai

SCANDINAVIA MAP

Barent[s]

Norwegian Sea

Hammerfest
Vadsø
Alta
Tromsø
Narvik
Kiruna
Bodø
Arctic Circle
Lapland Boundary
Rovaniemi
Boden
Tornio
Lulea
Kemi
Piteå
Oulu

Faroe Islands
(Denmark)

Finland

Russia

Sweden
Bay of
Bothnia

Steinkjer
Vaasa
Kuopio
Joensuu
Trondheim
Östersund
Jyväskylä
Molde
Norway
Härnösand
Ny-Ålesund
Sundsvall
Gulf of
Bothnia
Pori
Tampere
Lappeenranta
Hämeenlinna
Lahti
Kouvola
Sognefjord
Lillehammer
Falun
Gävle
Turku
Vantaa
Hamar
Espoo
★ **Helsinki**
Bergen
Archipelago
Sea
Gulf of Finland
Oslo ★
Uppsala
Drammen
Västerås
Stockholm
Estonia
Tønsberg
Moss
Eskilstuna
Skien
Fredrikstad
Örebro
Huddinge
Porsgrunn
Vättern
Lake
Stavanger
Norrköping
Sandnes
Linköping
Latvia
Kristiansand
Borås
Jönköping
Gotland
Gothenburg
Aalborg
Växjö
Lithuania
North Sea
Denmark
Halmstad
Kalmar
Aarhus
Helsingborg
Karlskrona
Baltic
Sea
Copenhagen ★
Lund
Esbjerg
Odense
Malmö

Poland

382 Scandinavian Map

A Child's Geography. Vol. 5: Explore Viking Realms

THE BRITISH ISLES MAP

Shetland Islands

Orkney Islands

Atlantic Ocean

North Sea

Outer Hebrides

Inner Hebrides

Inverness

Aberdeen

Scotland

Dundee

Glasgow
Paisley
Edinburgh

Londonderry

Northern Ireland

Lough Neagh

Belfast

Antrim

Sligo

Carlisle

Newcastle upon Tyne
Sunderland

Cumbrian Lake District

Middlesbrough

England

Isle of Man

Drogheda

Irish Sea

Lake Windermere

Blackpool
Preston

Bradford

York

Leeds
Huddersfield

Kingston upon Hull

Galway

Ireland

Liverpool

Manchester
Sheffield

Dublin

Holyhead

Anglesey

Stoke-on-Trent
Derby

Nottingham

Caernarfon

Kilkenny

Wales

Wolverhampton

Leicester

Peterborough

Norwich

Limerick

Birmingham

Coventry

Tralee

Waterford

Saint George Channel

Swansea

Cardiff

Northampton

Cambridge
Luton

Ipswich

Cork

Oxford

London

Southend-on-Sea

Thames River

Swindon

Reading

Bristol

Celtic Sea

Southampton
Bournemouth

Portsmouth

Brighton

Newquay

Plymouth

Isle of Wight

France

Isles of Scilly

English Channel

Jan Mayen
(Norway)

Greenland

Greenland Sea

Denmark Strait

Grimsey   Raufarhöfn

Ísafjördhur

Húnaflói   Húsavik

Dalvik

Blönduós   Sauðárkrókur   Akureyri

Iceland

Egilsstaðir
Neskaupstaður
Eskifjörður
Fjarðabyggð

Breiðafjörður

Stykkisholmur

Hofsjökull

Borgarnes   Langjökull

Faxaflói

Akranes   Vatnajökull

Kópavogur
Reykjanesbær   Mosfellsbær   Höfn
Keflavik   ★ Reykjavik
Hafnarfjördhur   ○ Selfoss

Myrdalsjökull

Vestmannaeyjar
Surtsey

Atlantic Ocean

Faroe Islands
(Denmark)